AF714717

THE AGI-READY CLASSROOM

Redefining Learning for the Next Generation

By

Susie Hala

Intelligloss Press

Legal Disclaimer

Educational Purpose Disclaimer

"This publication is part of the IntelliGloss AI Education Series, a structured curriculum support system for AI literacy in grades 6–12."

The information presented in this publication is provided for educational and informational purposes only. This book is intended to support educators, administrators, parents, and learners in understanding the concepts, opportunities, and challenges associated with artificial intelligence in education. It is not intended to serve as legal, technical, policy, cybersecurity, or professional advice.

Readers should consult qualified professionals, institutional guidelines, and local regulations before implementing any educational programs, technologies, or policies described in this book.

Technology and Accuracy Disclaimer
Artificial intelligence is a rapidly evolving field. While every effort has been made to ensure the accuracy and reliability of the information presented at the time of publication, technologies, policies, research findings, and best practices may change over time. The author and publisher make no guarantees that all information will remain current or applicable in future technological environments.

Readers are encouraged to verify tools, platforms, and recommendations independently before using them in educational settings.

Implementation Responsibility
Schools, educators, and institutions are solely responsible for determining how and whether to implement artificial intelligence tools, strategies, or classroom activities discussed in this book. Educational environments vary widely, and policies regarding technology use, student privacy, and curriculum development differ by district, state, and country.

The author and publisher assume no responsibility for outcomes resulting from the implementation of ideas, examples, or frameworks described in this book.

Student Safety and Data Privacy
Artificial intelligence tools may involve the collection or processing of data. Educators and institutions are responsible for ensuring that any technology used complies with applicable student privacy laws, data protection regulations, and school policies, including but not limited to FERPA, COPPA, GDPR, or other relevant regulations depending on jurisdiction.

The author and publisher are not responsible for the privacy practices, security policies, or data handling procedures of third-party platforms or software mentioned in this book.

Third-Party Tools and References
This book may reference third-party technologies, organizations, research studies, or platforms for illustrative and educational purposes. Such references do not constitute endorsements or guarantees regarding the performance, reliability, safety, or suitability of those tools for educational use.

Educators and institutions should conduct their own evaluations and risk assessments before adopting any technology.

No Professional Liability
The author and publisher shall not be held liable for any direct, indirect, incidental, or consequential damages resulting from the use or misuse of the information contained in this book. This includes but is not limited to decisions related to curriculum design, technology adoption, classroom instruction, institutional policies, or educational outcomes.

Educational Interpretation
The concepts and examples provided in this book are intended to support discussion and learning. They should not be interpreted as official standards, mandatory guidelines, or universally applicable policies for artificial intelligence education.

Schools and educators are encouraged to adapt the ideas presented here according to their local policies, cultural context, educational standards, and student needs.

Author's Intent
The goal of this book is to promote responsible AI literacy, thoughtful discussion, and ethical awareness as schools prepare students for a world increasingly shaped by intelligent technologies.

The author encourages readers to approach artificial intelligence education with curiosity, caution, and a commitment to responsible learning.

Title: THE AGI-READY CLASSROOM : Redefining Learning for the Next Generation

ISBN: 978-1-972925-23-2

Copyright © 2026 by Susie Hala
All rights reserved.

No part of this publication may be reproduced, stored in a retrieval system, transmitted, or distributed in any form or by any means—electronic, mechanical, photocopying, recording, or otherwise—without the prior written permission of the author, except in the case of brief quotations used in reviews, educational discussions, or scholarly references.`

Published by
IntelliGloss Press
United States of America

This book is intended for educational and informational purposes. Artificial intelligence technologies and policies evolve rapidly, and the author makes no guarantee regarding the completeness, accuracy, or continued applicability of the information presented. Educators, schools, and institutions are responsible for evaluating and implementing technologies in accordance with their own policies, legal requirements, and educational standards.

Unauthorized reproduction of this work may result in legal action.

Dedication

This book is dedicated to the next generation of learners—
the students who will grow up in a world shaped by intelligent technology,
and who deserve to understand it with clarity, confidence, and purpose.

To the educators who show up every day with dedication and heart,
guiding students through a rapidly changing world—
your role has never been more important.

To the parents and families who support learning at home,
encouraging curiosity, responsibility, and growth—
you are the foundation of every child's success.

And to my granddaughters,
whose curiosity, imagination, and future inspire me to do this work—
this book is for you.

May you not only learn how to use technology,
but understand it, question it, and shape it for the good of others.

About the Author

Susie Hala
Founder of the IntelliGloss AI Education Series

Susie Hala is an author, educator, and curriculum developer dedicated to advancing artificial intelligence literacy in education. Her work focuses on helping schools, educators, and students understand how intelligent technologies are shaping modern society—and why that understanding is essential for the next generation.

Hala is the creator of the IntelliGloss AI Education Series, a comprehensive and growing collection of educational books designed to make complex artificial intelligence concepts accessible, structured, and practical for classroom use. Her work emphasizes clarity, organization, and responsible implementation, enabling schools to introduce AI literacy without requiring advanced technical backgrounds.

In addition to her work in education, Hala brings hands-on experience working with artificial intelligence systems, including early exposure to rule-based AI technologies during her time working with AT&T. She has also developed modern digital platforms that integrate artificial intelligence, automation, and online systems, building e-commerce solutions and AI-driven applications that connect payment platforms, hosting environments, and conversational AI tools into real-world, functional systems.

This combination of foundational understanding and practical experience allows her to translate complex AI concepts into clear, accessible language for both educators and students.

Recognizing that artificial intelligence is rapidly transforming how information is created, interpreted, and used, Hala advocates for equipping students with the ability not only to use AI tools, but to understand, question, and evaluate them. Her work emphasizes critical thinking, ethical awareness, and responsible digital citizenship.

The IntelliGloss AI Education Series supports schools in teaching key areas such as artificial intelligence foundations, algorithms, machine learning concepts, and AI ethics, as well as the broader evolution of intelligent systems—from Artificial Narrow Intelligence (ANI) to Artificial General Intelligence (AGI) and Artificial Superintelligence (ASI). These resources are designed for students in grades 6–12 and for educators seeking structured, classroom-ready approaches to AI literacy.

In addition to her work in education publishing, Hala has a strong background in entrepreneurship, having built and managed multiple businesses and educational initiatives. Her experience across industries reinforces her belief that technology education must remain grounded in human values, critical thinking, and ethical responsibility.

Her mission is clear: to ensure that the next generation understands intelligent technology—not just how to use it, but how it truly works.

Preface

Two Students. Two Paths. One Future.

Before we begin, it is important to understand why learning how artificial intelligence works—not just how to use it—matters for every student.

Imagine two students who have just graduated from high school and are preparing for a job interview. The first student knows how to use artificial intelligence tools. This student can generate answers, complete assignments quickly, and rely on AI to assist with tasks. However, this student does not understand how artificial intelligence works behind the scenes.

The second student also knows how to use AI tools, but in addition, understands the foundational concepts behind them. This student has learned about data, algorithms, tokens, models, and how intelligent systems are trained and operate. This student can think critically about AI, recognize its limitations, and adapt when needed.

At first, the first student may appear faster and more efficient. However, over time, the second student demonstrates a deeper level of understanding, independence, and problem-solving ability. The second student is not only able to use artificial intelligence but also to question it, improve it, and grow with it.

This book is written for the second student.

In a world where artificial intelligence is becoming part of everyday life, students must not only learn how to use intelligent systems—they must learn how they work. True understanding leads to confidence, responsibility, and the ability to lead in an AI-driven future.

This perspective is not just theoretical—it is personal.

There was a time when I was the first student.

I knew how to use systems. I followed processes, completed tasks, and worked within structured environments that required accuracy and consistency. At the time, I did not think of these systems as artificial intelligence. They were simply part of the job—tools that had to be learned, followed, and mastered.

But looking back, I now understand something much deeper. I was working within rule-based systems—the earliest foundation of what we now recognize as artificial intelligence.

That realization changed everything.

As I began studying modern AI, including machine learning, deep learning, and intelligent systems, I started to see a clear connection between the past and the present. The structured systems I once worked in, the logic behind decision-making, and the step-by-step processes all still exist today. They have simply evolved.

Artificial intelligence did not appear overnight. It grew from rule-based systems into systems that can now learn, adapt, and assist in ways we never imagined.

I made a decision to move from simply using systems to understanding them.

That journey—from student one to student two—is the reason these books exist.

My mission is to help others bridge that same gap.

I believe that artificial intelligence should be understandable for everyone. It should not feel intimidating or out of reach. Students should feel confident exploring it. Teachers should feel prepared to introduce it. Everyday learners should have access to clear, structured explanations that make sense.

You do not need a background in technology. You do not need to know how to code. You only need the right explanation.

A Note from the Author

AI Is a Tool — Not a Decision Maker

Artificial Intelligence is becoming part of everyday life. Students use it to complete assignments, teachers use it to support instruction, and businesses use it to improve efficiency. While these tools are powerful and useful, there is an important truth that must remain clear from the very beginning:

Artificial Intelligence does not make decisions—people do.

One of the main purposes of this book is to help readers understand how AI works, what it can do, and—just as importantly—what it cannot do. AI systems are designed to process information, identify patterns, and generate responses based on data. They can assist with thinking, but they do not think independently. They can provide answers, but they do not understand consequences. They can suggest ideas, but they do not choose actions.

Every outcome that involves AI begins and ends with human involvement. A person asks the question. A person reviews the response. A person decides what to do next. Responsibility does not transfer to the machine.

In today's world, it is easy to confuse speed with intelligence and automation with authority. Because AI can respond quickly and confidently, it may appear as though it is making decisions. In reality, it is performing a task based on patterns it has learned—not exercising judgment.

This distinction matters. When people begin to rely on AI without understanding its role, they risk misunderstanding information, misusing technology, or placing trust in a system that is not capable of accountability. Clear understanding leads to responsible use.

This book was written to remove confusion and provide clarity. It is designed to help students and educators move beyond simply using AI tools and begin understanding the structure behind them. By learning how AI supports human thinking—rather than replacing it—readers can approach technology with confidence, awareness, and responsibility.

Artificial Intelligence is a powerful assistant. It can enhance learning, support creativity, and improve productivity. But it remains a tool.

The decisions, the actions, and the responsibility will always belong to the human.

— **Susie Hala**

Bringing Clarity to Artificial Intelligence

During a recent meeting with a school district, it became clear that one of the biggest challenges in artificial intelligence education is not the technology itself—but the way it is explained.

In that discussion, terms such as **chatbots, generative AI, agentic AI, autonomy, tools, hallucinations, and AI usage levels** were all mentioned together. While each term represents a distinct concept, they were often blended into one conversation without clear distinctions. The result was confusion, even among those who were actively trying to understand and make informed decisions.

This experience revealed an important truth:
Without clear definitions and structure, artificial intelligence becomes difficult to teach, difficult to learn, and difficult to use responsibly.

This book is designed to provide that structure.

Understanding the Core Concepts

To build a strong foundation, it is essential to separate and define the key ideas that are often confused.

Chatbot
A chatbot is a conversational interface that allows users to interact with an AI system through questions and prompts. It responds to input but does not act beyond what is directly requested.

Generative AI (Gen AI)
Generative AI refers to systems that create new content, including text, images, audio, and code. These systems generate outputs based on patterns learned from large datasets. While powerful, generative AI does not truly understand information and may occasionally produce inaccurate results.

Agentic AI
Agentic AI describes systems that can take action toward a goal. Rather than responding to a single prompt, these systems can plan, make decisions within defined limits, and carry out multi-step tasks. This introduces a higher level of functional independence.

Autonomy
Autonomy refers to how independently an AI system operates. Some systems require constant human guidance, while others can perform multiple steps with minimal input. Autonomy is not a separate type of AI, but a measure of how much control the system has in completing tasks.

Additional Terms That Shape Understanding

AI Tools
AI tools are the applications people use to interact with artificial intelligence, such as writing assistants, design platforms, and data analysis systems. These tools make AI accessible in everyday tasks.

Hallucination
A hallucination occurs when an AI system generates information that appears correct but is inaccurate or unsupported. This is a known limitation of generative systems and highlights the need for human verification.

The AI Use Continuum

Another important concept is how AI is used at different levels. Rather than viewing AI as a single capability, it is more accurate to understand it as a continuum of use:

Assistive Use
AI supports simple tasks such as answering questions, correcting grammar, or providing suggestions.

Augmented Use
AI helps expand human capability by generating ideas, organizing content, and assisting in problem-solving.

Agentic Use
AI begins to take on multi-step responsibilities, planning and completing tasks with reduced human input.

This continuum shows that AI can range from a helpful assistant to a more independent system, depending on how it is applied.

The Moment Everything Sounded Like One Conversation

During a recent discussion on artificial intelligence, I listened closely as different experts spoke about the future of AI. One referenced advanced systems beyond human intelligence, another discussed goal-driven AI systems, and the conversation shifted quickly between topics like autonomy, tools, and system behavior. At first, it sounded like a single, unified discussion. But the more I listened, the more I realized something important.

They were not all talking about the same thing.

One part of the conversation focused on future possibilities—high-level systems that do not yet exist. Another part focused on current technologies that are already being used today. At the same time, different terms were being used to describe how AI behaves, how it makes decisions, and how much independence it may have. These ideas were layered together in a way that made them sound connected, even when they were not.

This experience revealed a major challenge in understanding artificial intelligence today. Many discussions combine different types of AI, different levels of intelligence, and different behaviors into one conversation. Without clear structure, these ideas begin to blur together. For someone trying to learn, this can feel overwhelming and confusing.

This book is built to solve that problem.

Artificial intelligence is not one single concept. It is a system made up of multiple layers. Some layers describe how intelligent a system is. Other layers describe how the system behaves. Still others describe how much control or independence the system has. When these layers are separated and explained clearly, AI becomes much easier to understand.

The goal of this book is to bring clarity where confusion often exists. Instead of mixing everything into one explanation, each concept is presented in a structured and organized way. This allows students, educators, and readers to see how the pieces fit together without losing sight of what each part actually means.

Understanding artificial intelligence begins with understanding its structure.

Once that structure is clear, the conversation becomes clearer as well.

Why Clarity Matters

When these concepts are not clearly defined, they merge into what can be described as a "conceptual blur." This can lead to misunderstandings about what AI can and cannot do, as well as unrealistic expectations or misuse in educational settings.

Clear understanding helps ensure that:

Students remain active learners, not passive users

Educators maintain control over instructional outcomes

AI is used as a support tool rather than a replacement for thinking

The Purpose of This Book

This book is built on a simple but essential principle:

Students should not only use artificial intelligence—they should understand it.

By clearly defining core concepts such as chatbots, generative AI, agentic AI, autonomy, and the continuum of AI use, this curriculum provides a structured pathway for developing both technical understanding and critical thinking.

Artificial intelligence is not a single tool or system. It is a collection of capabilities that must be understood in context.

Clarity is the foundation of responsible innovation.

Structuring Artificial Intelligence to Create Clarity and Understanding

Why Structure Is Necessary

Artificial intelligence is often presented as one unified concept. In many discussions, different ideas such as intelligence level, system behavior, and autonomy are combined into a single explanation. This can make AI appear more complex and confusing than it actually is.

Clarity begins when these ideas are separated and organized.

Structuring artificial intelligence allows each concept to be understood on its own before being connected to the larger system.

The Problem Without Structure

When AI is not structured, conversations may include multiple terms that sound related but describe entirely different things. For example, a discussion may move quickly between advanced future systems, current tools, and system behaviors without clearly distinguishing between them.

This creates the impression that all forms of AI operate at the same level and in the same way, which is not accurate.

Without structure, understanding becomes difficult.

The Solution: A Structured Approach

Artificial intelligence becomes clearer when it is organized into distinct categories.

Level explains how intelligent a system is.
Behavior explains how the system operates.
Control explains how much independence the system has.

Each category answers a different question. Together, they form a complete picture of how AI systems function.

Clarity Through Separation

A system can operate at a current level of intelligence while demonstrating different behaviors or levels of independence. For example, a system that generates responses and a system that takes steps toward completing a task may operate at the same intelligence level but differ in how they behave.

This distinction becomes clear only when structure is applied.

Instructional Insight

When teaching artificial intelligence, it is important to avoid presenting all concepts at once. Separating ideas into categories allows learners to focus on one dimension at a time, building understanding step by step.

Structured learning leads to deeper comprehension.

Key Takeaway

Artificial intelligence is not one single idea. It is a system made up of multiple parts. Structuring those parts creates clarity, improves understanding, and allows learners to see how the system truly works.

Reflection Question

How does separating intelligence level, behavior, and control make artificial intelligence easier to understand?

The IntelliGloss Instructional Approach

The IntelliGloss AI Education Series is designed to help students move beyond simply using AI tools and begin understanding artificial intelligence as a complete system.

Students learn how AI is built, how it operates, and how it connects to the real world.

A Message to Students and Readers

If you have ever felt that technology was too complicated…
If you have ever been confused by systems that were never clearly explained…

I want you to know:

You are capable of understanding artificial intelligence.

Sometimes, the challenge is not the concept itself—it is how it has been presented.

This series was created to change that.

A Message to Educators

To the educators using this material:

These books are designed to support you in introducing artificial intelligence in a way that is clear, structured, and meaningful for students.

AI is becoming part of every industry, and students deserve more than just exposure to tools—they deserve understanding.

This series aims to provide that foundation.

Final Reflection

Every experience we have—especially the challenging ones—prepares us for something greater.

The systems I once worked in taught me discipline, structure, and attention to detail. Today, those same lessons allow me to break down complex ideas and make them understandable for others.

That is what this series represents:

Turning complexity into clarity.

Why Artificial Intelligence Education Matters for Every Student

Why AI Literacy Is Essential for Every Student

Artificial intelligence is no longer a future concept or a specialized technology used only by experts. It is already part of everyday life for students of all ages. From smartphones and search engines to navigation apps, social media, streaming platforms, and educational tools, AI systems influence how information is accessed, decisions are made, and learning takes place.

Because AI is embedded in daily life, understanding it is no longer optional. It is a foundational skill, similar to digital literacy and critical thinking. Students do not need to become programmers or engineers, but they do need to understand what AI is, how it works at a basic level, and how it affects their lives.

AI education should not be limited to computer science classrooms. Every student interacts with AI systems daily. Teaching students how these systems function empowers them to become informed users rather than passive consumers of technology.

This book is designed to make artificial intelligence understandable, approachable, and relevant. It focuses on clarity, responsibility, and real-world understanding to help students prepare for a future where humans and intelligent systems work side by side.

IntelliGloss AI Education Series

Teaching how AI actually works—from hardware to power to global systems.

Why AI Education Matters

Artificial intelligence is already shaping how students learn, write, research, and solve problems.

Yet many students—and educators—are using AI tools without understanding how these systems actually work.

Schools need more than access to technology.
They need structured, responsible AI education.

Our Approach

The IntelliGloss AI Education Series is designed to help students move beyond simply using AI tools and begin understanding artificial intelligence as a complete system.

Students learn how AI is built, how it operates, and how it connects to the real world.

The IntelliGloss Framework

Our books introduce AI through a clear and connected system:

- **Chip Family** — the hardware that powers AI
- **Watts Family** — the rate at which AI uses power
- **Energy Family** — the total power AI consumes over time
- **Infrastructure Family** — the global systems that support AI

This framework helps students understand AI from the inside out.

Built for the Classroom

Each book includes:

Structured chapters aligned with semester learning

Clear explanations designed for student understanding

Reflection sections with learning objectives

Worksheets, quizzes, and answer keys

Teacher Implementation Guides

Supporting Schools and Educators

The IntelliGloss series supports:

Responsible and ethical AI use

Student data awareness and safety

Critical thinking and digital literacy

Classroom-ready instruction for grades 6–12 and beyond

What This Book Is—and What It Is Not

Many people today are becoming familiar with artificial intelligence through tools like ChatGPT, Microsoft Copilot, Canva, and other AI-powered applications. These tools can help with writing, answering questions, creating images, and completing everyday tasks.

In addition to these tools, you may also hear terms such as **AI agents, agentic AI, autonomous systems, and generative AI**. While these may sound complex, they are all part of the same evolving landscape of artificial intelligence technologies.

This book is not a guide on how to use those tools.

Instead, it explains what makes those tools possible.

Behind every AI tool is a system made up of multiple layers working together. At the most basic level, information is represented as bits and processed through powerful computer chips. That information is organized into data, broken into tokens, and then processed by algorithms and models that allow the system to recognize patterns, generate responses, and perform tasks.

These components—chips, bits, tokens, data, algorithms, and models—work together as a complete system. While users may only see the tool, the real intelligence comes from how these underlying parts interact behind the scenes.

Artificial intelligence can also be understood in terms of different levels of capability. Most of the AI systems used today fall under **Artificial Narrow Intelligence (ANI)**, which is designed to perform specific tasks, such as answering questions or generating content. More advanced forms, such as **Artificial General Intelligence (AGI)** and **Artificial Superintelligence (ASI)** represent future possibilities where AI could match or exceed human-level thinking. While these advanced levels are still theoretical, understanding the differences helps provide a broader view of where AI is today and where it may be heading.

For students, parents, and educators, this distinction is important. Learning how to use AI tools is helpful, but understanding how they work—and where they fit within the larger AI landscape—builds stronger thinking, better decision-making, and more responsible use.

Most importantly, artificial intelligence does not make decisions on its own. It does not take responsibility for actions or outcomes. AI systems generate responses based on data and patterns, but it is always the human who decides what to do with that information.

This book is designed to make these underlying systems clear and accessible, even for readers who are new to artificial intelligence.

Artificial intelligence is still in its early stages of development. As these technologies continue to grow, those who understand the foundation behind them will be better prepared to adapt, question, and use them wisely.

Who This Book Is For

This book is designed for educators, school leaders, and curriculum developers guiding students in an age of rapidly advancing technology.

Artificial intelligence is already influencing how students learn, research, and communicate. Yet many educators have not received formal training in how these systems work or how they should be addressed in the classroom.

This book helps bridge that gap by providing clear explanations and practical frameworks for understanding artificial intelligence in an educational setting.

How Schools Can Use This Book

This book supports schools in developing a structured approach to artificial intelligence literacy.

It can be used for:

Professional development for educators

Classroom discussions and activities

Curriculum support across subject areas

Policy and academic integrity conversations

Rather than focusing on specific tools, this book emphasizes lasting principles that help students understand, evaluate, and use AI responsibly.

Closing Perspective

Artificial intelligence will continue to evolve. With the right knowledge and leadership, schools can ensure that students not only use these technologies, but understand them, question them, and apply them responsibly.

IntelliGloss is more than a book series. It is a structured approach to preparing students for a future shaped by artificial intelligence.

Rather than focusing only on how to use AI tools, this series helps students understand how AI actually works—from its foundational building blocks to real-world applications.

"Before exploring the technical structure of artificial intelligence, it is equally important to understand the human principles that guide its use."

Human Values Family

Definition

The Human Values Family in artificial intelligence represents the guiding principles that shape how AI systems are created, used, and integrated into society. These values include ethics, responsibility, trust, and human well-being.

Artificial intelligence may be built on data, algorithms, and computational systems, but its true impact is measured by how it affects people. For this reason, AI is not only a technical system—it is a human-centered system.

Key Concepts

The Human Values Family exists to ensure that artificial intelligence serves humanity in a positive and responsible way. While AI systems can process information and generate outcomes, they do not possess judgment, empathy, or moral understanding.

This means that human values must guide every stage of AI development—from design to deployment.

AI reflects the intentions, decisions, and assumptions of the people who build and use it. If those values are not carefully considered, AI systems can unintentionally produce biased, harmful, or misleading results.

Understanding human values in AI is not optional—it is essential.

Core Elements of the Human Values Family

Ethics
Ethics in AI refers to making decisions that are fair, just, and respectful of human rights. This includes minimizing bias, protecting privacy, and ensuring transparency in how systems operate.

Responsibility
Responsibility means that humans remain accountable for AI systems. Developers, educators, organizations, and users must take ownership of how AI is used and the outcomes it produces.

Trust
Trust is critical for the successful adoption of AI. People must feel confident that AI systems are reliable, safe, and aligned with their best interests.

Human Well-Being
AI should enhance human life—not replace, harm, or diminish it. This includes supporting learning, improving access to information, and creating opportunities while maintaining human dignity.

Real-World Connection

Artificial intelligence is already influencing how people learn, communicate, and make decisions. From search engines to classroom tools, AI is shaping daily experiences.

Without clear human values guiding these systems, there is a risk of reinforcing misinformation, bias, or unrealistic expectations.

For students, this means learning not only how to use AI tools, but how to question them, evaluate their outputs, and understand their limitations.

Applications in Education

In the classroom, the Human Values Family helps students develop critical thinking and ethical awareness. Teachers can use this framework to guide discussions about fairness, responsibility, and the impact of technology on society.

Students can explore questions such as:

How should AI be used responsibly?

What makes an AI system fair?

How does technology influence human behavior?

This approach supports both technical understanding and responsible decision-making.

Benefits

Teaching human values in AI helps students:

Develop ethical awareness

Strengthen critical thinking

Understand the societal impact of technology

Become responsible users and future creators of AI

It ensures that learning about AI goes beyond functionality and includes responsibility.

Challenges

Human values are not always universal. Different cultures, communities, and individuals may have different perspectives on what is considered fair or ethical.

Additionally, AI technology is evolving rapidly, often faster than policies and guidelines can keep up. This makes it essential for educators and students to stay informed and adaptable.

Summary

The Human Values Family reminds us that artificial intelligence is not just about machines—it is about people.

By focusing on ethics, responsibility, trust, and human well-being, students can learn to use AI thoughtfully and responsibly.

Understanding these principles helps prepare learners to navigate a world where artificial intelligence plays an increasingly important role in everyday life.

Executive Summary

IntelliGloss AI Education Series

Teaching How Artificial Intelligence Actually Works

Artificial intelligence is already shaping how students learn, write, research, and make decisions. Yet in many classrooms, students are being introduced to AI tools without understanding how these systems actually function.

This creates a critical gap.

Students may become efficient users of technology, but without foundational knowledge, they are not equipped to think critically, evaluate outputs, or use AI responsibly. As AI continues to expand across every industry, this gap will only grow more significant.

The **IntelliGloss AI Education Series** was created to address this challenge.

The Problem

Most current approaches to AI in education focus on tool usage rather than system understanding. As a result:

- Students rely on AI without understanding its limitations
- Educators lack structured frameworks for teaching AI concepts
- Key terms such as generative AI, agentic AI, and autonomy are often introduced without clear definitions
- Responsibility and ethical use are not consistently emphasized

Without clarity, artificial intelligence becomes difficult to teach, difficult to learn, and difficult to manage in a school environment.

The Solution

The IntelliGloss AI Education Series provides a structured, classroom-ready approach to artificial intelligence literacy for grades 6–12.

Rather than focusing on individual tools, this series teaches students how AI works as a complete system—from foundational components to real-world applications.

Students learn to move beyond surface-level interaction and develop true understanding.

The IntelliGloss Framework

The series introduces AI through a clear and connected structure, including:

- Foundational building blocks such as data, algorithms, tokens, and models
- System-level understanding through categories such as intelligence level, behavior, and control
- Real-world context through applications, limitations, and responsible use
- Human-centered learning through ethics, responsibility, trust, and student safety

This structured approach transforms artificial intelligence from a confusing concept into an understandable system.

Instructional Design

Each book in the series is designed for practical classroom use and includes:

- Structured chapters aligned with instructional pacing
- Clear, student-friendly explanations
- Reflection sections to reinforce understanding
- Worksheets, quizzes, and answer keys
- Teacher implementation support

No prior technical background is required for educators or students.

Guiding Principle

A central message of the IntelliGloss series is:

Artificial Intelligence is a tool—not a decision maker.

Students learn that while AI can support thinking and provide information, all decisions, actions, and responsibilities remain with humans. This principle reinforces critical thinking, accountability, and responsible technology use.

Why It Matters

AI literacy is no longer optional. It is a foundational skill.

Students who understand how AI works will be better prepared to:

Think critically about information

Adapt to emerging technologies

Use AI responsibly and ethically

Succeed in an increasingly AI-driven world

Our Goal

The IntelliGloss AI Education Series is designed to help schools move beyond simply using artificial intelligence tools and toward a deeper understanding of how these systems actually work.

By providing clear structure, defined concepts, and real-world context, this series equips students and educators with the knowledge needed to think critically, evaluate information, and use AI responsibly.

The goal is not just to introduce technology—but to build understanding, confidence, and accountability in an AI-driven world.

This is not just about learning to use AI—it is about preparing students to understand it, question it, and lead with it.

Clarity leads to confidence.
Understanding leads to responsible use.

Mission Statement

The mission of the IntelliGloss AI Education Series is to make artificial intelligence clear, structured, and accessible for every student and educator.

In a world where AI is rapidly transforming how information is created, used, and understood, this series is designed to move beyond surface-level interaction and provide a deeper understanding of how intelligent systems actually work.

Through clear explanations, organized frameworks, and real-world context, IntelliGloss equips learners with the ability to think critically, evaluate information, and engage with technology responsibly.

This mission is grounded in a simple belief:
students should not only learn how to use artificial intelligence—they should understand it.

By building both technical awareness and human-centered understanding, the IntelliGloss AI Education Series prepares students to navigate, question, and shape a future increasingly influenced by intelligent technologies.

The goal is not just to keep up with artificial intelligence—but to understand it, guide it, and use it responsibly.

Vision Statement

The vision of the IntelliGloss AI Education Series is to create a future where artificial intelligence is clearly understood, responsibly used, and thoughtfully integrated into education and everyday life.

In this future, students are not passive users of technology, but informed thinkers who understand how intelligent systems work, recognize their limitations, and apply them with purpose and responsibility.

Educators are equipped with clear frameworks and structured resources that make artificial intelligence accessible, teachable, and meaningful across all subjects—not just in technical fields.

Schools become environments where technology is not simply adopted, but understood—where students are encouraged to question, evaluate, and engage with AI in ways that support learning, creativity, and ethical awareness.

As artificial intelligence continues to evolve, this vision supports a generation that is prepared not only to adapt to change, but to lead it with knowledge, confidence, and integrity.

The future of artificial intelligence will not be defined by technology alone—but by the understanding and responsibility of those who use it.

Connecting AI Understanding to Cybersecurity Awareness

Definition

Understanding artificial intelligence is the first step toward understanding cybersecurity. While cybersecurity focuses on protecting systems, data, and users, artificial intelligence explains how those systems are built, how they function, and where they may be vulnerable.

The Connection

Every AI system is made up of components such as data, algorithms, models, and infrastructure. These same components are also the targets of cybersecurity threats.

When students understand:

- How data is collected and stored
- How algorithms make decisions
- How AI models process information
- How systems operate across frontend and backend layers

They begin to recognize where risks can exist and how systems can be misused.

Why This Matters

In today's digital world, students are not just users of technology—they are participants in complex systems powered by artificial intelligence.

Without understanding how these systems work:

- Technology becomes something they trust without question
- Risks become harder to recognize
- Decisions are made without awareness of consequences

With understanding:

- Students become more aware of how their data is used
- They recognize how systems can be manipulated
- They make more informed and responsible choices

Building Digital Readiness

Digital readiness is not only about using tools. It is about understanding the systems behind those tools.

By learning how AI works, students develop:

Awareness of digital environments

Confidence in navigating technology

A foundation for future learning, including cybersecurity

Conclusion

Cybersecurity begins with understanding.

Before students can protect systems, they must first understand how those systems are built and how they operate. This is why learning artificial intelligence is not only about innovation—it is also about responsibility.

The Foundation of Artificial Intelligence

Definition

The foundation of Artificial Intelligence (AI) refers to the core building blocks that allow AI systems to function. These building blocks work together to help machines learn from information, recognize patterns, and make decisions. AI is not magic—it is a system built on structured components that operate behind the scenes.

Understanding the Foundation in Simple Terms

Artificial Intelligence can be compared to a house. Before a house is complete, it must be built on a strong foundation. This foundation includes concrete, wiring, plumbing, and support structures that are not always visible but are essential for the house to function properly.

In the same way, AI systems rely on foundational components that are not visible to users but are necessary for AI tools to work. When people use AI applications such as chatbots or design tools, they are interacting with the surface. The true power of AI comes from what is underneath.

Key Components of the AI Foundation

1. Data (The Information)

Data is the starting point of all AI systems. It includes text, images, numbers, audio, and other forms of information. AI systems learn by analyzing patterns within this data.

2. Algorithms (The Instructions)

Algorithms are step-by-step instructions that tell the AI system how to process data. They guide how the system learns, identifies patterns, and produces results.

3. Models (The Trained System)

A model is created when data and algorithms are combined through a training process. The model acts as the "brain" of the AI system, allowing it to make predictions and generate responses.

4. Computing Power (The Engine)

AI systems require powerful computers to process large amounts of data. This includes specialized hardware such as processors and graphics processing units (GPUs) that allow AI to function efficiently.

5. Infrastructure (The Environment)

Infrastructure refers to the systems that support AI operations, including servers, storage, networks, and energy systems. Data centers are a key part of this infrastructure, providing the physical space where AI systems operate.

How These Components Work Together

AI systems function by combining all foundational components into a single process. Data is collected and analyzed using algorithms. This process creates a model that can recognize patterns and make decisions. The entire system is powered by computing machines and supported by infrastructure.

Why Understanding the Foundation Matters

Many people use AI tools without understanding how they work. This can lead to confusion, misuse, or over-reliance on technology. By understanding the foundation of AI, students and educators can:

Develop critical thinking skills

Use AI tools more responsibly

Recognize the limitations of AI systems

Build a deeper understanding of modern technology

Real-World Example

When a student asks a chatbot a question, the response does not come from "thinking" like a human. Instead, the AI system uses a trained model that has learned patterns from large amounts of data. It follows algorithms to predict the most appropriate answer, using powerful computers and infrastructure to deliver the response quickly.

This process is also influenced by how the question is asked. The words, structure, and clarity of a question—often referred to as a *prompt*—can affect the quality of the response. Learning how to communicate effectively with AI systems is an important skill known as prompt engineering. For further understanding, students and educators may explore *What to Say When You Talk to Yourself: A Guide to Prompt Engineering* by Susie Hala, which explains how carefully structured prompts can guide AI responses more effectively.

Conclusion

The foundation of Artificial Intelligence is built on data, algorithms, models, computing power, and infrastructure. These components work together to create systems that can learn, predict, and assist humans. Understanding this foundation helps students move beyond simply using AI tools and toward truly understanding how artificial intelligence works.

The Foundational Families of Artificial Intelligence

Introduction

Artificial intelligence is often described as a powerful technology, but in reality, it is not a single system. It is a combination of multiple components working together to create intelligent behavior.

To better understand how artificial intelligence works, it is helpful to break it down into organized groups. In the IntelliGloss framework, these groups are called **Foundational Families of Artificial Intelligence**.

Each family represents a key part of how AI systems are built and operate. Some families focus on how information is created and stored. Others focus on how machines learn, make decisions, process language, or perform tasks. Additional families represent the physical hardware, energy systems, and global infrastructure that make artificial intelligence possible.

When these families work together, they form a complete AI system.

This approach allows students and educators to move beyond simply using artificial intelligence tools and begin to understand what is happening behind the scenes. Instead of viewing AI as a mystery, learners can see it as a structured system made up of clearly defined components.

The diagram on the next page provides a visual overview of these families and how they connect to form the foundation of artificial intelligence.

By learning each family step by step, students develop a deeper understanding of how AI systems process information, learn from data, and interact with the world.

Understanding the Foundational Families of Artificial Intelligence is the first step toward true AI literacy.

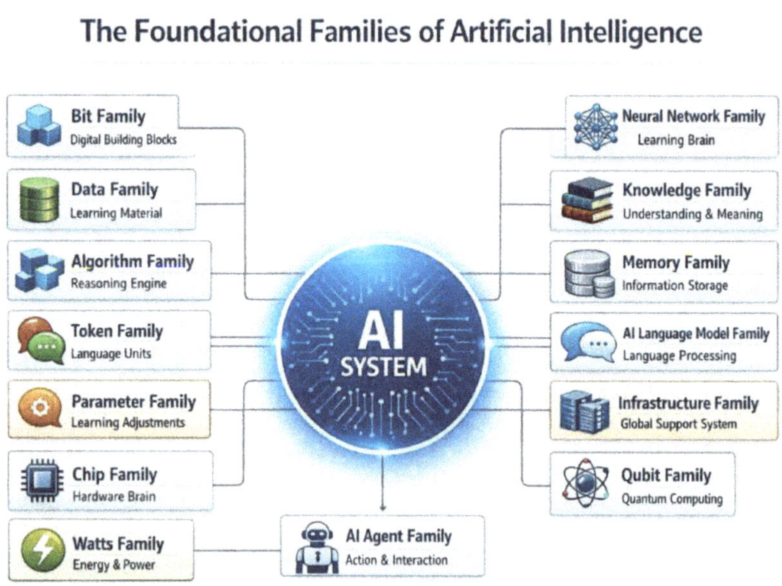

The Foundational Families of Artificial Intelligence

Family	Role	Description
Bit Family	Digital Building Blocks	The smallest unit of digital information (0 or 1). All computing systems begin with bits.
Algorithm Family	Reasoning Engine	Step-by-step instructions that tell computers how to solve problems and process information.
Token Family	Language Units	Pieces of text used by AI models to understand and generate human language.
Parameter Family	Learning Adjustment System	Adjustable numerical values inside AI models that allow them to learn patterns from data.
Data Family	Learning Material	The information AI studies in order to learn patterns, relationships, and knowledge.

Family	Role	Description
Logic Family	Decision Rules	The reasoning structures that allow AI systems to make decisions and evaluate conditions.
Memory Family	Information Storage	Systems that store and retrieve information so AI models can access past knowledge and context.
Knowledge Family	Understanding & Meaning	Structured information that allows AI to represent facts, relationships, and concepts.
Neural Network Family	Learning Brain	Interconnected layers of artificial neurons that enable AI systems to recognize patterns, learn from data, and make predictions.
AI Model Family	Intelligence Engine	The trained system that uses data, parameters, and neural networks to perform tasks such as prediction, classification, and generation.
AI Translator Architecture Family	Language Conversion System	Systems that transform input into output, enabling AI to convert text, speech, or images into meaningful responses.
AI Agent Family	Action and Task Execution System	AI systems designed to perceive information, make decisions, and carry out tasks autonomously or semi-autonomously.
Chip Family	Hardware Brain	Physical processors (GPUs, TPUs, CPUs, NPUs) that perform AI computations.
Watts Family	Energy Power	The electrical power required to run AI hardware and data centers.
AI Energy Family	Energy Source System	The total energy consumed over time to operate AI systems, including training and real-time usage.
Infrastructure Family	Global Support System	Data centers, internet networks, cloud systems, and global infrastructure that allow AI to operate and scale.
Ingredient Family	System Composition	The essential components that come together to create an AI system, including data, algorithms, models, hardware, and energy.
Qubit Family	Quantum Information Units	Quantum bits that can represent multiple states simultaneously, forming the foundation of quantum computing.

The Bit Family

Introduction

The Bit Family represents the starting point of all digital technology. Every computer system, application, and artificial intelligence model is built from bits—the smallest unit of information in computing.

A bit can hold one of two values: 0 or 1. While this may seem simple, these two values form the foundation of everything digital. When bits are combined and organized, they create larger units of data that allow computers to store text, display images, play videos, and run complex systems.

From a single bit to massive data systems, all digital information follows this same structure. This is how computers are able to represent and process the world in a form they can understand.

In artificial intelligence, bits are essential because they store the data that models learn from, process the calculations that drive decision-making, and support the systems that generate responses.

Understanding the Bit Family helps students see how simple binary signals grow into powerful technologies. It reveals that behind every advanced AI system is a foundation built from the most basic building blocks of information.

Bit Family — Visual Understanding of Data Size

How Much Data Can Each Unit Hold? (Simple Examples)

Unit	Size	Photos (Approx.)	Video (Approx. Hours)
Bit	1 bit	N/A	N/A
Byte	8 bits	1 character	N/A
Kilobyte (KB)	~1,000 bytes	Part of a paragraph	N/A
Megabyte (MB)	~1,000 KB	~1 photo	~1 minute of video
Gigabyte (GB)	~1,000 MB	~250 photos	~1–2 hours of video
Terabyte (TB)	~1,000 GB	~250,000 photos	~1,000–2,000 hours of video
Petabyte (PB)	~1,000 TB	~250 million photos	~1–2 million hours of video
Exabyte (EB)	~1,000 PB	~250 billion photos	~1–2 billion hours of video
Zettabyte (ZB)	~1,000 EB	~250 trillion photos	~1–2 trillion hours of video
Yottabyte (YB)	~1,000 ZB	~250 quadrillion photos	~1–2 quadrillion hours of video

---

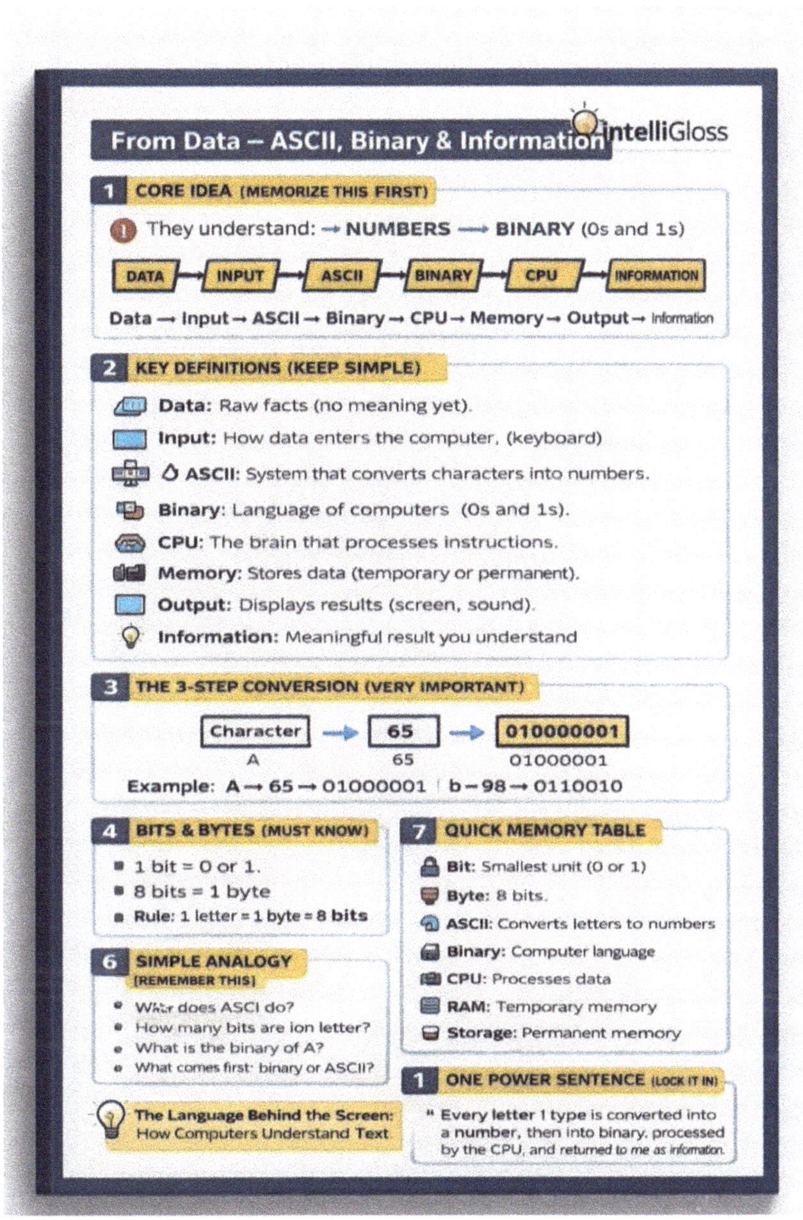

The Algorithm Family

Definition and Overview

The **Algorithm Family** represents the *thinking engine* of artificial intelligence — the set of mathematical instructions that guide how AI analyzes data, learns patterns, and makes decisions.

An **algorithm** is a sequence of steps designed to solve a problem or complete a task. In AI, algorithms tell the system *how to learn*, *how to predict*, and *how to improve* with every iteration.

In simple terms:

The Algorithm Family is the *logic of intelligence* — the invisible code that transforms data into decisions and predictions into progress.

How Algorithms Power AI

Every AI system — from simple chatbots to large-scale deep learning models — relies on algorithms as its foundation.
They determine how the model:

Processes and cleans data,

Identifies relationships between variables,

Learns from feedback, and

Improves over time.

Without algorithms, even the most powerful dataset or neural network would remain static and lifeless.

In essence, **algorithms are the teachers** that train AI how to think.

Why the Algorithm Family Matters

Algorithms are what separate automation from intelligence.
They allow machines to **reason**, **adapt**, and **learn** — not just follow commands.
For prompt engineers, understanding algorithmic behavior helps explain *why* AI sometimes misunderstands a question, repeats patterns, or changes tone after feedback.

Every AI response you receive follows an underlying process — a pattern recognition journey from input to output.

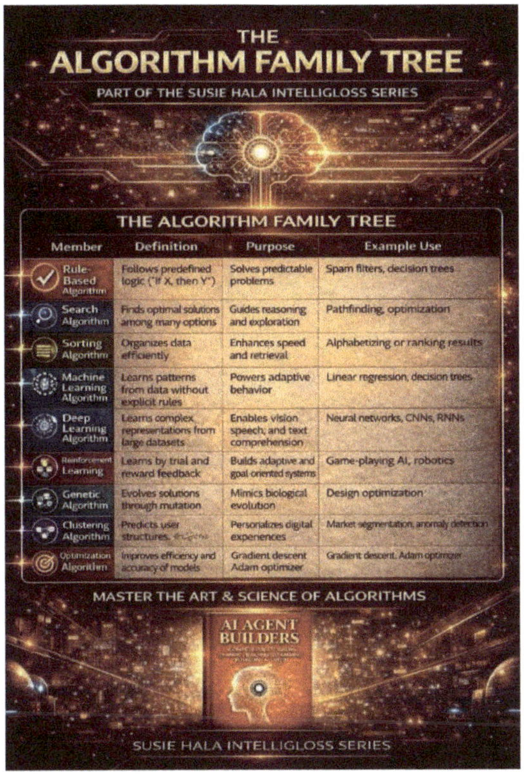

Analogy for Everyday Readers

Imagine AI as a chef in a kitchen:

> The **Data Family** provides the ingredients.
>
> The **Knowledge Family** gives the recipes.
>
> The **Algorithm Family** is the *cooking process* — mixing, heating, tasting, and adjusting until the dish is perfect.

Just as cooking methods determine the quality of food, algorithms determine the quality of intelligence.

Algorithm Efficiency and Energy Use

Not all algorithms are equal.
Some are **fast but shallow**, while others are **deep but energy-intensive**.
Training large AI models requires algorithms that can handle billions of calculations per second — powered by the **Watts Family** (energy) and executed through the **Chip Family** (hardware).

The design of efficient algorithms directly affects sustainability in AI — minimizing power consumption while maximizing accuracy and speed.

Algorithms and Prompt Engineering

For prompt engineers, algorithms explain *how* the AI arrives at its answers.
When a model gives inconsistent or off-topic results, it's often due to:

Misinterpretation of input signals (input encoding),

Bias in training algorithms, or

Overfitting to certain data patterns.

Knowing this helps you craft prompts that guide the AI's decision-making — not just its output.

Quick Takeaway: The Algorithm Family is the reasoning heart of AI.
It transforms information into understanding and enables machines to think, learn, and evolve like digital problem-solvers.

Token Family Introduction

The Token Family represents one of the most important bridges between human language and artificial intelligence. While humans communicate using words, sentences, and meaning, AI systems do not understand language in the same way. Instead, they rely on tokens—small units of text that allow machines to process, analyze, and generate language step by step.

A token can be a word, part of a word, a character, or even punctuation. When a student types a sentence into an AI system, that sentence is not read as a whole idea. It is first broken down into tokens. These tokens become the input that the AI model uses to recognize patterns, predict outcomes, and generate responses.

The Token Family works closely with several other foundational families in artificial intelligence. It connects directly with the Data Family, which provides the text used for training, and the Neural Network Family, which processes token patterns to produce intelligent outputs. It also plays a key role in the AI Translator Architecture Family, where tokens are transformed, analyzed, and reassembled into meaningful responses.

Understanding tokens helps students see what is happening behind the scenes when they interact with AI tools. Instead of viewing AI as a "magic system," they begin to understand that every response is built from sequences of tokens processed through mathematical models.

In simple terms, if language is what humans speak, tokens are what AI understands.

Token Family Breakdown Chart

Component	Role	Description	Example
Tokenization	Input Conversion	The process of breaking text into smaller units (tokens) that AI can process	"Artificial Intelligence" → "Artificial" + "Intelligence"
Tokens	Language Units	The individual pieces of text used by AI models for understanding and generation	"AI", "learn", "ing", "."
Subword Tokens	Efficiency Units	Words split into smaller parts to handle unknown or complex vocabulary	"unbelievable" → "un", "believ", "able"
Character Tokens	Fine-Grained Units	Text broken down into individual characters for detailed processing	"AI" → "A" + "I"
Vocabulary (Token Set)	Token Library	The complete set of tokens an AI model recognizes and uses	GPT models have thousands to millions of tokens
Encoding	Token Mapping	Converting tokens into numerical representations for computation	"AI" → [1234, 5678] (example IDs)
Decoding	Output Reconstruction	Converting numerical outputs back into readable text	[1234, 5678] → "AI system"
Context Window	Memory Limit	The number of tokens an AI can process at one time	Example: 8,000 tokens ≈ several pages of text
Token Embeddings	Meaning Representation	Mathematical vectors that capture relationships between tokens	"king" and "queen" have similar embeddings
Token Prediction	Language Generation	The process of predicting the next token in a sequence	"AI is" → predicts "powerful"

The Token Family reminds us that behind every intelligent response is a structured sequence of tokens working together. What feels like natural conversation to humans is, for AI, a carefully processed stream of language units transformed into meaning.

The AI Ecosystem Family

The AI Ecosystem Family is a connected group of artificial intelligence technologies, systems, behaviors, and applications that work together to help machines perform intelligent tasks. This ecosystem includes core AI systems, AI agents, agentic AI, AI autonomy, autonomous AI workers, and generative AI. Each part plays a different role in how modern AI systems think, learn, create, make decisions, solve problems, and interact with the world.

At the center of the ecosystem is artificial intelligence itself — the broad field focused on building machines and software that can perform tasks that normally require human intelligence. AI agents act as the systems that carry out goals and actions. Agentic AI describes the ability of

AI systems to plan, reason, adapt, and pursue objectives with limited human guidance. AI autonomy represents the level of independence an AI system has while making decisions and taking actions. AI autonomous workers apply these capabilities to perform real-world tasks like digital employees or assistants. Generative AI adds the ability to create new content such as text, images, music, video, code, and designs.

The AI Ecosystem Family demonstrates that modern artificial intelligence is no longer just one single technology. Instead, it is an interconnected environment of systems, tools, intelligence, automation, creativity, and human collaboration. As AI continues to evolve, these technologies are becoming increasingly integrated into education, business, healthcare, communication, cybersecurity, research, and everyday life.

Understanding the AI Ecosystem Family helps students, educators, and readers see how the different parts of AI connect together to shape the future of intelligent systems and the digital world.

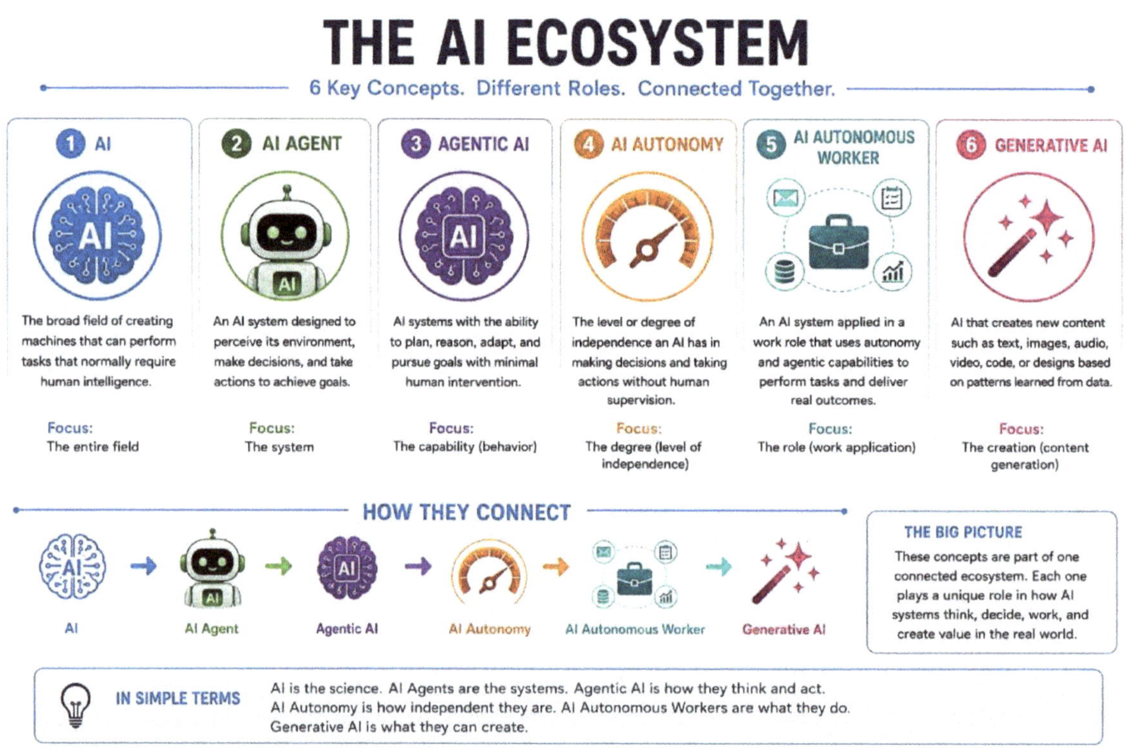

Parameter Family Introduction

The Parameter Family represents the internal learning system of artificial intelligence. While tokens provide the language and data provides the learning material, parameters are what allow AI systems to adjust, improve, and make intelligent decisions over time.

In simple terms, parameters are numerical values inside an AI model that change as the system learns. These values are not visible to users, but they play a critical role in how the model understands patterns, relationships, and meaning. Every time an AI system is trained, it adjusts its parameters to better predict outcomes and generate accurate responses.

Parameters exist throughout neural networks, where they act as the connections between artificial neurons. Each connection has a weight, which determines how important a particular piece of information is. During training, these weights are continuously adjusted based on data, allowing the system to improve its performance.

The Parameter Family works closely with the Data Family, which provides the information needed for learning, and the Neural Network Family, which organizes how parameters are structured and applied. It also supports the Token Family by helping the model interpret and predict sequences of language.

Understanding parameters helps students recognize that AI is not simply programmed with fixed rules. Instead, it learns by adjusting internal values that guide how it processes information. These adjustments are what allow AI systems to evolve from simple pattern recognition to complex reasoning and decision-making.

In essence, if data is what AI learns from, parameters are how AI learns.

Parameter Family Breakdown Chart

Component	Role	Description	Example
Parameters	Learning Values	Numerical values inside an AI model that are adjusted during training	Millions or billions of values inside a model
Weights	Connection Strength	Values that determine how strongly one neuron influences another	A higher weight = stronger influence
Bias	Adjustment Factor	A value added to help the model shift and fine-tune outputs	Helps improve accuracy in predictions
Training Process	Learning Mechanism	The process of adjusting parameters using data to improve performance	Model improves after analyzing many examples
Loss Function	Error Measurement	Measures how far the model's prediction is from the correct answer	Lower loss = better performance

Component	Role	Description	Example
Optimization Algorithm	Adjustment Strategy	Method used to update parameters efficiently	Gradient Descent adjusts weights step by step
Gradient	Direction of Change	Indicates how parameters should change to reduce error	Shows whether to increase or decrease a value
Backpropagation	Learning Process	System that sends error signals backward to update parameters	Adjusts earlier layers based on output error
Hyperparameters	Control Settings	External settings that guide how training happens (not learned)	Learning rate, batch size
Model Size	Capacity Indicator	The total number of parameters in a model	Larger models = more learning capacity

The Parameter Family is the hidden engine of learning in artificial intelligence. While users interact with outputs, it is the continuous adjustment of parameters behind the scenes that makes intelligent behavior possible.

Data Family Introduction

The Data Family represents the foundation of learning in artificial intelligence. Every AI system depends on data to develop knowledge, recognize patterns, and make decisions. Without data, artificial intelligence cannot learn, adapt, or function effectively.

Data can take many forms, including text, images, audio, video, and numerical information. These inputs provide the raw material that AI systems analyze during training. By studying large amounts of data, AI models begin to identify patterns, relationships, and structures that allow them to make predictions and generate responses.

The quality and diversity of data play a critical role in how well an AI system performs. Accurate, balanced, and relevant data helps models produce reliable results, while poor or biased data can lead to incorrect or unfair outcomes. This is why data collection, preparation, and evaluation are essential steps in the development of responsible AI systems.

The Data Family works closely with the Parameter Family, which adjusts internal values based on data, and the Neural Network Family, which processes and organizes data through layers of computation. It also supports the Token Family when dealing with language, as text data is converted into tokens for analysis.

Understanding the Data Family helps students recognize that AI does not "know" things on its own. Instead, it learns from the information it is given. The more meaningful and well-prepared the data, the more capable the AI system becomes.

In simple terms, data is the source of knowledge, and it is the starting point for all artificial intelligence.

Data Family Breakdown Chart

Component	Role	Description	Example
Data	Learning Material	Raw information used by AI systems to learn patterns and relationships	Text, images, audio, numbers
Dataset	Organized Collection	A structured group of data used for training and evaluation	A folder of labeled images
Training Data	Learning Input	Data used to teach the AI model during training	Thousands of sentences for a language model
Validation Data	Performance Check	Data used to tune the model during training without directly learning from it	Helps prevent overfitting
Test Data	Final Evaluation	Data used to measure how well the model performs after training	New unseen examples
Structured Data	Organized Format	Data arranged in tables with clear categories	Spreadsheets, databases
Unstructured Data	Flexible Format	Data without a predefined structure	Text documents, images, videos
Labeled Data	Guided Learning	Data tagged with correct answers to guide training	Image labeled “cat” or “dog”
Unlabeled Data	Self-Learning Input	Data without labels, used in unsupervised learning	Raw text without categories
Data Quality	Accuracy Measure	The reliability and correctness of data	Clean, complete, and consistent data
Data Bias	Imbalance Issue	When data does not represent all groups fairly	Skewed or incomplete datasets
Data Preprocessing	Preparation Step	Cleaning and organizing data before training	Removing errors, formatting text

The Data Family reminds us that artificial intelligence is only as strong as the information it learns from. High-quality data leads to meaningful insights, while poor data can limit or misguide intelligent systems.

Memory Family Introduction

The Memory Family represents how artificial intelligence systems store, retain, and retrieve information. Just as humans rely on memory to recall past experiences, learn new concepts, and make decisions, AI systems depend on memory to access previously processed information and maintain context.

In artificial intelligence, memory is not a single component but a collection of mechanisms that allow systems to handle information over time. Some forms of memory are short-term, holding information temporarily while a task is being completed. Other forms are long-term, storing learned knowledge that can be used across different tasks and interactions.

Memory plays a critical role in enabling AI systems to understand sequences, maintain context in conversations, and improve decision-making. For example, when a user interacts with a language model, the system uses memory to keep track of previous words, sentences, or prompts in order to generate coherent and relevant responses.

The Memory Family works closely with the Data Family, which provides the information to be stored, and the Parameter Family, which encodes learned knowledge within the model. It also supports the Neural Network Family by enabling systems to process sequences and retain important patterns over time.

Understanding the Memory Family helps students see that AI is not simply reacting to individual inputs in isolation. Instead, it relies on stored information and contextual awareness to produce meaningful and consistent outputs.

In simple terms, if data is what AI learns from, memory is how AI remembers and uses what it has learned.

Memory Family Breakdown Chart

Component	Role	Description	Example
Memory	Information Storage	The ability of an AI system to store and access information	Retaining previous inputs in a task
Short-Term Memory	Temporary Storage	Holds information for immediate processing	Keeping track of words in a sentence
Long-Term Memory	Persistent Storage	Stores learned knowledge for future use	Knowledge embedded in model parameters
Context Memory	Conversation Tracking	Maintains information within a specific interaction	Remembering earlier parts of a prompt
Working Memory	Active Processing	Handles information currently being used in computation	Processing a sequence step by step
External Memory	Extended Storage	Memory stored outside the model for retrieval	Databases, vector stores
Internal Memory	Embedded Knowledge	Information stored within the model itself	Learned patterns inside neural networks
Sequence Memory	Order Awareness	Tracks the order of inputs over time	Understanding sentence structure

Component	Role	Description	Example
Retrieval Mechanism	Access System	Retrieves stored information when needed	Searching relevant past data
Attention Mechanism	Focus System	Highlights important parts of memory for processing	Focusing on key words in a sentence
Memory Capacity	Storage Limit	The amount of information the system can handle at once	Context window size

The Memory Family shows that intelligence is not just about processing information in the moment, but about retaining, organizing, and using knowledge over time to create meaningful understanding.

Knowledge Family Introduction

The Knowledge Family represents how artificial intelligence organizes, connects, and uses information to create understanding. While data provides raw information and memory stores it, knowledge is what gives that information meaning and structure.

In artificial intelligence, knowledge is not simply a collection of facts. It is the result of identifying relationships, patterns, and connections within data. AI systems use knowledge to recognize concepts, make decisions, and generate meaningful responses. This allows machines to move beyond simple data processing and toward more intelligent behavior.

Knowledge can be represented in different ways within AI systems. Some forms are structured, such as databases and knowledge graphs, where relationships between concepts are clearly defined. Other forms are learned implicitly through neural networks, where patterns are encoded within parameters and used to guide predictions.

The Knowledge Family works closely with the Data Family, which provides the information needed to build knowledge, and the Memory Family, which stores and retrieves that information. It also connects with the Parameter Family, where learned knowledge is embedded within the model, and the Neural Network Family, which processes and organizes that knowledge.

Understanding the Knowledge Family helps students recognize that AI systems do not simply memorize information. Instead, they learn how pieces of information relate to one another, allowing them to interpret meaning, solve problems, and respond intelligently.

In simple terms, if data is information and memory stores it, knowledge is the understanding that makes it useful.

Knowledge Family Breakdown Chart

Component	Role	Description	Example
Knowledge	Understanding System	Organized information that allows AI to interpret meaning and make decisions	Recognizing relationships between concepts
Facts	Basic Information	Individual pieces of information stored within a system	“Water freezes at 0°C”
Relationships	Connection Mapping	Links between pieces of information that create meaning	“Teacher teaches student”
Knowledge Representation	Structure System	Methods used to organize and store knowledge in AI	Knowledge graphs, semantic networks
Knowledge Graph	Network Mapping	A structured representation of entities and their relationships	Google Knowledge Graph
Semantic Understanding	Meaning Interpretation	The ability to understand meaning behind words and data	Understanding synonyms and context
Inference	Reasoning Process	Drawing conclusions based on known information	If A = B and B = C, then A = C
Rules	Decision Framework	Logical guidelines used to make decisions	If temperature < 0°C → freeze
Ontology	Concept Framework	A structured system defining categories and relationships	Classification of animals
Explicit Knowledge	Direct Information	Clearly defined and stored knowledge	Rules, databases
Implicit Knowledge	Learned Patterns	Knowledge learned through experience and data	Patterns learned by neural networks
Knowledge Integration	System Coordination	Combining information from multiple sources	Merging text, images, and data

The Knowledge Family transforms information into understanding, allowing artificial intelligence to move beyond data and memory into meaningful reasoning and intelligent decision-making.

AI Model Family Introduction

The AI Model Family represents the core system within artificial intelligence that performs tasks such as prediction, classification, and content generation. It is the part of AI that users interact with, whether they are asking questions, generating images, or analyzing data.

An AI model is a trained system that has learned patterns from data. During training, the model processes large amounts of information and adjusts its internal parameters to improve accuracy. Once trained, the model can take new input and produce meaningful output based on what it has learned.

AI models can take many forms depending on their purpose. Some models are designed to recognize images, others to understand language, and others to make decisions or predictions. Large Language Models (LLMs), for example, are designed to process and generate human language by predicting sequences of tokens.

The AI Model Family works closely with the Data Family, which provides the learning material, and the Parameter Family, which stores learned patterns. It also relies on the Neural Network Family for structure and the Chip and Infrastructure Families for execution and deployment.

Understanding the AI Model Family helps students see that AI is not just a concept, but a working system that has been trained to perform specific tasks. It is the engine that transforms input into output.

In simple terms, if AI is the system, the model is the part that actually does the thinking and producing.

AI Model Family Breakdown Chart

Component	Role	Description	Example
AI Model	Core System	The trained system that performs tasks	Chatbot, image generator
Training	Learning Process	Process of teaching the model using data	Learning from datasets
Inference	Output Generation	Using the trained model to produce results	Answering a question
Model Architecture	Structural Design	Defines how the model is built	Neural networks, transformers
Parameters	Learned Values	Internal values adjusted during training	Billions of weights
Input Data	Entry Information	Data provided to the model for processing	User prompt
Output Data	Result	The response or prediction generated	AI-generated text
Model Types	Functional Categories	Different kinds of models for different tasks	Classification, generation
Fine-Tuning	Model Adjustment	Improving a model for specific tasks	Custom-trained AI
Pretrained Model	Base System	A model trained on large datasets before use	General-purpose AI
Evaluation	Performance Check	Measuring how well the model performs	Accuracy, loss metrics

The AI Model Family represents the working core of artificial intelligence, where learned patterns are transformed into meaningful actions, predictions, and responses.

Neural Network Family Introduction

The Neural Network Family represents the structural foundation of how artificial intelligence learns and processes information. Inspired by the human brain, neural networks are systems of interconnected units, often called neurons, that work together to analyze data, recognize patterns, and make decisions.

In artificial intelligence, a neural network is made up of layers. The input layer receives data, the hidden layers process that data, and the output layer produces a result. As information flows through these layers, the network applies mathematical transformations that allow it to detect patterns and relationships within the data.

Neural networks rely heavily on the Parameter Family, where weights and biases determine how strongly information flows between neurons. During training, these parameters are adjusted to improve the network's performance. The more the network learns, the better it becomes at recognizing patterns and making accurate predictions.

The Neural Network Family works closely with the Data Family, which provides the information needed for learning, and the Memory and Knowledge Families, which help store and organize learned information. It also supports the Token Family when processing language, allowing AI systems to interpret sequences of tokens in meaningful ways.

Understanding neural networks helps students see that AI is not simply following instructions. Instead, it is learning from examples and improving over time through layered processing and pattern recognition.

In simple terms, neural networks are the systems that allow AI to think, learn, and make sense of information.

Neural Network Family Breakdown Chart

Component	Role	Description	Example
Neural Network	Learning Structure	A system of interconnected neurons that processes data and learns patterns	Image recognition system
Neuron (Node)	Processing Unit	A basic unit that receives input, processes it, and passes output forward	A single calculation point

Component	Role	Description	Example
Input Layer	Data Entry Point	The first layer that receives raw data	Pixels of an image
Hidden Layers	Processing Layers	Intermediate layers that transform data and detect patterns	Feature detection layers
Output Layer	Result Generator	The final layer that produces predictions or decisions	"Cat" vs "Dog" classification
Weights	Signal Strength	Values that determine how strongly inputs influence outputs	Higher weight = stronger impact
Bias	Adjustment Value	Helps shift outputs to improve learning accuracy	Fine-tuning predictions
Activation Function	Decision Function	Determines whether a neuron should activate based on input	ReLU, Sigmoid
Forward Propagation	Data Flow	The process of passing input data through the network to produce output	Input → Hidden → Output
Backpropagation	Learning Process	Adjusts weights and biases based on error to improve performance	Correcting mistakes
Loss Function	Error Measurement	Calculates how far the output is from the correct answer	Prediction vs actual
Deep Neural Network	Advanced Structure	A network with many hidden layers for complex learning	Deep learning models

The Neural Network Family provides the structure that allows artificial intelligence to transform data into understanding, making it possible for machines to learn from experience and improve over time.

Dual Language System in Artificial Intelligence

Definition

The Dual Language System in Artificial Intelligence refers to the way AI communicates using two different forms of language at the same time: human language for interaction and machine language for internal processing.

Key Components

Human Language (Natural Language)
This is the language people use to communicate with AI, such as English, Spanish, Tongan, or Fijian. It includes words, sentences, and questions that users type or speak.

Machine Language (Numerical Representation)
This is how AI understands information internally. Words are converted into numbers called tokens and processed using mathematical models and algorithms.

How It Works (Step-by-Step)

A user enters a question in human language

The AI converts the words into numerical tokens

The AI processes the tokens using a neural network

The AI generates a response based on patterns and probabilities

The response is converted back into human language

Example

User Input:
"What is Artificial Intelligence?"

AI Process:

Converts words into numbers

Analyzes patterns from training data

Predicts the best possible answer

Output:
"Artificial Intelligence is the ability of machines to perform tasks that normally require human intelligence."

Why This Matters

Understanding the dual language system helps students realize that:

AI does not "think" like humans

AI translates language into math and back into language

Every interaction with AI is based on patterns, not emotions or understanding

Applications

Chatbots and virtual assistants

Language translation systems

Search engines

Voice recognition tools

Challenges

Misinterpretation of human language

Bias in language data

Lack of true understanding or reasoning

Summary

Artificial Intelligence works by translating human language into machine-readable data and then converting the results back into human language. This dual system allows AI to interact with people while operating through mathematical processes behind the scenes.

AI Translator Architecture Family Introduction

The AI Translator Architecture Family represents the system that transforms input into meaningful output in artificial intelligence. It acts as the bridge between what humans provide and what AI produces. Whether a user types a question, uploads an image, or speaks a command, this architecture is responsible for interpreting that input and generating a response.

In artificial intelligence, translation does not only mean converting one language to another. It refers to the broader process of transforming one form of information into another. For example, text can be translated into a response, speech can be converted into text, and images can be interpreted into descriptions. This transformation process is at the core of how modern AI systems function.

The AI Translator Architecture is built on multiple foundational families. It relies on the Token Family to break input into manageable units, the Neural Network Family to process patterns, and the Parameter Family to guide learning. It also uses knowledge and memory to maintain context and produce coherent results.

At the center of this architecture is the ability to encode and decode information. Encoding transforms input into a format the model can understand, while decoding converts processed information back into human-readable output. This continuous transformation allows AI systems to interact with users in a natural and meaningful way.

Understanding the AI Translator Architecture Family helps students see that AI is not simply responding randomly. Instead, it is systematically translating input into output through structured processes and learned patterns.

In simple terms, if tokens are the language pieces and neural networks are the brain, the AI Translator Architecture is the system that turns understanding into communication.

AI Translator Architecture Family Breakdown Chart

Component	Role	Description	Example
AI Translator Architecture	Transformation System	Converts input into meaningful output	Question → Answer
Input Processing	Data Intake	Receives and prepares user input for analysis	Text prompt entered by a user
Encoding	Input Conversion	Transforms input into numerical representations	Words → token IDs
Context Building	Meaning Formation	Organizes input into a structured understanding	Sentence context tracking
Sequence Processing	Order Handling	Maintains the correct order of information	Word sequence in a sentence
Attention Mechanism	Focus System	Identifies important parts of input data	Highlighting key words
Representation Layer	Feature Mapping	Converts data into internal representations for processing	Embeddings
Decoding	Output Generation	Converts processed data back into human-readable form	Token IDs → words
Output Generation	Response Creation	Produces the final answer or result	AI-generated response
Multimodal Translation	Cross-Format Processing	Translates between different types of data	Image → text description
Feedback Loop	Improvement Cycle	Uses results to refine future outputs	Model learning over time

The AI Translator Architecture Family shows that artificial intelligence is not just about understanding information, but about transforming it into meaningful communication that humans can use and interact with.

AI Architecture Family Introduction

The AI Architecture Family represents the overall design and structure of an artificial intelligence system. While individual families such as Data, Parameters, and Neural Networks explain how AI learns and processes information, the AI Architecture Family shows how all these components are organized and work together as a complete system.

In artificial intelligence, architecture refers to the blueprint that defines how data flows through a system, how components interact, and how decisions are produced. It determines how input is received, how it is processed, and how output is generated. A well-designed architecture allows AI systems to operate efficiently, scale to large problems, and produce reliable results.

AI architectures can vary depending on the type of system being built. Some are designed for image recognition, others for language processing, and others for decision-making or automation. Despite these differences, most architectures share common elements such as input layers, processing layers, memory components, and output mechanisms.

The AI Architecture Family connects all foundational families. It integrates the Data Family for input, the Token Family for language processing, the Neural Network Family for computation, the Parameter Family for learning, and the Memory and Knowledge Families for storing and organizing information. It also works closely with the AI Translator Architecture Family to transform input into meaningful output.

Understanding the AI Architecture Family helps students see the "big picture" of artificial intelligence. Instead of viewing AI as separate parts, they begin to understand it as a coordinated system where each component plays a specific role.

In simple terms, if individual families are the parts of AI, the AI Architecture Family is the blueprint that brings everything together into one working system.

AI Architecture Family Breakdown Chart

Component	Role	Description	Example
AI Architecture	System Blueprint	The overall design that defines how an AI system is structured and operates	ChatGPT system design
Input Layer	Data Entry Point	Receives raw input from users or external sources	Text prompt, image upload
Preprocessing Layer	Data Preparation	Cleans and organizes input data before processing	Tokenization, normalization
Processing Core	Computation Engine	The main system where data is analyzed and transformed	Neural networks, transformers
Parameter System	Learning Core	Stores adjustable values that guide learning and predictions	Model weights and biases

Component	Role	Description	Example
Memory System	Context Storage	Maintains and retrieves information during processing	Context window, external memory
Knowledge System	Understanding Layer	Organizes relationships and meaning within the system	Knowledge graphs, learned patterns
Decision Layer	Output Logic	Determines the final output based on processed data	Selecting the best response
Output Layer	Result Delivery	Presents results to the user in a usable format	Text, image, or audio response
Feedback Loop	Improvement System	Uses outcomes to refine future performance	Model updates and retraining
Scalability System	Expansion Capability	Allows the system to handle increasing data and complexity	Cloud-based AI systems
Integration Layer	System Connection	Connects AI with external tools and platforms	APIs, databases, applications

The AI Architecture Family reveals that artificial intelligence is not a single technology, but a coordinated system of interconnected components working together to transform data into intelligent outcomes.

Chip Family Introduction

The Chip Family represents the physical hardware that powers artificial intelligence systems. While software components such as data, algorithms, and neural networks define how AI works, none of these systems can function without the computing chips that perform the actual calculations.

Chips are specialized electronic components designed to process information at extremely high speeds. In artificial intelligence, these chips handle the complex mathematical operations required for training models and generating outputs. Every prediction, calculation, and response produced by an AI system is executed by hardware within the Chip Family.

Different types of chips are used depending on the needs of the system. Central Processing Units (CPUs) handle general-purpose tasks, while Graphics Processing Units (GPUs) are optimized for parallel processing, making them ideal for training neural networks. More specialized chips, such as Tensor Processing Units (TPUs) and Neural Processing Units (NPUs), are designed specifically for AI workloads, enabling faster and more efficient computation.

The Chip Family works closely with the Neural Network Family, which defines the structure of computation, and the Parameter Family, which stores the values being processed. It also connects to the Infrastructure Family, where large-scale systems of chips are organized in data centers and cloud environments.

Understanding the Chip Family helps students recognize that artificial intelligence is not purely abstract. It depends on physical machines that require power, resources, and engineering to operate. These chips are the engines that bring AI models to life.

In simple terms, if AI is the intelligence, chips are the machines that make that intelligence possible.

Chip Family Breakdown Chart

Component	Role	Description	Example
Chip (Processor)	Computation Engine	Electronic hardware that performs calculations required for AI	CPU, GPU
CPU (Central Processing Unit)	General Processor	Handles a wide range of computing tasks	Running basic applications
GPU (Graphics Processing Unit)	Parallel Processor	Processes many calculations at once, ideal for AI training	Training neural networks
TPU (Tensor Processing Unit)	AI Accelerator	Specialized chip designed for machine learning tasks	Google TPU
NPU (Neural Processing Unit)	Edge AI Processor	Optimized for running AI on devices like phones	Smartphone AI features
AI Accelerator	Performance Booster	Hardware designed to speed up AI computations	Dedicated AI chips
Memory (Hardware)	Data Storage	Stores data and instructions for processing	RAM, VRAM
Parallel Processing	Speed Mechanism	Ability to perform multiple calculations simultaneously	GPUs processing thousands of operations
Throughput	Processing Capacity	Amount of data processed over time	High-performance computing systems
Latency	Response Time	Time it takes to process a request	Faster chips = lower latency
Power Consumption	Energy Usage	Amount of energy required to run the chip	High-performance GPUs use more power
Edge Devices	Local Processing	Devices that run AI locally without cloud support	Phones, smart cameras

The Chip Family reminds us that behind every intelligent system is powerful hardware performing millions or billions of calculations, turning abstract models into real-world functionality.

Watts Family Introduction

The Watts Family represents the measurement of power used by artificial intelligence systems. While the Chip Family provides the hardware that performs computations, the Watts Family explains how much energy those systems consume while operating.

A watt is a unit of power that measures the rate at which energy is used. In artificial intelligence, watts help us understand how much electricity is required to run processors, train models, and generate responses. Every time an AI system processes data, performs calculations, or produces output, it consumes power.

Different AI systems require different levels of power depending on their size and complexity. Small systems, such as those running on mobile devices, use relatively low amounts of power. In contrast, large-scale AI models operating in data centers can require significant amounts of electricity, especially during training, where billions of calculations are performed continuously.

The Watts Family works closely with the Chip Family, which determines how efficiently computations are performed, and the Infrastructure Family, where large networks of machines operate together. It also connects to the overall design of AI systems, as more efficient models can reduce power consumption while maintaining performance.

Understanding the Watts Family helps students recognize that artificial intelligence is not only about intelligence and computation, but also about energy use and resource management. As AI continues to grow, managing power efficiently becomes an important part of building responsible and sustainable systems.

In simple terms, if chips perform the work, watts measure how much power it takes to do that work.

Watts Family Breakdown Chart

Component	Role	Description	Example
Watt (W)	Power Measurement	Unit that measures the rate of energy use	A device using 100 watts
Power Consumption	Energy Usage Rate	Amount of power used during operation	AI model running on GPUs
Energy Efficiency	Performance Balance	How effectively a system uses power to perform tasks	More output with less power
High-Performance Computing	Intensive Power Use	Systems that require large amounts of power for complex tasks	AI training clusters

Component	Role	Description	Example
Idle Power	Standby Usage	Power consumed when systems are not actively processing	Servers waiting for requests
Peak Power	Maximum Usage	Highest level of power used during heavy workloads	Training large AI models
Thermal Output	Heat Generation	Heat produced as a result of power usage	Cooling systems in data centers
Cooling Systems	Temperature Control	Systems used to manage heat from high power usage	Air or liquid cooling
Power Supply	Energy Source	Provides electricity to AI systems	Electrical grid, batteries
Edge Power Usage	Local Energy Use	Power consumption on smaller devices	Smartphones, IoT devices
Data Center Power	Large-Scale Usage	Power required for large AI operations	Server farms running AI models
Sustainable Energy	Efficiency Goal	Use of renewable energy to reduce environmental impact	Solar-powered data centers

The Watts Family highlights that intelligence comes with a cost—every AI system requires power, and understanding that power is essential for building efficient and sustainable technologies.

Watts Family (AI Power Usage Scale)

Definition

The **Watts Family** represents the real-time power usage of artificial intelligence systems, measured in watts (W). It shows how much power AI systems consume at a given moment as they process data and perform computations.

Watts Scale

1 Watt
10 Watts
100 Watts
500 Watts
1,000 Watts (1 Kilowatt)
10,000 Watts (10 Kilowatts)
100,000 Watts (100 Kilowatts)
1,000,000 Watts (1 Megawatt)
10,000,000 Watts (10 Megawatts)
100,000,000+ Watts (100+ Megawatts)

Key Characteristics

Measured in real-world electrical power

Higher watt values indicate higher processing demand

Used to represent the scale of AI systems from small devices to large infrastructures

Closely connected to the Chip Family, Energy Family, and Infrastructure Family

Examples

Low watts → small devices and basic AI functions

Medium watts → computers and advanced applications

High watts → data centers and large AI systems

Summary

The **Watts Family** provides a numerical representation of how much power artificial intelligence systems use in real time, helping to illustrate the scale and intensity of AI operations.

Student Insight

Watts show how much power AI is using right now.

AI Energy Family Introduction

The AI Energy Family represents the total amount of energy consumed by artificial intelligence systems over time. While the Watts Family measures the rate at which power is used at any given moment, the Energy Family focuses on the accumulated energy required to perform tasks, run systems, and sustain operations.

In artificial intelligence, energy is used every time a model is trained, a system processes data, or a response is generated. Large-scale AI systems, especially those operating in data centers, can consume significant amounts of energy due to the continuous processing of massive datasets and complex computations.

Energy is typically measured over time using units such as kilowatt-hours (kWh), which reflect how much power has been used during a specific period. For example, running a high-performance AI system for several hours or days results in a total energy cost that goes beyond the moment-to-moment power usage measured in watts.

The AI Energy Family works closely with the Watts Family, which provides the rate of power consumption, and the Chip Family, which determines how efficiently computations are performed. It also connects to the Infrastructure Family, where large-scale systems operate continuously and require long-term energy management.

Understanding the AI Energy Family helps students recognize that artificial intelligence has real-world resource implications. It is not only about performance and speed, but also about sustainability, efficiency, and responsible use of technology.

In simple terms, if watts measure how fast energy is used, energy measures how much is used over time.

AI Energy Family Breakdown Chart

Component	Role	Description	Example
Energy	Total Consumption	The total amount of power used over a period of time	Running an AI system for hours or days
Kilowatt-hour (kWh)	Energy Measurement	Unit used to measure energy consumption over time	1 kWh = using 1,000 watts for 1 hour
Energy Usage	Consumption Tracking	Total energy required for AI operations	Training a large model
Training Energy	Learning Cost	Energy used during model training processes	Weeks of GPU usage
Inference Energy	Response Cost	Energy used when AI generates outputs	Answering a user prompt
Energy Efficiency	Optimization Goal	Reducing energy use while maintaining performance	Efficient AI models
Energy Scaling	Growth Impact	Increase in energy use as systems grow larger	Bigger models = more energy
Data Center Energy	Infrastructure Demand	Total energy used by large AI facilities	Server farms operating 24/7
Cooling Energy	Temperature Control	Energy required to cool systems and prevent overheating	Air conditioning in data centers
Renewable Energy	Sustainability Source	Use of clean energy to power AI systems	Solar, wind-powered data centers
Carbon Impact	Environmental Effect	Emissions associated with energy consumption	AI training carbon footprint
Energy Management	Resource Control	Strategies to monitor and reduce energy use	Efficient scheduling, hardware optimization

The AI Energy Family reminds us that artificial intelligence operates within the physical world, where every computation consumes energy and every system has an impact on resources and sustainability.

Energy Family (Total Power Consumption of Artificial Intelligence)

Definition

The **Energy Family** represents the total amount of electricity used by artificial intelligence systems over time. It is measured in watt-hours (Wh) or kilowatt-hours (kWh) and shows how much energy AI systems consume while running.

Energy Scale

1 Watt-hour (Wh)
10 Watt-hours (Wh)
100 Watt-hours (Wh)
500 Watt-hours (Wh)
1,000 Watt-hours (1 Kilowatt-hour, kWh)
10,000 Watt-hours (10 kWh)
100,000 Watt-hours (100 kWh)
1,000,000 Watt-hours (1 Megawatt-hour, MWh)
10,000,000 Watt-hours (10 MWh)
100,000,000+ Watt-hours (100+ MWh)

Key Characteristics

Measured over time (not instant like watts)

Represents total electricity consumption

Increases the longer AI systems run

Directly related to cost and energy usage

Closely connected to Watts Family, Chip Family, and Infrastructure Family

Examples

Low energy → short AI tasks or small devices

Medium energy → daily AI usage on computers

High energy → training AI models and running data centers

Summary

The **Energy Family** provides a numerical representation of the total electricity consumed by artificial intelligence systems over time, helping to illustrate the overall cost and impact of AI operations.

Student Insight

Energy shows how much total power AI has used over time.

AI Infrastructure Family Introduction

The AI Infrastructure Family represents the large-scale systems and environments that support, power, and connect artificial intelligence technologies. While individual components such as chips, data, and models explain how AI works, infrastructure explains where and how these systems operate in the real world.

AI infrastructure includes data centers, cloud platforms, networking systems, and storage environments that allow artificial intelligence to function at scale. These systems provide the computing power, data access, and connectivity needed to train models, process information, and deliver results to users around the world.

Modern AI systems rely heavily on cloud-based infrastructure, where thousands of machines work together to handle massive workloads. This allows AI to scale efficiently, making it possible to process large datasets, run complex models, and serve millions of users simultaneously. Infrastructure also ensures reliability, security, and continuous availability of AI services.

The AI Infrastructure Family works closely with the Chip Family, which provides the hardware, the Watts and Energy Families, which manage power consumption, and the Data Family, which supplies the information being processed. It also supports the AI Architecture Family by providing the environment where all system components are deployed and connected.

Understanding the AI Infrastructure Family helps students recognize that artificial intelligence is not contained within a single device. Instead, it operates across global systems that require coordination, resources, and engineering to function effectively.

In simple terms, if AI is the system and chips are the engines, infrastructure is the environment that allows everything to run at scale.

AI Infrastructure Family Breakdown Chart

Component	Role	Description	Example
AI Infrastructure	System Environment	The physical and digital systems that support AI operations	Global AI platforms
Data Center	Processing Hub	Facilities that house servers and computing equipment	Large server farms
Cloud Computing	Scalable Platform	Remote systems that provide computing resources over the internet	AWS, Azure, Google Cloud
Servers	Compute Units	Machines that process data and run AI models	Rack-mounted servers
Networking	Connectivity System	Systems that allow communication between machines	Internet, fiber networks
Storage Systems	Data Management	Systems that store large volumes of data	Databases, cloud storage
Distributed Computing	Workload Sharing	Splitting tasks across multiple machines for efficiency	Parallel processing across clusters
Edge Infrastructure	Local Processing	Running AI closer to the user or device	Smart devices, IoT systems
Load Balancing	Traffic Control	Distributes workloads to prevent overload	Managing user requests
Security Systems	Protection Layer	Safeguards data and systems from threats	Encryption, firewalls
Redundancy	Reliability System	Backup systems to ensure continuous operation	Failover servers
Scalability	Growth Capability	Ability to expand resources as demand increases	Adding more servers dynamically

The AI Infrastructure Family reveals that artificial intelligence operates on a global scale, relying on interconnected systems that provide the power, storage, and connectivity needed to support intelligent technologies.

AI Agent Family Introduction

The AI Agent Family represents systems that can take action, make decisions, and perform tasks on behalf of users or other systems. Unlike traditional AI models that only respond to input, AI agents are designed to operate with a level of autonomy, allowing them to plan, execute, and adapt to achieve specific goals.

An AI agent receives input from its environment, processes that information, and takes actions based on predefined objectives or learned behaviors. These actions can include answering questions, automating workflows, retrieving information, or interacting with other systems. Some agents operate in simple environments, while others function in complex systems that require continuous decision-making.

AI agents often combine multiple foundational families. They use the Data Family to gather information, the Memory and Knowledge Families to retain and understand context, and the Neural Network and Parameter Families to process and learn from interactions. They also rely on the AI Architecture and Infrastructure Families to operate reliably at scale.

Modern AI agents can work independently or as part of larger systems. For example, a customer support agent can respond to inquiries automatically, while a more advanced agent can complete multi-step tasks such as scheduling, research, or system management.

Understanding the AI Agent Family helps students see that artificial intelligence is not only about generating responses, but also about taking meaningful action in real-world scenarios.

In simple terms, if AI models think and respond, AI agents act and execute.

AI Agent Family Breakdown Chart

Component	Role	Description	Example
AI Agent	Action System	An AI system that can make decisions and perform tasks	Virtual assistant
Environment	Operating Context	The space where the agent interacts and gathers information	Web, apps, databases
Input Perception	Data Intake	Receives information from the environment	User query or sensor input
Decision Engine	Action Selection	Determines what action to take based on input	Choosing a response or task
Action Execution	Task Performance	Carries out decisions in the environment	Sending an email, retrieving data
Goal System	Objective Setting	Defines what the agent is trying to achieve	Complete a task or solve a problem
Planning Module	Strategy Builder	Breaks down tasks into steps	Multi-step problem solving
Feedback Loop	Learning Cycle	Improves performance based on outcomes	Adjusting actions over time
Autonomy Level	Independence Scale	Degree of independence in decision-making	Fully automated vs assisted

Component	Role	Description	Example
Multi-Agent System	Collaboration Network	Multiple agents working together	Coordinated AI systems

Ingredient Family Introduction

The Ingredient Family represents the essential components that come together to create an artificial intelligence system. Just as a recipe requires specific ingredients to produce a final dish, AI systems rely on a combination of foundational elements working together to function effectively.

Artificial intelligence is not built from a single component. It requires data to learn from, algorithms to guide processing, models to perform tasks, hardware to execute computations, and energy to power the entire system. Each of these elements plays a critical role, and the absence of any one component would prevent the system from operating properly.

The Ingredient Family provides a simplified way for students to understand AI as a system made up of interconnected parts. Instead of viewing AI as complex or mysterious, learners can begin to see it as something constructed from identifiable and understandable components.

This family connects directly with all other foundational families, including Data, Algorithm, Neural Network, Parameter, Chip, and Energy Families. It serves as an overview that brings these elements together into a unified perspective.

Understanding the Ingredient Family helps students recognize that artificial intelligence is built, not magical. It is the result of carefully combining the right components in the right way.

In simple terms, if AI is the final product, the Ingredient Family represents everything needed to build it.

Ingredient Family Breakdown Chart

Component	Role	Description	Example
Data	Learning Input	Provides the information AI uses to learn patterns	Text, images, audio
Algorithms	Instruction Set	Guides how data is processed and decisions are made	Sorting, classification
AI Models	Execution System	Performs tasks such as prediction or generation	Language models
Neural Networks	Processing Structure	Organizes how data is processed through layers	Deep learning models
Parameters	Learning Adjustments	Fine-tune how the model learns and makes predictions	Weights and biases

Component	Role	Description	Example
Tokens	Language Units	Breaks text into smaller pieces for processing	Words or subwords
Hardware (Chips)	Computation Engine	Executes calculations required by AI systems	GPUs, CPUs
Energy	Power Source	Supplies the energy needed to run systems	Electricity usage
Infrastructure	Support System	Provides the environment for AI to operate at scale	Cloud systems, data centers
Memory	Storage System	Stores and retrieves information for processing	Context memory
Knowledge	Understanding Layer	Represents meaning and relationships within data	Knowledge graphs

The Ingredient Family shows that artificial intelligence is built from a combination of essential components, each playing a vital role in creating intelligent systems.

The Frontend and Backend Family of Artificial Intelligence

How AI Systems Connect User Interaction to Intelligent Processing

Introduction

Every artificial intelligence system operates through two essential layers: the frontend and the backend. These layers work together to transform human interaction into intelligent responses, allowing AI systems to function smoothly and effectively.

The frontend is the part of the system that users see and interact with. It includes screens, input tools, and the display of results. Whether a user is typing a question, speaking a command, or uploading an image, all interaction begins at the frontend.

Behind the scenes, the backend serves as the processing engine of the system. It receives input from the frontend, manages data, connects to the AI model, and performs the computations needed to generate a response. The backend is where the intelligence of the system operates, using models, algorithms, and infrastructure to interpret and respond to user requests.

This visual illustrates how these two layers work together as a complete system. It shows the flow of information from user input to AI processing and back to the user as a result. By understanding this structure, students can see that AI is not a single tool, but a coordinated system of layers working together.

In simple terms, the frontend is where interaction happens, and the backend is where intelligence is created.

Every AI system has two sides: what you see and what actually does the thinking.

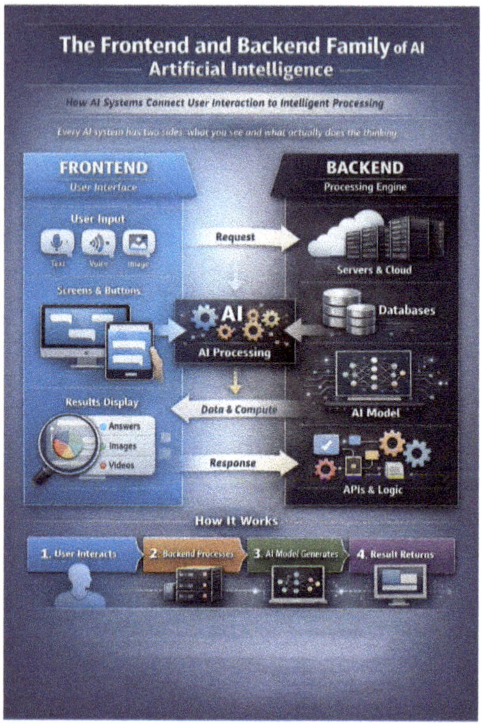

AI Qubit Family Introduction

The AI Qubit Family represents the foundation of quantum computing as it relates to artificial intelligence. While traditional computing relies on bits, which can exist as either 0 or 1, quantum computing uses qubits, which can exist in multiple states simultaneously.

A qubit is the basic unit of quantum information. Unlike classical bits, qubits can take advantage of properties such as superposition and entanglement, allowing quantum systems to process complex computations more efficiently in certain scenarios. This opens new possibilities for solving problems that are difficult or impossible for traditional computers.

In the context of artificial intelligence, qubits have the potential to accelerate learning processes, optimize large-scale systems, and improve complex simulations. Although quantum AI is still in development, it represents a future direction where computational power can expand beyond current limitations.

The AI Qubit Family connects with the Chip Family, as quantum processors are specialized hardware, and with the Algorithm Family, where new types of quantum algorithms are designed.

It also relates to the Parameter and Neural Network Families, as researchers explore quantum-enhanced learning models.

Understanding the AI Qubit Family helps students see that artificial intelligence is continuously evolving. It introduces the idea that the foundations of computing themselves can change, leading to new forms of intelligence and problem-solving.

In simple terms, if bits are the foundation of today's computing, qubits represent the foundation of tomorrow's possibilities.

AI Qubit Family Breakdown Chart

Component	Role	Description	Example
Qubit	Quantum Unit	Basic unit of quantum information	Quantum bit in a quantum computer
Superposition	Multi-State Ability	Ability to exist in multiple states at once	0 and 1 simultaneously
Entanglement	Connection Property	Linking qubits so they influence each other	Paired quantum states
Quantum Gate	Operation System	Performs operations on qubits	Quantum logic gates
Quantum Circuit	Processing Structure	Sequence of quantum operations	Quantum algorithms
Quantum Processor	Hardware Engine	Specialized chip for quantum computing	Quantum computer hardware
Quantum Algorithm	Computation Method	Algorithm designed for quantum systems	Optimization problems
Quantum Speedup	Performance Advantage	Faster processing for certain problems	Complex simulations
Quantum Noise	Stability Challenge	Errors caused by environmental interference	Qubit instability
Quantum Error Correction	Stability Solution	Techniques to reduce errors in quantum systems	Fault-tolerant computing

The AI Qubit Family introduces a new frontier in computing, where the limits of traditional systems are expanded, opening the door to more powerful and advanced forms of artificial intelligence.

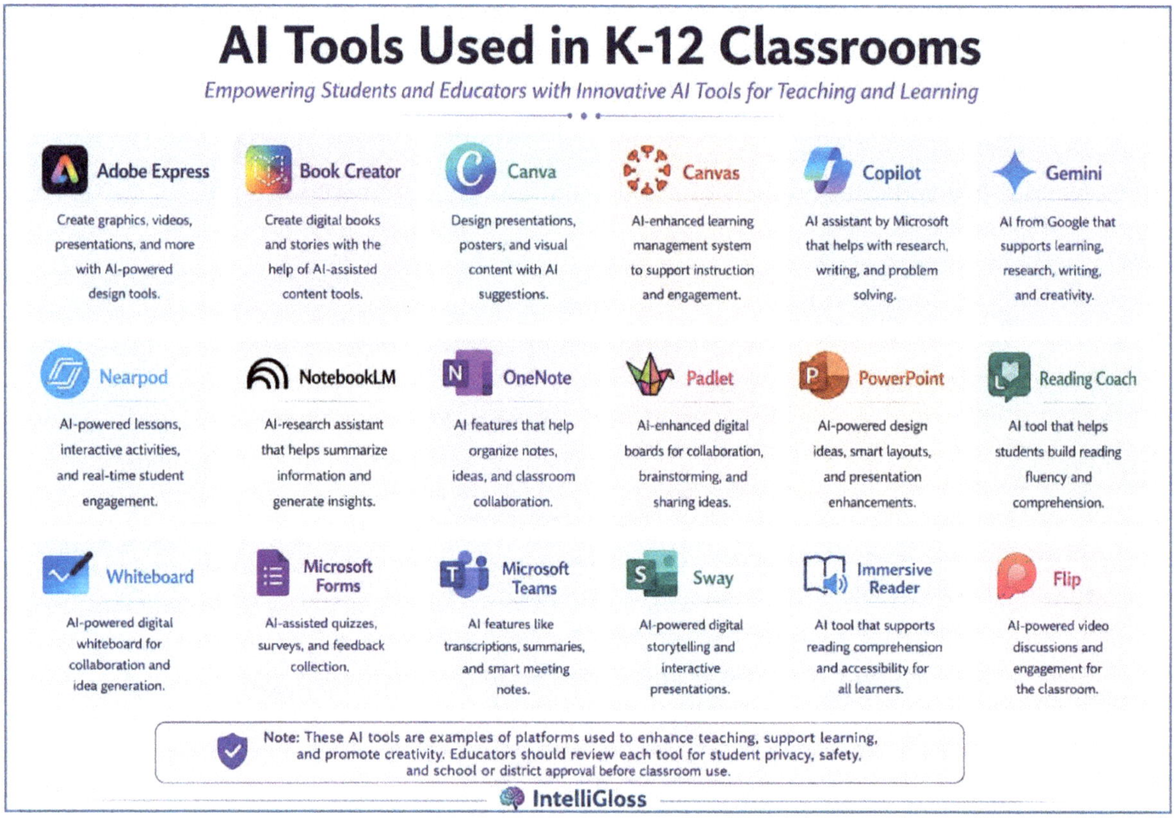
AI Tools Used in K-12 Classrooms
Empowering Students and Educators with Innovative AI Tools for Teaching and Learning
Adobe Express
Create graphics, videos, presentations, and more with AI-powered design tools.
Book Creator
Create digital books and stories with the help of AI-assisted content tools.
Canva
Design presentations, posters, and visual content with AI suggestions.
Canvas
AI-enhanced learning management system to support instruction and engagement.
Copilot
AI assistant by Microsoft that helps with research, writing, and problem solving.
Gemini
AI from Google that supports learning, research, writing, and creativity.
Nearpod
AI-powered lessons, interactive activities, and real-time student engagement.
NotebookLM
AI-research assistant that helps summarize information and generate insights.
OneNote
AI features that help organize notes, ideas, and classroom collaboration.
Padlet
AI-enhanced digital boards for collaboration, brainstorming, and sharing ideas.
PowerPoint
AI-powered design ideas, smart layouts, and presentation enhancements.
Reading Coach
AI tool that helps students build reading fluency and comprehension.
Whiteboard
AI-powered digital whiteboard for collaboration and idea generation.
Microsoft Forms
AI-assisted quizzes, surveys, and feedback collection.
Microsoft Teams
AI features like transcriptions, summaries, and smart meeting notes.
Sway
AI-powered digital storytelling and interactive presentations.
Immersive Reader
AI tool that supports reading comprehension and accessibility for all learners.
Flip
AI-powered video discussions and engagement for the classroom.
Note: These AI tools are examples of platforms used to enhance teaching, support learning, and promote creativity. Educators should review each tool for student privacy, safety, and school or district approval before classroom use.
IntelliGloss

TABLE OF CONTENTS

Introduction

Preparing Education for the Age of Artificial General Intelligence

Education has always evolved alongside human innovation. From the invention of the printing press to the arrival of computers and the internet, every major technological breakthrough has changed how people learn, communicate, and prepare for the future. Today, schools around the world are experiencing another transformation through Artificial Intelligence (AI). AI is helping teachers create lesson plans, personalize instruction, automate routine tasks, analyze student progress, and introduce new ways of learning that were once unimaginable.

While today's AI systems are powerful, they are designed to perform specific tasks. They can generate text, recognize images, translate languages, solve mathematical problems, and answer questions, but each system operates within a defined area of expertise. Artificial General Intelligence (AGI) represents the next stage in this technological journey. AGI refers to intelligent systems that may one day learn across many subjects, reason through unfamiliar problems, adapt to new situations, and apply knowledge in ways that more closely resemble human thinking.

Whether AGI arrives sooner or later than many experts predict, one fact is already clear: education cannot afford to wait until the technology is fully developed before beginning the conversation. Schools have a responsibility to prepare students not only to use future technologies but also to understand them, evaluate them critically, and apply them responsibly. The classroom has always been the place where society prepares the next generation for the world they will inherit. That responsibility becomes even more important as intelligent technologies continue to advance.

This book was written for teachers, school leaders, curriculum specialists, students, parents, policymakers, and anyone interested in the future of education. You do not need a technical background or computer science degree to understand the ideas presented in these pages. The goal of this book is to explain AGI in plain English, making complex concepts understandable and relevant to everyday teaching and learning. Throughout the book, technical language is translated into practical examples that connect directly to real classrooms and real educational challenges.

Preparing for AGI is not about replacing teachers. It is not about allowing machines to make educational decisions on behalf of students. Instead, it is about understanding how increasingly capable intelligent systems can support learning while preserving the qualities that make education deeply human. Teachers inspire curiosity, encourage perseverance, build meaningful relationships, recognize emotional needs, and help students develop character. These qualities cannot simply be programmed into a machine. As technology becomes more capable, the human role in education becomes even more valuable.

The AGI-ready classroom is built on partnership rather than competition. Intelligent systems may help analyze information, personalize instruction, identify learning gaps, and provide immediate feedback. Educators, however, continue to provide wisdom, ethical guidance, creativity, empathy, encouragement, and professional judgment. Students benefit most when technology enhances—not replaces—the relationships that make learning meaningful.

Preparing classrooms for AGI also requires schools to think beyond technology itself. Educational leaders must consider student privacy, cybersecurity, responsible data use, fairness, accessibility, digital citizenship, and the ethical use of intelligent systems. Families must understand both the opportunities and the limitations of emerging technologies so they can support healthy learning habits at home. Policymakers must develop thoughtful guidelines that encourage innovation while protecting students and educators. Successful implementation depends on collaboration among teachers, administrators, parents, communities, and technology developers.

The future workforce will also look different. Many careers will evolve as intelligent systems become more capable, while entirely new professions will emerge. Students will need strong communication skills, adaptability, creativity, critical thinking, collaboration, ethical decision-making, and lifelong learning habits. These human-centered abilities will remain essential regardless of how advanced technology becomes. Schools that prepare students only to memorize information may leave them unprepared for a rapidly changing world. Schools that cultivate curiosity, resilience, sound judgment, and problem-solving will help students succeed in whatever future awaits.

Throughout this book, we will explore how AGI could influence curriculum design, classroom instruction, school leadership, student learning, assessment, professional development, educational policy, and community engagement. We will examine both the exciting possibilities and the important challenges. Rather than focusing on speculation alone, we will emphasize practical preparation that educators and families can begin today.

No one can predict every detail of the future. Technology will continue to evolve, and new discoveries will reshape our understanding of intelligence. However, one principle remains constant: education exists to help people grow, think independently, solve meaningful problems, and contribute positively to society. AGI may transform many aspects of teaching and learning, but it should always serve these larger educational goals rather than replace them.

The journey toward an AGI-ready classroom begins with knowledge. By understanding the technology, asking thoughtful questions, embracing innovation responsibly, and keeping people at the center of every educational decision, schools can prepare students not only to live in the age of Artificial General Intelligence but also to lead it with wisdom, integrity, compassion, and purpose.

Learn AGI. Understand AGI. Shape the Future.

— Susie Hala
IntelliGloss Press

Chapter 1

From AI to AGI

Understanding the Next Evolution of Intelligence

Human history has always been shaped by the ability to learn, adapt, and solve problems. Thousands of years ago, people relied on observation and experience to survive. They learned how to build shelters, grow food, create tools, communicate through language, and work together in communities. Every generation passed knowledge to the next, allowing civilization to progress. This ability to learn from experience is one of the defining characteristics of intelligence. As societies grew more advanced, people developed mathematics, science, engineering, medicine, and technology. Each discovery expanded what humans could accomplish. Today, humanity stands at another important turning point. The development of Artificial Intelligence has already begun changing the way people work, communicate, and learn. Now, researchers around the world are working toward an even more ambitious goal known as Artificial General Intelligence, or AGI. Understanding this next step is becoming increasingly important for students, teachers, parents, and school leaders because the decisions made today will influence classrooms for many years to come.

To understand AGI, it is helpful to first understand intelligence itself. Intelligence is much more than memorizing facts or solving difficult equations. It includes the ability to recognize patterns, think critically, reason through unfamiliar situations, communicate ideas, make informed decisions, learn from mistakes, and apply knowledge to new problems. Human intelligence combines logic with creativity, curiosity, emotions, ethics, and social understanding. A child who learns to ride a bicycle, a teacher who adjusts a lesson after recognizing student confusion, a doctor diagnosing an unfamiliar illness, and an engineer designing a safer bridge all demonstrate different forms of intelligence. These abilities require observation, learning, adaptation, and sound judgment. Human intelligence is flexible because it can transfer knowledge from one situation to another. This remarkable ability has inspired scientists and engineers to ask an important question for decades: Can machines also learn to think, reason, and adapt?

Artificial Intelligence was created to answer part of that question. AI refers to computer systems designed to perform tasks that normally require human intelligence. These tasks include recognizing speech, identifying images, translating languages, recommending movies, answering questions, detecting fraud, driving vehicles, and analyzing enormous amounts of information. During the past several decades, AI has become part of everyday life, even if many people do not realize it. Students use AI-powered search engines and educational software. Teachers use AI to help create lesson plans, quizzes, presentations, and classroom activities. Parents interact with AI through online shopping, navigation systems, digital assistants, and customer service chatbots. Hospitals use AI to assist doctors in identifying diseases. Banks use AI to detect unusual financial transactions. Farmers use AI to monitor crops, while manufacturers use AI to improve production. Artificial Intelligence has quietly become one of the most influential technologies of the twenty-first century.

Although AI has achieved remarkable success, today's systems remain specialized. Most AI programs are designed to perform specific tasks exceptionally well but cannot easily transfer their knowledge to completely different situations. A chess-playing AI may defeat world champions but cannot teach a history lesson. A language model may explain scientific concepts but cannot independently repair a broken engine. A medical imaging system may detect signs of disease with impressive accuracy but cannot suddenly become an architect. Each system is trained for particular objectives using carefully prepared data and algorithms. This type of AI is commonly called Artificial Narrow Intelligence because its abilities are focused within defined boundaries. Even the most advanced AI systems available today do not possess the broad, flexible understanding that humans demonstrate every day.

Imagine asking a fifth-grade student to solve a math problem, write a short story, explain the water cycle, recognize a friend's emotions, organize a science project, and learn a new board game—all within the same afternoon. Most students can attempt each task because human intelligence naturally transfers knowledge between different subjects and experiences. People do not need to be rebuilt every time they encounter a new challenge. Instead, they draw upon previous learning, common sense, reasoning, and creativity. This ability to move from one type of problem to another is one of the greatest differences between humans and today's AI systems. Scientists believe that creating machines capable of similar flexibility represents one of the biggest challenges in computer science.

This challenge has led researchers to pursue Artificial General Intelligence. AGI describes a future generation of intelligent systems that could learn across many different subjects instead of remaining limited to one specialty. Rather than requiring separate programs for each task, an AGI system would be expected to understand unfamiliar situations, apply knowledge gained in one area to another, solve problems it has never encountered before, and continue learning throughout its operation. While researchers continue debating exactly how AGI should be defined and when it might become possible, the central idea remains consistent: AGI aims to build systems with broad, adaptable intelligence rather than narrow expertise. It is important to recognize that AGI does not yet exist as a confirmed technology in everyday use. Instead, it represents an active area of research and development that continues to evolve through advances in computing, machine learning, neuroscience, robotics, and cognitive science.

For students, understanding the difference between AI and AGI is not simply an academic exercise. It is preparation for a future that may look very different from the world their parents experienced. Many students entering elementary school today will graduate into careers that have not yet been invented. They may work alongside intelligent systems capable of assisting with research, engineering, medicine, business, scientific discovery, environmental protection, and creative design. Success in this future will require more than learning how to use technology. Students will need to understand how intelligent systems make decisions, where their strengths and weaknesses lie, and how humans can continue providing creativity, ethical judgment, leadership, empathy, and responsibility. Schools play a vital role in developing these uniquely human abilities while helping students become confident users of emerging technologies.

The transition from AI to AGI should not be viewed as a competition between humans and machines. Throughout history, technology has often expanded human capabilities rather than replacing them completely. Calculators did not eliminate mathematics education. Computers did not eliminate teachers. The internet did not eliminate libraries, although it changed how information is accessed. Similarly, AGI should be understood as a tool that may help people solve increasingly complex problems while leaving important human responsibilities in human hands. Teachers will continue inspiring students, encouraging curiosity, recognizing emotional needs, building confidence, and creating meaningful learning experiences. Parents will continue teaching values, responsibility, compassion, and character. Technology can support these efforts, but it cannot replace the relationships that define education.

As you begin this journey through *The AGI-Ready Classroom*, remember that learning about AGI is not about predicting every invention of the future. Instead, it is about preparing to think critically, ask thoughtful questions, embrace innovation responsibly, and remain adaptable in a rapidly changing world. Every generation has faced technological change, but few have witnessed advances as significant as those taking place today. By understanding the evolution from Artificial Intelligence to Artificial General Intelligence, students, educators, and parents can become informed participants in shaping the future rather than simply reacting to it. The classroom of tomorrow begins with the knowledge we choose to build today, and that journey starts by understanding the remarkable evolution of intelligence itself.

Chapter 1 Summary

From AI to AGI: Understanding the Next Evolution of Intelligence

Artificial Intelligence (AI) has become an important part of everyday life, helping people complete tasks such as searching for information, recognizing images, translating languages, and assisting with education. However, today's AI systems are designed for specific purposes and are considered Artificial Narrow Intelligence (ANI). They perform specialized tasks extremely well but cannot easily apply what they learn to completely different situations.

Artificial General Intelligence (AGI) represents the next stage in the evolution of intelligent systems. Unlike today's AI, AGI is designed to learn across multiple subjects, adapt to unfamiliar situations, reason through complex problems, and transfer knowledge from one task to another in ways that resemble human learning. Although AGI has not yet been achieved, researchers around the world continue working toward this goal.

This chapter explained that intelligence involves much more than memorizing information. Human intelligence includes reasoning, creativity, curiosity, communication, ethical judgment, problem-solving, and emotional understanding. These uniquely human qualities remain essential regardless of how advanced technology becomes.

Students, educators, and parents all have important roles in preparing for the future. Schools must continue teaching critical thinking, creativity, collaboration, communication, ethics, and lifelong learning while helping students understand how intelligent technologies work. Rather than viewing AGI as a replacement for people, education should prepare students to work alongside intelligent systems responsibly and effectively.

The journey toward an AGI-ready classroom begins with knowledge. By understanding the differences between AI and AGI, learners become better prepared for the opportunities and challenges of tomorrow's world.

Chapter 1 Reflection

Take a few moments to think about what you learned in this chapter. Write your answers in complete sentences.

1. Before reading this chapter, what did you think Artificial Intelligence was? Has your understanding changed? Explain your answer.
2. Why is it important to understand the difference between Artificial Intelligence and Artificial General Intelligence?
3. Which human qualities do you believe will remain valuable even if AGI becomes highly advanced? Why?
4. How might AGI change the way students learn in the future?
5. What responsibilities do teachers have as intelligent technologies continue to develop?
6. Why should parents learn about AGI along with their children?
7. What concerns do you have about AGI? What opportunities excite you the most?
8. If you could help design an AGI-powered classroom, what features would you include to improve learning while protecting students?
9. How can schools prepare students for careers that may not exist yet?
10. After reading this chapter, what is one new idea you want to learn more about as you continue reading this book?

Chapter 1 Worksheet

Vocabulary Matching

Match each term with the correct definition.

A. Artificial Intelligence (AI)

B. Artificial General Intelligence (AGI)

C. Intelligence

D. Critical Thinking

E. Adaptability

F. Ethics

G. Creativity

H. Lifelong Learning

1. _____ The ability to continue learning throughout life.
2. _____ The ability to adjust successfully to new situations.
3. _____ The process of carefully analyzing information before making decisions.
4. _____ Intelligent computer systems designed to perform specific tasks.
5. _____ Moral principles that help guide responsible decisions.
6. _____ The ability to produce original ideas and solve problems in new ways.
7. _____ The ability to learn, reason, solve problems, and apply knowledge.
8. _____ A future form of intelligent systems capable of learning across many different subjects.

Short Answer

1. What is the main difference between AI and AGI?

____

2. Give three examples of AI that people use every day.

____
____

3. Why is AGI considered the next evolution of intelligent systems?

____
____

4. Name four human skills that technology cannot easily replace.

____
____

5. Why should schools begin preparing for AGI today?

____
____
____

Critical Thinking

Imagine you are the principal of a school opening ten years from now.

Describe three ways you would prepare your teachers and students for an AGI-powered future while keeping education safe, ethical, and student-centered.

____
____
____
____
____

Chapter 1 Quiz

Multiple Choice

1. What does AGI stand for?

A. Advanced Global Intelligence

B. Artificial General Intelligence

C. Automated General Information

D. Applied General Innovation

2. Today's AI systems are generally designed to:

A. Perform many different jobs equally well.

B. Replace all human workers.

C. Perform specialized tasks.

D. Think exactly like humans.

3. Which statement best describes AGI?

A. A calculator.

B. A future intelligent system capable of learning across many different subjects.

C. A search engine.

D. A social media application.

4. Which of the following is considered a uniquely human strength?

A. Empathy

B. Ethical judgment

C. Creativity

D. All of the above

5. Why should schools prepare for AGI?

A. Because technology is becoming more advanced.

B. To help students develop future-ready skills.

C. To understand both opportunities and challenges.

D. All of the above.

True or False

6. _____ Today's AI can easily perform every task a human can do.
7. _____ AGI has already replaced teachers in schools worldwide.
8. _____ Critical thinking is an important skill in an AGI future.
9. _____ Parents should also understand emerging technologies.
10. _____ Learning about AGI helps students prepare for future careers.

Chapter 1 Quiz

Multiple Choice

1. What does AGI stand for?

A. Advanced Global Intelligence

B. Artificial General Intelligence

C. Automated General Information

D. Applied General Innovation

2. Today's AI systems are generally designed to:

A. Perform many different jobs equally well.

B. Replace all human workers.

C. Perform specialized tasks.

D. Think exactly like humans.

3. Which statement best describes AGI?

A. A calculator.

B. A future intelligent system capable of learning across many different subjects.

C. A search engine.

D. A social media application.

4. Which of the following is considered a uniquely human strength?

A. Empathy

B. Ethical judgment

C. Creativity

D. All of the above

5. Why should schools prepare for AGI?

A. Because technology is becoming more advanced.

B. To help students develop future-ready skills.

C. To understand both opportunities and challenges.

D. All of the above.

True or False

6. _____ Today's AI can easily perform every task a human can do.
7. _____ AGI has already replaced teachers in schools worldwide.
8. _____ Critical thinking is an important skill in an AGI future.
9. _____ Parents should also understand emerging technologies.
10. _____ Learning about AGI helps students prepare for future careers.

Chapter 1 Answer Key

Worksheet Answers

Vocabulary Matching

1. H
2. E
3. D
4. A
5. F
6. G
7. C
8. B

Short Answer (Suggested Responses)

1. AI performs specialized tasks, while AGI aims to learn and reason across many different subjects.
2. Possible answers include virtual assistants, navigation apps, language translators, recommendation systems, facial recognition, educational software, and chatbots.
3. AGI seeks to develop flexible intelligence that can adapt, reason, and solve unfamiliar problems across multiple areas.

4. Possible answers include empathy, creativity, ethical judgment, leadership, communication, collaboration, and critical thinking.
5. Schools should prepare students with the knowledge, skills, and ethical understanding needed to work responsibly alongside increasingly capable intelligent technologies.

Quiz Answers

1. **B**
2. **C**
3. **B**
4. **D**
5. **D**
6. **False**
7. **False**
8. **True**
9. **True**
10. **True**

Chapter 2

Why Every Classroom Must Prepare for AGI

Education has never remained the same for very long. Every generation has experienced changes that required schools to adapt, teachers to learn new methods, and students to develop new skills. Long before computers existed, students learned almost entirely from printed textbooks, handwritten notes, and face-to-face instruction. The arrival of calculators changed mathematics education. Personal computers introduced digital learning. The internet opened access to information from around the world. Smartphones placed enormous amounts of knowledge into the hands of students within seconds. More recently, Artificial Intelligence has begun helping educators create lesson plans, analyze student performance, generate educational resources, and personalize instruction. Each technological advancement created questions, challenges, and opportunities. Some people worried that new technologies would replace traditional learning, while others recognized that schools could use these tools to improve education. History has shown that successful schools are not those that resist change but those that learn how to adapt while keeping students at the center of every decision. Artificial General Intelligence represents another important stage in this continuing journey.

Preparing classrooms for AGI does not mean that schools expect intelligent machines to replace teachers or make educational decisions independently. Instead, preparation means understanding how education may evolve as intelligent technologies become more capable. Schools have always prepared students for the future rather than only teaching about the past. A student entering elementary school today may graduate into a world where intelligent systems assist scientists in discovering new medicines, engineers in designing safer cities, doctors in improving patient care, and environmental researchers in protecting natural resources. Future careers may involve working alongside intelligent systems every day. Students who understand how these technologies function will be better prepared to make informed decisions, solve meaningful problems, and contribute responsibly to society. Waiting until AGI becomes commonplace before discussing it in classrooms would leave many students unprepared for the opportunities and responsibilities they may encounter.

One of the greatest strengths of education is its ability to help students develop skills that remain valuable even as technology changes. Facts can often be found within seconds using digital tools, but understanding how to evaluate information, identify trustworthy sources, recognize misinformation, and think critically requires human guidance. As intelligent systems continue improving, students will need more than technical knowledge. They will need curiosity to ask thoughtful questions, creativity to imagine new possibilities, communication skills to explain complex ideas, collaboration to work effectively with others, and ethical judgment to make responsible decisions. These abilities cannot simply be downloaded into a computer. They develop through meaningful classroom experiences, thoughtful discussions, problem-solving activities, teamwork, and supportive relationships with teachers and classmates. Preparing for AGI means strengthening these human abilities rather than allowing technology to weaken them.

Many people imagine future classrooms filled with advanced computers, interactive displays, intelligent tutoring systems, and personalized learning platforms. While these technologies may become increasingly common, the most important feature of an AGI-ready classroom is not the equipment inside the room. The most important feature is the mindset of the people who learn there. Students who are willing to explore new ideas, ask questions, adapt to change, and continue learning throughout their lives will succeed regardless of which technologies become available. Teachers who remain curious, continue developing professionally, and embrace innovation thoughtfully will continue making a tremendous difference in students' lives. School leaders who encourage responsible experimentation while maintaining high educational standards will help their communities navigate technological change with confidence. Preparing for AGI begins with preparing people rather than simply purchasing new devices.

Another reason every classroom should prepare for AGI is that technology continues evolving much faster than educational systems traditionally change. Schools often spend years updating curriculum, selecting textbooks, training teachers, and implementing new instructional programs. By the time these changes are fully adopted, technology may have advanced significantly. This does not mean schools should chase every new innovation. Instead, educators should develop flexible learning environments that emphasize transferable knowledge and lifelong learning. Students who understand how to learn independently will remain prepared even as technologies continue changing throughout their careers. Rather than teaching students only how to use today's software, schools should teach them how to evaluate new technologies, understand their capabilities, recognize their limitations, and use them responsibly. These habits prepare students not only for AGI but also for future innovations that have not yet been imagined.

Preparing for AGI also requires schools to expand the meaning of digital literacy. In the past, digital literacy often meant learning how to use computers, create documents, search the internet, or communicate online. While these skills remain important, tomorrow's students will need a broader understanding of intelligent technologies. They should understand that AI systems learn from data, that algorithms influence recommendations, that information generated by machines should always be verified, and that intelligent systems can sometimes produce inaccurate or biased results. Students should learn how to ask better questions, compare multiple sources of information, recognize ethical concerns, and understand the importance of human oversight. These skills help students become informed users of technology rather than passive consumers of automated answers.

Teachers also benefit from preparing early rather than waiting for technology to become widespread. Professional learning allows educators to explore new instructional strategies, understand emerging technologies, and develop confidence before major changes occur. Teachers who understand AGI concepts will be better prepared to answer students' questions, evaluate educational tools thoughtfully, and integrate new resources in ways that strengthen learning rather than distract from it. Professional development should not focus only on technical skills. It should also help educators discuss ethics, student privacy, academic integrity, responsible technology use, and the continuing importance of human relationships in education. As technology becomes increasingly sophisticated, teachers remain the trusted guides who help students understand not only how to use powerful tools but also when and why they should be used responsibly.

Preparing every classroom for AGI is ultimately an investment in people. Technology will continue changing throughout the lives of today's students, but qualities such as integrity, compassion, perseverance, adaptability, creativity, wisdom, and critical thinking will remain essential regardless of how intelligent machines become. Schools have always served a greater purpose than simply delivering information. They help young people develop character, confidence, responsibility, and hope for the future. These human qualities become even more valuable in a world where intelligent technologies can perform many technical tasks. An AGI-ready classroom recognizes that the future belongs not only to those who understand advanced technology but also to those who understand how to use it ethically, responsibly, and in service to others.

Chapter 2 (Part 2)

As schools begin thinking about AGI, it is helpful to imagine how learning might change over the next decade. Consider a science classroom where every student is investigating the same topic but learning in different ways. One student understands best by watching animations, another prefers reading detailed explanations, while another learns most effectively through hands-on experiments and classroom discussions. An advanced AGI learning assistant could recognize these differences and recommend learning activities that match each student's needs without changing the educational goals. Students who master concepts quickly could receive more challenging assignments, while those needing additional support could receive extra explanations and practice. The teacher would continue leading the classroom, encouraging collaboration, answering questions, and ensuring that every student remains engaged. In this environment, technology becomes a powerful teaching assistant rather than the teacher itself.

Imagine another classroom where students are working on a project to solve a real-world environmental problem. Instead of simply searching the internet for information, students collaborate with intelligent systems to analyze climate data, compare possible solutions, examine historical trends, and evaluate the advantages and disadvantages of different approaches. The AGI system provides information, simulations, and suggestions, but students remain responsible for asking questions, evaluating evidence, discussing ideas with classmates, and presenting their own conclusions. The technology accelerates research, but human reasoning determines the final decisions. This type of learning encourages students to think independently instead of simply accepting the first answer they receive.

One of the greatest opportunities presented by AGI is the possibility of making education more personalized than ever before. Every classroom contains students with different interests, backgrounds, abilities, learning speeds, and personal goals. Traditional instruction often requires teachers to balance the needs of many learners within limited class time. Intelligent educational systems may eventually help teachers identify learning gaps more quickly, monitor student progress continuously, recommend targeted practice activities, and provide immediate feedback. These capabilities could allow teachers to spend more time mentoring students, leading discussions, encouraging creativity, and building meaningful relationships instead of performing repetitive administrative tasks. Technology should create more opportunities for human interaction, not fewer.

At the same time, schools must recognize that every powerful technology brings important responsibilities. Students should never assume that every answer generated by an intelligent system is automatically correct. Like today's AI systems, future AGI technologies may occasionally produce inaccurate information, misunderstand complex situations, or present incomplete explanations. Students must continue verifying facts, consulting reliable sources, asking thoughtful questions, and applying critical thinking before accepting any conclusion. Learning how to question information respectfully and responsibly is one of the most valuable skills education can provide. The goal is not to distrust technology but to understand that good judgment remains essential regardless of how advanced intelligent systems become.

Privacy will become another important responsibility for schools preparing for AGI. Educational technologies often process information about student learning, classroom performance, and instructional activities. Schools must carefully protect this information while following privacy laws and ethical standards. Students and parents should understand what information is collected, how it is used, who has access to it, and how it is protected. Transparency builds trust between schools, families, and technology providers. Responsible educational innovation depends not only on advanced technology but also on clear communication, accountability, and respect for every learner.

Equity must also remain at the center of educational planning. Every student deserves access to high-quality learning opportunities regardless of family income, geographic location, language, or disability. As AGI technologies become more common, school leaders must work to prevent a digital divide in which some students benefit from advanced educational tools while others are left behind. Equal access to technology, reliable internet connections, teacher support, and high-quality instructional resources helps ensure that innovation benefits entire communities rather than only a small group of learners. Preparing for AGI means creating opportunities that are inclusive, fair, and accessible for everyone.

Teachers will continue serving as the heart of every successful classroom. While intelligent systems may assist with organizing information, generating practice activities, analyzing data, and providing personalized recommendations, they cannot replace the trust that develops between teachers and students. A teacher recognizes when a student feels discouraged, celebrates personal achievements, encourages perseverance after failure, and inspires confidence during difficult moments. These human relationships motivate students to continue learning even when challenges become difficult. Technology may improve efficiency, but meaningful education continues to depend upon compassion, encouragement, and genuine human connection.

School leaders also play an essential role in preparing their communities for the future. Principals, district administrators, curriculum specialists, and school boards must develop thoughtful plans for introducing emerging technologies responsibly. Successful implementation requires ongoing professional learning, clear policies, community involvement, cybersecurity planning, ethical guidelines, and continuous evaluation. Rather than adopting technology simply because it is new, educational leaders should ask important questions. Does this technology improve learning? Does it protect student privacy? Does it support teachers instead of replacing their professional judgment? Does it help every student succeed? Responsible leadership ensures that innovation serves educational goals rather than distracting from them.

Parents remain valuable partners throughout this journey. The conversations that begin in the classroom should continue at home where families discuss responsible technology use, online safety, honesty, kindness, and digital citizenship. Children benefit when parents ask questions about what they are learning, encourage curiosity, monitor technology use appropriately, and help young people develop healthy habits that balance digital experiences with face-to-face relationships, physical activity, creativity, and family interaction. Preparing for AGI is not solely the responsibility of schools. It is a shared responsibility among educators, families, communities, and students themselves.

Perhaps the most important lesson of all is that preparing for AGI is not primarily about machines. It is about preparing people to think wisely, act ethically, solve meaningful problems, and improve society. Technology will continue changing throughout the lives of today's students. Some careers will evolve, while entirely new professions will emerge. New discoveries will create opportunities that cannot yet be predicted. Students who develop adaptability, resilience, curiosity, communication skills, creativity, collaboration, leadership, and lifelong learning habits will remain prepared regardless of how technology evolves. These qualities have always been valuable, and they will become even more important in an increasingly intelligent world.

Every classroom has the opportunity to become an AGI-ready classroom—not by filling every desk with advanced technology, but by building a culture of learning, curiosity, responsibility, innovation, and ethical leadership. Schools that encourage students to ask thoughtful questions, embrace lifelong learning, work collaboratively, and use technology responsibly will prepare graduates who are ready not only to adapt to the future but also to help shape it. The future of education is not defined by the intelligence of machines. It is defined by the wisdom, character, creativity, and purpose of the people who use them. As we continue our journey through this book, we will discover that the most successful classrooms of tomorrow will always place human learning, human values, and human potential at the center of every technological advancement.

Chapter 2 Summary

Why Every Classroom Must Prepare for AGI

Education has always evolved as society has changed. From printed books and calculators to computers, the internet, and Artificial Intelligence, every generation has adapted to new technologies while continuing to focus on helping students learn and grow. Artificial General Intelligence (AGI) represents the next major step in this evolution, making it important for schools to begin preparing today rather than waiting until the technology becomes commonplace.

Preparing for AGI is not about replacing teachers with machines. Instead, it is about helping students understand how intelligent technologies work, how they can be used responsibly, and how human skills such as creativity, empathy, critical thinking, communication, and ethical decision-making will remain essential in the future. Schools that prepare students for AGI are also preparing them for careers, technologies, and challenges that may not yet exist.

An AGI-ready classroom focuses on developing lifelong learners who can adapt to change, evaluate information carefully, solve complex problems, and collaborate with both people and intelligent technologies. Teachers remain the leaders of the classroom by guiding students, encouraging curiosity, building relationships, and helping learners develop sound judgment.

The chapter also emphasized the importance of privacy, cybersecurity, equity, digital citizenship, and responsible technology use. School leaders, teachers, parents, and students all share responsibility for ensuring that AGI supports education while protecting the well-being of every learner.

Preparing classrooms for AGI is ultimately about preparing people. Technology will continue to evolve, but human character, wisdom, integrity, compassion, and lifelong learning will always remain the foundation of a successful education.

Chapter 2 Reflection

Reflect on what you learned in this chapter. Answer each question using complete sentences.

1. Why do you think schools should begin preparing for AGI before it becomes widely available?
2. How has education changed because of technology during your lifetime?

3. Which human qualities do you believe will become even more important in an AGI-powered world? Explain your answer.
4. How could AGI help students learn more effectively without replacing teachers?
5. Why is critical thinking important when using intelligent technologies?
6. What responsibilities do schools have when protecting student privacy?
7. How can parents support children as intelligent technologies become part of everyday learning?
8. Why should every student develop lifelong learning habits?
9. If you were a school principal, what would be your first priority in preparing your school for AGI?
10. After completing this chapter, what excites you most about the future of education, and what concerns you the most?
11.
12.

Chapter 2 Worksheet

Part A – Vocabulary Matching

Match each term with the correct definition.

A. AGI-Ready Classroom

B. Digital Citizenship

C. Lifelong Learning

D. Critical Thinking

E. Student Privacy

F. Equity

G. Adaptability

H. Personalized Learning

1. _____ Treating others responsibly and safely when using digital technology.
2. _____ Protecting personal information collected about students.
3. _____ The ability to adjust successfully to new situations.
4. _____ Learning experiences designed to meet each student's individual needs.
5. _____ A classroom prepared for the responsible use of future intelligent technologies.
6. _____ Continuing to learn throughout life.
7. _____ Providing fair opportunities for every learner.
8. _____ Carefully analyzing information before making decisions.

Part B – Short Answer

1. Why should schools begin preparing for AGI today instead of waiting until it becomes common?

2. List four human skills that will continue to be valuable even as AGI develops.

3. Explain why teachers remain important in an AGI-ready classroom.

4. Why should students verify information provided by intelligent systems?

5. Why is equity important when schools adopt new technologies?

Part C – Critical Thinking

Imagine your school is introducing AGI-powered learning tools next year.

Write one paragraph explaining three rules you would recommend to ensure these technologies are used responsibly, ethically, and fairly for every student.

Chapter 2 Quiz

Multiple Choice

1. Why should schools prepare for AGI now?

A. Because every school already uses AGI.

B. Because preparing early helps students develop future-ready skills.

C. Because teachers will no longer be needed.

D. Because textbooks will disappear.

2. What is one of the most important goals of an AGI-ready classroom?

A. Replacing teachers.

B. Developing human skills alongside technology.

C. Eliminating homework.

D. Using computers all day.

3. Which human skill remains essential in an AGI-powered future?

A. Ethical judgment.

B. Creativity.

C. Critical thinking.

D. All of the above.

4. Why should students evaluate information generated by intelligent systems?

A. Technology may sometimes provide incomplete or inaccurate information.

B. Machines never make mistakes.

C. Students should never use technology.

D. There is no need to verify information.

5. Which group shares responsibility for preparing students for AGI?

A. Teachers only.

B. Parents only.

C. School administrators only.

D. Teachers, parents, students, and school leaders.

True or False

6. _____ Preparing for AGI means replacing teachers with machines.
7. _____ Student privacy should remain a priority as educational technology evolves.
8. _____ Lifelong learning helps students adapt to future changes.
9. _____ Every student should have fair access to educational opportunities.
10. _____ Human relationships will continue to be important in education.

Chapter 2 Answer Key

Worksheet Answers

Part A – Vocabulary Matching

1. **B**
2. **E**
3. **G**
4. **H**
5. **A**
6. **C**
7. **F**
8. **D**

Part B – Suggested Responses

1. Schools should prepare now so students and teachers can gradually develop the knowledge and skills needed to use future intelligent technologies responsibly.
2. Possible answers include creativity, empathy, communication, collaboration, leadership, ethical judgment, critical thinking, adaptability, and problem-solving.
3. Teachers guide learning, build relationships, encourage students, provide ethical leadership, and help learners think critically about technology.
4. Intelligent systems can occasionally provide inaccurate, incomplete, or biased information, so students should verify facts using reliable sources.
5. Equity ensures that every student has access to high-quality learning opportunities regardless of background, income, or location.

Quiz Answers

1.B

2.B

3.D

4.A

5.D

7.False

8.True

9.True

10.True

11.True

Chapter 3

The Future Role of Teachers in an AGI World

Throughout history, teachers have remained one of the most important influences in the lives of students. Long before computers, smartphones, or Artificial Intelligence existed, teachers inspired curiosity, shared knowledge, encouraged perseverance, and helped young people discover their potential. While classrooms have changed over the centuries, the purpose of education has remained remarkably consistent: to help students develop the knowledge, skills, values, and confidence needed to succeed in life. As Artificial General Intelligence (AGI) continues to evolve, many people wonder whether intelligent systems will eventually replace teachers. It is an understandable question because AGI is expected to perform increasingly complex tasks, analyze enormous amounts of information, and provide personalized assistance. However, the future of education is not about replacing teachers with intelligent machines. Instead, it is about redefining the teacher's role so that educators can focus even more on the uniquely human aspects of learning that technology cannot duplicate.

Teaching has never been limited to delivering information. If education were simply about presenting facts, students could learn everything from books or online resources without entering a classroom. Yet schools continue to exist because learning involves much more than collecting information. Great teachers motivate students to ask questions, challenge assumptions, overcome obstacles, build confidence, develop character, and discover interests that shape their futures. A teacher notices when a student feels discouraged after struggling with a difficult assignment. A teacher recognizes hidden talents that students may not yet see in themselves. A teacher creates an environment where mistakes become opportunities to learn rather than reasons to give up. These responsibilities require empathy, emotional intelligence, patience, encouragement, and professional judgment. They are deeply human qualities that cannot simply be programmed into a machine.

As AGI develops, many routine classroom tasks may become easier to manage. Intelligent systems could assist teachers by organizing lesson materials, suggesting instructional activities, creating personalized practice exercises, summarizing student progress, identifying learning gaps, translating instructional materials into multiple languages, and generating visual explanations for difficult concepts. Instead of spending hours preparing repetitive classroom materials, teachers may have more time to work directly with students, facilitate discussions, mentor individuals, communicate with families, and design creative learning experiences. Rather than replacing teachers, AGI has the potential to reduce administrative burdens and allow educators to devote more attention to the personal interactions that have always defined excellent teaching.

One of the most important responsibilities of future teachers will be helping students learn how to think instead of simply telling them what to think. As intelligent systems become increasingly capable of generating information instantly, students will have access to more knowledge than any previous generation. However, having access to information does not automatically produce understanding. Students must learn how to evaluate evidence, distinguish facts from opinions, recognize misinformation, compare different perspectives, ask thoughtful questions, and make responsible decisions based on reliable information. Teachers guide students through this process by encouraging discussion, challenging assumptions, and helping learners develop independent judgment. In an AGI-powered world, critical thinking becomes even more valuable because intelligent technologies can produce both remarkable insights and convincing mistakes. Students need teachers who help them understand not only the answers they receive but also how those answers should be evaluated.

The classroom of the future will likely place greater emphasis on collaboration than memorization. While students will continue learning important facts and foundational knowledge, they will also spend more time solving authentic problems, working in teams, designing creative solutions, and applying what they learn to real-life situations. Teachers will become facilitators of discovery, creating meaningful learning experiences that encourage students to investigate, experiment, communicate, and reflect. AGI may provide information, simulations, and immediate feedback, but teachers will continue helping students connect ideas, build confidence, resolve disagreements, and understand the broader purpose behind their learning. These experiences develop communication skills, leadership, empathy, adaptability, and resilience—qualities that remain essential regardless of technological advancement.

Another important role for teachers will involve helping students develop ethical judgment. Every new technology raises important questions about responsibility, fairness, privacy, security, and appropriate use. Students will need guidance as they learn when to rely on intelligent systems, when to verify information independently, and when human judgment should take priority over automated recommendations. Teachers create opportunities for thoughtful conversations about honesty, academic integrity, bias, digital citizenship, intellectual property, and the ethical responsibilities that accompany powerful technologies. These discussions help students become responsible users of AGI rather than simply skilled operators of advanced software.

Teachers will also serve as lifelong learners themselves. Education has always required continuous professional growth, but the pace of technological change will make ongoing learning even more important. Future educators will regularly explore emerging technologies, evaluate new instructional strategies, attend professional development programs, collaborate with colleagues, and adapt their teaching practices as educational research continues to evolve. This willingness to learn models an important lesson for students. When teachers demonstrate curiosity, adaptability, and a commitment to lifelong learning, they encourage students to develop those same habits. In many ways, the most effective teachers of the future will not be those who claim to know everything but those who show students how to continue learning throughout their lives.

Perhaps the greatest strength of teachers is their ability to build meaningful relationships. Every student enters the classroom with unique experiences, strengths, challenges, dreams, and concerns. Some students learn quickly, while others require additional time and encouragement. Some feel confident speaking in front of others, while some struggle with anxiety or self-doubt. Teachers recognize these differences and respond with compassion, patience, and understanding. They celebrate achievements, provide encouragement after setbacks, and create learning environments where students feel respected, valued, and safe. These relationships form the foundation upon which academic success is built. No matter how advanced AGI becomes, it cannot replace the trust that develops between a caring teacher and a student who knows someone genuinely believes in their potential.

The future role of teachers will not become smaller because of AGI—it will become even more significant. As intelligent systems assume routine tasks, educators will have greater opportunities to focus on mentorship, creativity, ethical leadership, communication, collaboration, emotional development, and personalized guidance. The classroom of tomorrow will continue to rely on technology as a valuable educational partner, but it will always depend on teachers to provide wisdom, inspiration, compassion, and purpose. The most successful schools will recognize that technology is at its best when it strengthens human relationships rather than replacing them. In the years ahead, students may remember the intelligent tools they used, but they will always remember the teachers who challenged them to think, encouraged them to dream, and inspired them to become their very best.

Chapter 3 (Part 2)

As classrooms continue evolving, the partnership between teachers and AGI will likely become one of the most significant developments in modern education. Instead of viewing intelligent systems as competitors, educators can think of them as highly capable assistants that support teaching while allowing teachers to concentrate on the work that only people can perform. Imagine beginning a school day where an AGI system has already organized instructional materials, analyzed student progress from the previous lesson, identified concepts that need additional review, and suggested activities based on each learner's strengths and challenges. The teacher enters the classroom with a clearer understanding of where students need support, but the decisions about instruction remain firmly in human hands. The educator determines which recommendations are useful, adjusts the lesson to fit the personalities and needs of the class, and creates opportunities for meaningful discussion. Technology supplies information, while teachers provide wisdom and professional judgment.

Consider a classroom studying the history of the Civil Rights Movement. An AGI system may quickly gather historical documents, create interactive timelines, translate primary sources into multiple languages, and answer factual questions. However, it cannot replace the thoughtful conversation that occurs when students discuss courage, fairness, justice, equality, and the responsibilities of citizenship. A skilled teacher encourages students to examine different viewpoints, ask respectful questions, support opinions with evidence, and reflect on how historical events continue to influence society today. These conversations develop empathy, ethical reasoning, communication skills, and civic responsibility. They remind students that education is not only about learning what happened but also about understanding why it matters. AGI can provide valuable resources, but only teachers can cultivate the human understanding that transforms information into wisdom.

Science classrooms offer another example of this partnership. Students investigating renewable energy might use AGI to compare solar, wind, hydroelectric, and geothermal technologies, analyze environmental data, and model possible solutions for reducing carbon emissions. While the technology helps students process complex information, teachers guide them in evaluating the reliability of data, considering economic and environmental trade-offs, working collaboratively in teams, and presenting evidence-based conclusions. Students learn that technology can accelerate research, but responsible decision-making still requires critical thinking, creativity, and ethical consideration. By combining intelligent tools with thoughtful instruction, classrooms become places where innovation and human judgment work together rather than competing with one another.

Professional growth will become even more important for teachers as AGI continues to develop. Effective educators have always adapted to changing curriculum, educational research, and instructional methods. The AGI era will continue this tradition of lifelong learning. Teachers will participate in professional development that helps them understand emerging technologies, evaluate educational software, interpret learning analytics responsibly, and design lessons that encourage higher-order thinking instead of simple memorization. Schools that invest in continuous learning for educators will be better prepared to introduce new technologies responsibly while maintaining high academic standards. Professional development should also include opportunities for teachers to collaborate, share successful classroom strategies, discuss ethical concerns, and learn from one another's experiences. Education has always been strongest when teachers learn together.

Teacher preparation programs at colleges and universities will also continue evolving. Future educators will study instructional design, classroom management, child development, assessment, and educational psychology while also learning about artificial intelligence, data literacy, digital citizenship, privacy protection, and responsible technology integration. They will practice evaluating AI-generated content, recognizing algorithmic bias, protecting student information, and using intelligent systems to strengthen learning without allowing technology to replace meaningful classroom interaction. Preparing future teachers for AGI means helping them become confident instructional leaders who understand both the possibilities and the limitations of advanced technologies.

One of the greatest responsibilities teachers will carry into the AGI era is helping students maintain their humanity in an increasingly digital world. Technology can provide immediate answers, but it cannot teach kindness by comforting a classmate who is struggling. It cannot demonstrate integrity by admitting a mistake and learning from it. It cannot inspire perseverance by encouraging a student to continue working after repeated failure. Teachers model these qualities every day through their words, actions, and relationships with students. Young people often remember how teachers made them feel long after they forget individual lessons or assignments. Feeling respected, encouraged, challenged, and believed in creates confidence that lasts far beyond the classroom. These experiences shape character as much as academic achievement.

The future classroom will also become more collaborative than ever before. Students will increasingly work on interdisciplinary projects that combine science, mathematics, technology, history, language arts, and the arts to solve authentic problems. AGI may assist by organizing information, generating simulations, or suggesting possible solutions, but teachers will help students divide responsibilities, resolve disagreements, appreciate diverse perspectives, communicate effectively, and evaluate ideas thoughtfully. Collaboration teaches students that the best solutions often emerge when people contribute different experiences and viewpoints. These interpersonal skills cannot be developed through technology alone; they require interaction with classmates and guidance from caring educators.

Parents will continue depending upon teachers as trusted partners throughout their children's education. As intelligent technologies become more common, families may have questions about privacy, academic honesty, responsible technology use, and balancing digital learning with healthy personal development. Teachers help build trust by communicating openly with families, explaining how educational technologies are used, listening to concerns, and working together to support student success. This partnership becomes especially important as children learn to navigate increasingly sophisticated digital environments. Strong relationships between schools and families provide students with consistent guidance both inside and outside the classroom.

Although AGI may dramatically change many aspects of education, one truth will remain unchanged: students learn best when they feel connected to teachers who care about their success. A classroom built on respect, encouragement, curiosity, and meaningful relationships creates an environment where students are willing to ask questions, take intellectual risks, learn from mistakes, and pursue excellence. Technology can enhance that environment, but it cannot create it on its own. Human relationships remain the foundation upon which all meaningful learning is built.

As we look toward the future, it becomes clear that the role of teachers is not disappearing—it is expanding. Educators will become mentors, learning designers, ethical guides, coaches, collaborators, innovators, and leaders who prepare students for a world filled with intelligent technologies while helping them preserve the qualities that define our humanity. AGI may change the tools used in education, but teachers will continue shaping lives through encouragement, wisdom, compassion, and high expectations. The most successful classrooms of the future will not be those with the most advanced technology. They will be the classrooms where exceptional teachers use intelligent tools wisely to help every student grow academically, socially, emotionally, and ethically. In an AGI-ready classroom, technology supports learning, but teachers continue to inspire the future.

Chapter 3 Summary

The Future Role of Teachers in an AGI World

Teachers have always been the foundation of education. While technology has changed the tools used in classrooms, it has never replaced the importance of human relationships, guidance, encouragement, and ethical leadership. Artificial General Intelligence (AGI) may transform many aspects of teaching and learning, but it will not replace the essential role of educators.

This chapter explained that teachers do much more than present information. They inspire curiosity, build confidence, recognize individual strengths, encourage perseverance, and help students develop critical thinking, communication, creativity, and strong character. These uniquely human qualities remain at the center of meaningful education.

As AGI becomes more advanced, teachers may use intelligent systems to assist with lesson planning, personalized learning, student progress monitoring, language translation, assessment support, and administrative tasks. By reducing routine work, AGI can allow teachers to spend more time mentoring students, leading discussions, providing feedback, and building positive classroom relationships.

The chapter also emphasized that teachers will become lifelong learners who continually develop new skills and adapt to emerging technologies. Professional development, collaboration with colleagues, and responsible technology integration will become increasingly important as education evolves.

Finally, the chapter reinforced that the future classroom will always depend on human leadership. AGI can provide information and support learning, but teachers provide wisdom, compassion, ethical guidance, and inspiration. The most successful AGI-ready classrooms will combine intelligent technology with exceptional educators who place students at the center of every learning experience.

Chapter 3 Reflection

Think carefully about the ideas presented in this chapter. Answer each question using complete sentences.

1. Why do you believe teachers will continue to play an important role even as AGI becomes more advanced?
2. Which human qualities discussed in this chapter do you think are most important for great teachers? Explain your answer.
3. How could AGI reduce the workload of teachers without replacing them?
4. Why is building positive relationships between teachers and students so important for learning?
5. How can teachers help students think critically instead of simply accepting information from intelligent systems?
6. Why should teachers continue learning throughout their careers?
7. If you were a teacher, how would you use AGI to improve learning while keeping students actively engaged?
8. What responsibilities do teachers have when helping students use AGI ethically and responsibly?
9. Describe one classroom activity where both a teacher and AGI work together successfully.
10. After reading this chapter, how has your opinion changed about the future role of teachers in education?

Chapter 3 Worksheet

Part A – Vocabulary Matching

Match each term with its correct definition.

A. Mentor

B. Critical Thinking

C. Lifelong Learning

D. Professional Development

E. Ethical Leadership

F. Collaboration

G. Personalized Learning

H. Emotional Intelligence

1. _____ Continuing to improve knowledge and skills throughout life.
2. _____ Working together to accomplish shared goals.
3. _____ Understanding and managing emotions while recognizing the feelings of others.
4. _____ A trusted guide who supports another person's growth and success.
5. _____ Improving teaching knowledge through ongoing education and training.
6. _____ Learning experiences designed around individual student needs.
7. _____ Making responsible decisions based on fairness, honesty, and integrity.
8. _____ Carefully analyzing information before making decisions.

Part B – Short Answer

1. List four responsibilities that teachers will continue to have in an AGI-ready classroom.

____

____

2. Why is empathy an important quality for teachers?

____

____

3. Name three ways AGI could assist teachers with their daily work.

____

____

4. Why should students verify information provided by intelligent systems?

5. How do teachers help students develop confidence?

Part C – Critical Thinking

Imagine you are designing the classroom of the future.

Write one paragraph describing how teachers and AGI could work together to create an exciting, safe, and effective learning environment while keeping students at the center of every decision.

Chapter 3 Quiz and Answer Key

Quiz

Multiple Choice

1. According to this chapter, the primary role of teachers in the future will be to:

A. Be replaced by AGI.

B. Focus only on grading assignments.

C. Mentor, guide, inspire, and support student learning.

D. Allow technology to make all classroom decisions.

2. Which task could AGI help teachers perform?

A. Organizing lesson materials.

B. Monitoring student progress.

C. Creating personalized learning activities.

D. All of the above.

3. Which quality is uniquely human and cannot easily be replaced by technology?

A. Empathy.

B. Compassion.

C. Ethical judgment.

D. All of the above.

4. Why is critical thinking important when students use AGI?

A. To evaluate information carefully.

B. To recognize possible errors or bias.

C. To make informed decisions.

D. All of the above.

5. Which statement best describes the partnership between teachers and AGI?

A. AGI replaces teachers completely.

B. Teachers and AGI work together to improve learning.

C. Teachers no longer need professional development.

D. Students no longer need teachers.

True or False

6. _____ Teachers only teach information.
7. _____ Human relationships remain important in education.
8. _____ Professional development helps teachers prepare for emerging technologies.
9. _____ AGI should support teachers rather than replace them.
10. _____ Lifelong learning is important for both teachers and students.

Answer Key

Worksheet Answers

Part A – Vocabulary Matching

1. **C**
2. **F**
3. **H**
4. **A**
5. **D**
6. **G**
7. **E**
8. **B**

Part B – Suggested Responses

1. Possible answers include mentoring students, providing ethical guidance, building relationships, encouraging critical thinking, supporting emotional growth, facilitating discussions, and inspiring lifelong learning.
2. Empathy helps teachers understand students' feelings, provide encouragement, and create a supportive learning environment.
3. Possible answers include lesson planning, generating instructional materials, analyzing student progress, creating personalized activities, translating content, and organizing classroom resources.
4. Students should verify information because intelligent systems can sometimes produce inaccurate, incomplete, or biased responses.
5. Teachers build confidence by encouraging effort, recognizing student strengths, providing constructive feedback, supporting perseverance, and celebrating progress.

Quiz Answers

1. **C**
2. **D**
3. **D**
4. **D**
5. **B**
6. **False**

7. **True**
8. **True**
9. **True**
10. **True**

Chapter 4

Personalized Learning Beyond Today's AI

Personalized learning has been one of the greatest goals of education for many decades. Every student enters the classroom with unique experiences, strengths, interests, talents, challenges, and dreams. Some students learn best by reading, while others understand concepts more easily through discussion, hands-on activities, visual demonstrations, or repeated practice. Some students master new ideas quickly, while others benefit from additional guidance and encouragement before feeling confident. Great teachers have always recognized these differences and worked hard to meet the individual needs of every learner. However, providing personalized instruction has never been an easy task. A single classroom may contain twenty-five or thirty students, each learning at a different pace and requiring different kinds of support. Even the most experienced teachers face the challenge of balancing individual attention with the needs of the entire class. Artificial General Intelligence has the potential to become an important educational partner by helping teachers personalize learning more effectively while preserving the human relationships that remain essential to successful education.

To understand how AGI could transform personalized learning, it is helpful to first understand what personalization truly means. Personalized learning is not simply allowing every student to work independently on a computer. Instead, it is an educational approach that recognizes every learner as an individual. It adjusts instruction, resources, pacing, feedback, and learning experiences to help each student reach meaningful academic goals. Effective personalization also encourages students to take ownership of their learning by understanding their strengths, identifying areas for improvement, setting goals, and reflecting on their progress. Personalized learning combines academic achievement with personal growth, helping students become confident, independent, and motivated learners.

Today's Artificial Intelligence has already introduced many forms of personalized education. Educational software can recommend practice questions based on previous answers, adjust the difficulty of assignments, provide immediate feedback, and identify concepts that require additional review. Language-learning applications adapt lessons based on student performance, while mathematics platforms recommend exercises that match individual skill levels. These technologies have improved learning opportunities for many students, but they remain limited because they focus on specific tasks or subjects. Artificial General Intelligence may eventually extend personalization far beyond these current capabilities by understanding learning across multiple disciplines, recognizing patterns in student development, and supporting teachers with a more complete picture of each learner's educational journey.

Imagine entering a classroom where every student begins the day with a learning plan designed specifically for their needs while still participating in shared classroom experiences. One student who excels in mathematics may receive more advanced problem-solving activities while another receives additional support with foundational concepts. A student who enjoys visual learning may receive interactive simulations, while another who prefers reading explores detailed explanations and historical examples. Students interested in engineering could connect science lessons with real-world design challenges, while students passionate about art explore creative projects that reinforce the same academic concepts. The teacher remains the leader of the classroom, ensuring that every student works toward common educational standards while using different pathways to reach those goals. AGI supports this process by organizing information and suggesting learning opportunities, but the teacher decides which recommendations best serve each student.

One of the most exciting possibilities of AGI is its ability to recognize patterns that may be difficult for people to identify quickly. Over time, an intelligent educational system could analyze classroom participation, assignment performance, project work, reading habits, writing development, and problem-solving strategies to help teachers understand how students learn most effectively. Rather than replacing teacher observations, this information provides another valuable resource that educators can use when making instructional decisions. A teacher might discover that a student consistently understands scientific concepts after participating in group discussions or that another student demonstrates stronger writing skills after creating visual outlines before beginning an essay. These insights allow teachers to provide more targeted support while continuing to use their professional judgment and classroom experience.

Personalized learning also extends beyond academic subjects. Every student develops socially and emotionally as they grow. Confidence, motivation, perseverance, resilience, communication, collaboration, and self-management all influence academic success. Teachers recognize when students become discouraged, celebrate personal achievements, encourage persistence after failure, and create supportive learning environments where every learner feels respected. Future AGI systems may help educators identify patterns related to student engagement, participation, or learning behaviors, but interpreting these patterns requires human understanding. Teachers know that students are more than data points or assessment scores. Every learner has a unique story, personal experiences, family background, cultural identity, interests, and aspirations that shape the learning process. Effective personalization always begins by seeing students as complete individuals rather than simply measuring academic performance.

Another important advantage of personalized learning is helping students develop ownership of their education. Instead of waiting for teachers to direct every activity, students gradually learn how to set goals, monitor their progress, reflect on their strengths, identify areas for improvement, and develop strategies for overcoming challenges. AGI may provide personalized recommendations, organize learning resources, and offer immediate feedback, but students remain active participants in their educational journey. Learning becomes something students do with purpose rather than something that simply happens to them. This sense of ownership encourages responsibility, independence, curiosity, and confidence—qualities that support lifelong learning long after students leave the classroom.

As education moves toward increasingly personalized learning environments, one principle must remain clear: technology should strengthen relationships rather than replace them. Students thrive when they know their teachers understand their goals, recognize their potential, and genuinely care about their success. Personalized learning is most effective when intelligent technology supports educators by providing useful insights while teachers continue making instructional decisions based on compassion, experience, professional expertise, and meaningful relationships. Artificial General Intelligence may expand the possibilities of personalized education, but the heart of learning will always remain the connection between dedicated teachers and the students they inspire every day.

Chapter 4 (Part 2)

As personalized learning continues to evolve, classrooms of the future may become far more flexible than those of today. Instead of every student completing the same assignment at the same pace, learning experiences may be adjusted to help each individual achieve the same educational goals through different pathways. For example, during a lesson about ecosystems, one student may explore an interactive virtual rainforest, another may conduct a local field investigation, another may analyze scientific data, while another creates a multimedia presentation explaining how living organisms depend upon one another. Although each student approaches the topic differently, everyone is working toward the same learning objectives. AGI may help organize these learning experiences by recommending resources, monitoring progress, and identifying areas where additional support is needed. The teacher remains responsible for ensuring that learning is accurate, meaningful, and aligned with educational standards.

Students with different learning needs may especially benefit from future AGI-supported classrooms. Some learners require additional practice before mastering new concepts, while others need greater challenges to remain engaged. Students learning English as a second language may receive translated explanations and vocabulary support. Learners with reading difficulties may benefit from text-to-speech technology or simplified explanations that gradually increase in complexity. Students with advanced abilities may explore enrichment projects that encourage deeper investigation without waiting for the rest of the class to finish routine assignments. Personalized learning creates opportunities for every student to experience growth, not by lowering expectations, but by providing the appropriate support needed to reach high standards.

One important advantage of AGI-assisted personalization is immediate feedback. Traditionally, students often waited hours or even days before receiving comments on assignments, quizzes, or classroom activities. Future intelligent systems may provide instant guidance as students work through problems, identify misunderstandings before they become habits, and recommend additional practice when necessary. Immediate feedback helps students correct mistakes while ideas remain fresh in their minds. However, not all feedback should come from technology. Teachers continue providing encouragement, asking thoughtful questions, recognizing creative thinking, and helping students understand why an answer is correct rather than simply telling them whether it is right or wrong. Human feedback builds confidence and deeper understanding in ways that automated responses alone cannot achieve.

Personalized learning also encourages students to become active participants in setting educational goals. Instead of viewing assignments as tasks to complete only for grades, students learn to reflect on their progress, identify strengths, recognize challenges, and develop strategies for improvement. Teachers help students establish realistic goals while encouraging perseverance and celebrating meaningful progress. AGI may assist by tracking achievements, organizing learning portfolios, and recommending resources, but the responsibility for learning continues to belong to the student. This shared partnership between student, teacher, and technology encourages independence while maintaining accountability.

Although personalized learning offers many exciting possibilities, schools must also address important challenges. One concern is ensuring that personalization does not become isolation. Students learn valuable lessons by working with classmates, participating in discussions, solving problems together, and appreciating different perspectives. Collaboration teaches communication, leadership, empathy, and teamwork—skills that remain essential regardless of technological advancement. Teachers play an important role in balancing individualized instruction with shared classroom experiences that help students build relationships and learn from one another. An AGI-ready classroom should strengthen both independent learning and collaborative learning rather than choosing one over the other.

Another important consideration involves fairness. Personalized learning should provide equal opportunities for every student, regardless of family income, language, disability, or geographic location. Schools must ensure that advanced educational technologies are available to all learners rather than creating new barriers between those who have access and those who do not. Equity means providing every student with the tools, support, and encouragement needed to reach their highest potential. Educational leaders must continue investing in reliable technology, teacher training, accessibility, and community partnerships so that innovation benefits every learner.

Privacy also remains a significant responsibility in personalized learning environments. Intelligent educational systems may collect information about student performance, learning preferences, classroom participation, and academic progress. Schools have an ethical responsibility to protect this information carefully, explain how it is used, and follow all applicable privacy laws and policies. Students and parents should understand what data is collected, why it is needed, and how it supports learning. Trust is built when schools communicate openly and use technology responsibly while respecting the rights of every learner.

Teachers will continue serving as the decision-makers throughout this process. While AGI may identify patterns and suggest instructional strategies, educators determine how those recommendations fit the needs of individual students. Professional judgment remains essential because learning involves factors that extend beyond academic data. Teachers understand classroom culture, family circumstances, student interests, emotional well-being, and personal motivation in ways that intelligent systems cannot fully measure. Technology provides valuable information, but teachers provide understanding. Together, they create learning environments that are both innovative and compassionate.

As students become more familiar with personalized learning, they will also develop important lifelong skills. They will learn how to manage their time, evaluate information carefully, accept constructive feedback, solve unfamiliar problems, and adapt to changing circumstances. These abilities prepare students not only for future careers but also for responsible citizenship in a rapidly evolving world. Personalized learning is not simply about improving test scores. It is about helping every learner discover their strengths, build confidence, and become capable of learning throughout life. Education becomes a continuous journey rather than a destination reached at graduation.

Looking ahead, personalized learning supported by AGI has the potential to transform education into an experience that is more responsive, engaging, and meaningful than ever before. Students may receive instruction that respects their individual abilities while encouraging collaboration, creativity, and critical thinking. Teachers may spend less time managing routine administrative tasks and more time inspiring, mentoring, and supporting learners. Parents may gain clearer insights into student progress while working more closely with schools to support educational success. Together, these partnerships can create learning environments where every student has the opportunity to thrive.

The future of personalized learning is not defined by how intelligent technology becomes. It is defined by how wisely educators choose to use it. The most successful AGI-ready classrooms will never measure success by the number of devices they own or the sophistication of their software. Instead, they will measure success by the growth of their students—their curiosity, confidence, compassion, creativity, resilience, and willingness to continue learning throughout their lives. Artificial General Intelligence may help personalize education, but it is the dedication of teachers, the determination of students, and the support of families that will continue shaping the future of learning for generations to come.

Chapter 4 Summary

Personalized Learning Beyond Today's AI

Personalized learning recognizes that every student learns differently. Each learner has unique strengths, interests, experiences, challenges, and goals. Instead of expecting every student to learn in exactly the same way or at the same pace, personalized learning adapts instruction to meet individual needs while maintaining high academic expectations for everyone.

Today's Artificial Intelligence already supports personalized learning by recommending lessons, adjusting the difficulty of assignments, and providing immediate feedback. Artificial General Intelligence (AGI) has the potential to expand these capabilities by helping teachers better understand how students learn, identifying learning patterns across multiple subjects, and recommending individualized learning experiences that support academic growth.

The chapter emphasized that personalized learning does not replace teachers. Instead, AGI serves as a valuable educational assistant by organizing information, monitoring student progress, and suggesting instructional strategies. Teachers continue making the important educational decisions while building relationships, encouraging students, providing ethical guidance, and supporting social and emotional development.

Students also have an important role in personalized learning. They become active participants by setting goals, reflecting on their progress, accepting feedback, and developing lifelong learning habits. Personalized learning encourages independence while helping students take greater responsibility for their education.

Finally, the chapter highlighted the importance of fairness, student privacy, accessibility, collaboration, and responsible technology use. The future of personalized learning depends not only on intelligent technology but also on teachers, parents, school leaders, and students working together to create learning environments where every learner has the opportunity to succeed.

Chapter 4 Reflection

Take time to reflect on the ideas presented in this chapter. Answer each question using complete sentences.

1. Why is personalized learning important for students with different learning styles?
2. How could AGI help teachers provide more individualized instruction?
3. Why should students continue taking responsibility for their own learning even when intelligent technologies are available?
4. What human qualities remain important in a personalized learning environment?
5. Why is collaboration still valuable even when learning becomes more personalized?
6. How can schools protect student privacy while using advanced educational technologies?
7. What role should parents play in supporting personalized learning?
8. If you could design your own personalized learning experience, what would it look like?
9. What benefits and challenges do you see in AGI-supported personalized learning?
10. After reading this chapter, how has your understanding of personalized learning changed?

Chapter 4 Worksheet

Part A – Vocabulary Matching

Match each term with its correct definition.

A. Personalized Learning

B. Learning Pathway

C. Feedback

D. Collaboration

E. Student Privacy

F. Adaptability

G. Lifelong Learning

H. Educational Equity

1. _____ Learning experiences designed around each student's individual needs.
2. _____ Information that helps students improve their performance.
3. _____ Working with others to achieve shared goals.
4. _____ Protecting personal educational information.
5. _____ Continuing to learn throughout life.
6. _____ A student's unique route toward mastering learning goals.
7. _____ The ability to adjust successfully to change.
8. _____ Providing fair educational opportunities for every learner.

Part B – Short Answer

1. Explain how AGI may improve personalized learning.

____

____

2. Why are teachers still necessary in personalized learning environments?

____

____

3. Name four human skills that remain essential even when AGI supports learning.

____

____

4. Why should students learn to set their own educational goals?

____

____

5. Why is protecting student data important?

____

Part C – Critical Thinking

Imagine you are designing an AGI-powered classroom where every student receives personalized instruction.

Describe three ways you would ensure that technology improves learning while protecting fairness, privacy, collaboration, and the important role of teachers.

Chapter 4 Quiz

Multiple Choice

1. What is the main goal of personalized learning?

A. Teaching every student exactly the same way.

B. Adjusting instruction to meet individual student needs.

C. Replacing teachers with computers.

D. Eliminating classroom discussions.

2. How could AGI support personalized learning?

A. By analyzing learning patterns.

B. By recommending individualized activities.

C. By helping teachers identify learning gaps.

D. All of the above.

3. Which person remains responsible for making educational decisions?

A. The AGI system.

B. The student only.

C. The teacher.

D. The computer programmer.

4. Which quality remains important in every personalized classroom?

A. Human relationships.

B. Empathy.

C. Collaboration.

D. All of the above.

5. Why should schools protect student information?

A. To respect privacy and build trust.

B. Because data has no value.

C. To eliminate teachers.

D. To prevent students from learning.

True or False

6. _____ Every student learns in exactly the same way.
7. _____ Personalized learning can help students become more independent learners.
8. _____ AGI should replace teacher judgment.
9. _____ Collaboration remains valuable in personalized learning.
10. _____ Lifelong learning prepares students for future changes.

Chapter 4 Answer Key

Worksheet Answers

Part A – Vocabulary Matching

1. **A**
2. **C**
3. **D**
4. **E**
5. **G**
6. **B**
7. **F**
8. **H**

Part B – Suggested Responses

1. AGI can analyze student progress, recognize learning patterns, recommend personalized activities, provide immediate feedback, and help teachers identify learning needs more efficiently.
2. Teachers continue guiding instruction, building relationships, encouraging students, providing ethical leadership, supporting emotional development, and making professional educational decisions.
3. Possible answers include creativity, empathy, communication, collaboration, ethical judgment, leadership, adaptability, resilience, and critical thinking.
4. Goal setting helps students take ownership of their learning, monitor progress, stay motivated, and become lifelong learners.
5. Student information must be protected to respect privacy, maintain trust, comply with school policies and laws, and ensure educational data is used responsibly.

1. **B**
2. **D**
3. **C**
4. **D**
5. **A**
6. **False**

7. **True**
8. **False**
9. **True**
10. **True**

Chapter 5

Intelligent Classrooms of the Future

For generations, classrooms have been places where students gather to learn, ask questions, solve problems, and prepare for life beyond school. Although the appearance of classrooms has changed over time, their purpose has remained remarkably consistent. Years ago, classrooms relied primarily on chalkboards, printed textbooks, handwritten assignments, and face-to-face instruction. As technology advanced, overhead projectors gave way to computers, interactive whiteboards, tablets, and online learning platforms. Today, many classrooms already use Artificial Intelligence to assist with lesson planning, language translation, adaptive learning, and student assessment. The next stage of educational innovation may introduce learning environments supported by Artificial General Intelligence (AGI), creating classrooms that are more responsive, collaborative, and personalized than ever before. However, the classroom of the future will not simply be defined by advanced technology. It will be defined by how effectively technology supports meaningful learning while preserving the human relationships that make education successful.

An intelligent classroom is not simply a room filled with computers or sophisticated digital equipment. Instead, it is a learning environment where technology works together with teachers and students to improve understanding, encourage creativity, solve problems, and support individual growth. In an AGI-ready classroom, technology becomes an educational partner rather than the center of attention. The teacher remains the instructional leader who guides discussions, encourages curiosity, builds relationships, and helps students connect knowledge to real-world experiences. AGI supports this process by organizing information, identifying learning patterns, recommending instructional resources, and helping educators respond more effectively to the needs of every learner. The classroom remains centered on people while technology quietly enhances the learning experience behind the scenes.

Imagine entering a classroom where the learning environment automatically adjusts to support both teaching and learning. Interactive displays present visual explanations that match the day's lesson. Students access learning materials through devices that remember previous progress while suggesting resources based on individual learning goals. Scientific simulations allow students to safely explore experiments that would otherwise be impossible because of cost, distance, or safety concerns. History lessons transport students through immersive digital recreations of important historical events, allowing learners to observe civilizations, cultures, and discoveries in engaging new ways. Mathematics becomes more interactive through visual demonstrations that help students understand abstract concepts, while literature comes alive through multimedia experiences that encourage discussion and critical analysis. These technologies do not replace thoughtful instruction; they provide additional opportunities for students to experience learning in deeper and more meaningful ways.

One of the greatest advantages of intelligent classrooms is their ability to support active learning. Traditional education sometimes relied heavily on memorization and repetition because information was difficult to access. Today's students have immediate access to enormous amounts of knowledge through digital technologies. As a result, future classrooms may spend less time asking students to memorize isolated facts and more time encouraging them to analyze information, solve authentic problems, conduct research, communicate ideas clearly, collaborate with classmates, and develop creative solutions to real-world challenges. AGI can assist by providing immediate access to reliable information, organizing complex data, generating simulations, and helping students explore multiple perspectives. Teachers then guide students in evaluating evidence, questioning assumptions, and applying knowledge responsibly.

Collaboration will become even more important in intelligent classrooms. Modern workplaces increasingly require people to work across disciplines, cultures, and geographic locations. Students therefore need opportunities to practice teamwork long before entering their future careers. Intelligent technologies may support collaboration by connecting students with classrooms around the world, translating conversations between different languages, organizing group projects, and helping teams share ideas efficiently. Students may work together to solve environmental challenges, design community improvement projects, investigate scientific questions, or develop creative business ideas while learning how to communicate respectfully, appreciate diverse viewpoints, and resolve disagreements constructively. These experiences prepare students for a future where human collaboration remains one of the most valuable skills despite continuing technological advancement.

An intelligent classroom also encourages curiosity by making learning more interactive. Rather than simply reading about the solar system, students might explore virtual space missions that demonstrate planetary motion and gravitational forces. Biology students could examine three-dimensional models of living cells, while engineering students design structures using advanced simulations that test strength and stability before construction begins. Geography students may investigate global climate patterns through interactive maps and live environmental data, while language arts students collaborate on digital storytelling projects that combine writing, visual design, and multimedia communication. AGI helps organize these learning opportunities while teachers ensure that students understand the underlying concepts rather than becoming distracted by technology itself. Effective learning always emphasizes understanding before entertainment.

As classrooms become increasingly intelligent, teachers continue serving as the leaders who shape classroom culture. Every learning environment reflects the expectations established by the educator. Respect, kindness, responsibility, perseverance, honesty, and curiosity do not automatically emerge because technology becomes more advanced. They develop through consistent guidance, positive relationships, thoughtful classroom management, and meaningful conversations. Teachers help students learn how to work respectfully with intelligent technologies while maintaining academic integrity, ethical decision-making, and responsible digital citizenship. These lessons become increasingly important as AGI becomes more capable because students must understand not only how to use advanced technology but also when, why, and under what circumstances it should be used responsibly.

Another important characteristic of intelligent classrooms is flexibility. Every school serves students with different backgrounds, interests, learning styles, languages, abilities, and career aspirations. Future classrooms should provide multiple pathways for learning without lowering academic expectations. Some students may demonstrate understanding through written reports, while others create presentations, scientific models, engineering prototypes, artistic projects, or multimedia demonstrations. AGI can recommend different learning resources and instructional strategies, but teachers determine which approaches best support each learner. Flexibility allows students to discover their strengths while ensuring that every individual continues progressing toward shared educational standards.

The intelligent classroom of the future is not a vision built around machines replacing people. Instead, it represents a learning environment where technology quietly supports teachers, empowers students, strengthens collaboration, and creates opportunities that were previously impossible. The classroom remains a place where relationships matter, questions are encouraged, mistakes become learning opportunities, and every student is challenged to reach their highest potential. As AGI continues developing, the schools that benefit most will be those that combine technological innovation with compassionate teaching, strong leadership, ethical responsibility, and a commitment to lifelong learning. Intelligent classrooms are ultimately not about creating smarter machines—they are about helping students become wiser, more capable, and more compassionate human beings.

Chapter 5 (Part 2)

As intelligent classrooms continue to evolve, the daily learning experience may become more organized, efficient, and responsive to student needs. Instead of spending valuable instructional time searching for resources, recording attendance, organizing assignments, or manually tracking academic progress, teachers may receive assistance from AGI systems that perform many routine administrative tasks automatically. Attendance records could be updated securely, assignments organized according to each student's learning plan, and classroom resources prepared before students arrive. These efficiencies do not reduce the importance of teachers. Instead, they give educators more time to do what they do best—teach, mentor, encourage, and build meaningful relationships with students. Every minute saved on repetitive administrative work becomes another opportunity to engage directly with learners.

Future intelligent classrooms may also support continuous assessment rather than relying primarily on occasional quizzes or major examinations. Instead of measuring learning only at the end of a lesson or grading period, AGI-assisted educational systems could help teachers recognize student understanding throughout the learning process. As students participate in discussions, complete projects, solve problems, conduct research, and demonstrate new skills, the system may organize observations that help teachers identify strengths, recognize misconceptions, and recommend timely interventions. This approach allows educators to address learning challenges before they become larger obstacles. Assessment becomes a tool for improving instruction rather than simply measuring performance. Teachers continue making final educational decisions while using technology to gain deeper insight into student growth.

Safety will remain one of the highest priorities in every intelligent classroom. While advanced technologies provide many educational benefits, schools must also protect students from cybersecurity threats, unauthorized access to personal information, inappropriate online content, and misuse of intelligent systems. School leaders, technology specialists, teachers, parents, and students all share responsibility for maintaining safe digital learning environments. Strong passwords, secure networks, responsible online behavior, and regular cybersecurity training become essential parts of modern education. Students should understand that digital safety is not only a technical issue but also a personal responsibility that requires honesty, respect, and good judgment every time technology is used.

Privacy is equally important as intelligent educational systems become more capable. Personalized learning often depends on information about student progress, learning preferences, and classroom performance. Schools must collect and use this information responsibly while protecting the rights of students and families. Parents deserve clear explanations about what information is collected, how it supports learning, who has access to it, and how long it is retained. Transparency builds confidence between schools and families while encouraging responsible innovation. Intelligent classrooms should never compromise trust in pursuit of technological advancement. Responsible technology use begins with protecting the dignity and privacy of every learner.

School leaders play a vital role in creating successful intelligent classrooms. Principals, curriculum directors, technology coordinators, and district administrators make decisions that influence how new technologies are introduced, supported, and evaluated. Effective leadership requires more than purchasing modern equipment. Leaders must develop long-term plans that include teacher training, technical support, cybersecurity, accessibility, ethical guidelines, and continuous evaluation of educational outcomes. They should regularly ask whether new technologies genuinely improve student learning, strengthen instruction, and support teachers in meaningful ways. Innovation should always serve educational goals rather than becoming an end in itself.

Students also have important responsibilities in intelligent classrooms. Advanced technology does not eliminate the need for effort, honesty, or self-discipline. Students remain responsible for completing assignments, participating actively in discussions, respecting classmates, asking thoughtful questions, and using intelligent systems ethically. They must learn when technology is appropriate, when independent thinking is required, and when collaboration with others leads to stronger solutions. Responsible students understand that AGI is a powerful educational tool, not a shortcut that replaces learning. They use technology to deepen understanding rather than avoiding the hard work that meaningful learning often requires.

Another important feature of intelligent classrooms is their ability to connect learning with real-world experiences. Future students may work on interdisciplinary projects that combine science, mathematics, engineering, history, literature, economics, and environmental studies to address authentic community challenges. AGI may help students analyze information, compare solutions, model possible outcomes, and organize research findings. Teachers guide students through the decision-making process by encouraging critical thinking, evaluating evidence, and considering ethical consequences. These learning experiences prepare students to solve complex problems while understanding that successful solutions require both technological knowledge and human wisdom.

Intelligent classrooms may also strengthen communication between schools and families. Parents could receive timely updates about classroom activities, learning goals, student progress, upcoming projects, and recommended ways to support learning at home. Instead of communication occurring only during report card periods or parent conferences, families become active educational partners throughout the school year. Teachers continue interpreting student progress while technology helps organize information in clear and meaningful ways. Strong partnerships between schools and families create consistent support systems that encourage student success both inside and outside the classroom.

As technology becomes increasingly capable, schools must also preserve opportunities for creativity, imagination, and human connection. Students should continue participating in music, art, theater, athletics, debate, community service, laboratory investigations, outdoor learning, and collaborative projects that develop social and emotional skills. AGI can enhance many of these experiences by providing additional resources, simulations, or creative suggestions, but it should never replace the joy of discovering ideas through direct human interaction. Education prepares students not only to perform academic tasks but also to become compassionate citizens, thoughtful leaders, and responsible members of their communities.

Looking toward the future, intelligent classrooms will continue changing as new discoveries reshape education. Some technologies that seem remarkable today may eventually become as common as calculators, laptops, or interactive whiteboards. What remains constant is the purpose of education itself: helping students develop knowledge, character, curiosity, resilience, and the confidence to contribute positively to society. Schools that successfully prepare for AGI will recognize that technology alone does not create outstanding education. Outstanding education occurs when dedicated teachers, supportive families, visionary leaders, motivated students, and responsible technologies work together toward a shared mission of lifelong learning.

The intelligent classroom of the future is ultimately a place where innovation serves humanity. It is a classroom where teachers continue inspiring, students continue discovering, families continue supporting, and technology quietly strengthens the learning experience without replacing the relationships that make education meaningful. AGI may transform many educational tools, but the true measure of an intelligent classroom will always be the growth of the students who learn within it. When schools combine advanced technology with compassion, wisdom, integrity, and a commitment to excellence, they prepare young people not only for the future of work but also for the future of responsible citizenship and lifelong learning.

Chapter 5 Summary

Intelligent Classrooms of the Future

Intelligent classrooms combine the knowledge and experience of teachers with the capabilities of Artificial General Intelligence (AGI) to create engaging, personalized, and effective learning environments. While advanced technologies can organize information, provide learning resources, and support classroom management, teachers remain the instructional leaders who guide learning, build relationships, and help students develop character and critical thinking skills.

This chapter explained that intelligent classrooms are not simply rooms filled with advanced technology. Instead, they are learning environments where technology supports teaching while keeping students at the center of every educational decision. AGI can assist teachers with lesson preparation, personalized instruction, continuous assessment, classroom organization, and administrative tasks, allowing educators to spend more time mentoring students and encouraging meaningful learning.

The chapter also explored how intelligent classrooms encourage collaboration, creativity, communication, and problem-solving through real-world learning experiences. Students may work on interdisciplinary projects, participate in interactive simulations, and develop future-ready skills while continuing to learn the importance of teamwork, ethical decision-making, and responsible technology use.

Privacy, cybersecurity, accessibility, and educational equity remain essential responsibilities as schools adopt increasingly advanced technologies. School leaders, teachers, students, and families all play important roles in ensuring that intelligent classrooms are safe, inclusive, and focused on student success.

The future classroom is not defined by technology alone. It is defined by how wisely people use technology to strengthen education, inspire curiosity, and prepare students to become knowledgeable, ethical, compassionate, and lifelong learners.

Chapter 5 Reflection

Think about what you learned in this chapter. Write your answers in complete sentences.

1. What makes an intelligent classroom different from a traditional classroom?
2. Why should teachers remain the leaders of intelligent classrooms?
3. How could AGI improve classroom learning without replacing human interaction?
4. Why are collaboration and communication still important in technology-rich classrooms?
5. What responsibilities do students have when using intelligent technologies?
6. Why should schools continue teaching creativity, ethics, and critical thinking even as AGI becomes more advanced?
7. How can intelligent classrooms improve communication between schools and families?
8. What challenges might schools face when creating intelligent classrooms?

9. If you designed an intelligent classroom, what features would you include to improve learning?
10. What is the most important lesson you learned from this chapter about the future of education?

Chapter 5 Worksheet

Part A – Vocabulary Matching

Match each term with the correct definition.

A. Intelligent Classroom

B. Collaboration

C. Cybersecurity

D. Continuous Assessment

E. Personalized Learning

F. Privacy

G. Educational Technology

H. Innovation

1. _____ Protecting computers, networks, and digital information from threats.
2. _____ A classroom where technology and teachers work together to improve learning.
3. _____ Working together toward shared goals.
4. _____ Using technology to support teaching and learning.
5. _____ Ongoing evaluation of student progress during learning.
6. _____ Protecting personal information.
7. _____ Creating new ideas, methods, or solutions.
8. _____ Learning experiences designed to meet individual student needs.

Part B – Short Answer

1. List four ways AGI may help teachers in intelligent classrooms.

___

___

2. Why is classroom collaboration important in the future of education?

____

____

3. Explain why cybersecurity is important in schools.

____

____

4. Why should teachers continue making educational decisions even when AGI is available?

____

____

5. Describe one real-world project that students could complete in an intelligent classroom.

____

____

____

Part C – Critical Thinking

Imagine your school is building a new intelligent classroom.

Write one paragraph describing how teachers, students, parents, and AGI should work together to create a safe, engaging, and effective learning environment.

____

____

____

____

____

____

Chapter 5 Quiz

Multiple Choice

1. What is the primary purpose of an intelligent classroom?

A. Replacing teachers.

B. Supporting teaching and improving student learning.

C. Eliminating classroom discussions.

D. Using technology for every activity.

2. Which responsibility remains with teachers in an intelligent classroom?

A. Building relationships with students.

B. Making instructional decisions.

C. Guiding classroom discussions.

D. All of the above.

3. Why is cybersecurity important in intelligent classrooms?

A. To protect digital systems and student information.

B. To replace school administrators.

C. To eliminate homework.

D. To reduce classroom discussions.

4. Which skill will continue to be valuable regardless of technology?

A. Critical thinking.

B. Communication.

C. Collaboration.

D. All of the above.

5. Which statement best describes AGI in an intelligent classroom?

A. AGI replaces teachers.

B. AGI supports teachers and enhances learning.

C. AGI eliminates student responsibility.

D. AGI makes ethics unnecessary.

True or False

6. _____ Intelligent classrooms are only about having more computers.
7. _____ Teachers remain essential in AGI-supported classrooms.
8. _____ Student privacy should always be protected.
9. _____ Families play an important role in supporting student learning.
10. _____ The purpose of technology is to strengthen education, not replace human relationships.

Chapter 5 Answer Key

Worksheet Answers

Part A – Vocabulary Matching

1. **C**
2. **A**
3. **B**
4. **G**
5. **D**
6. **F**
7. **H**
8. **E**

Part B – Suggested Responses

1. Possible answers include organizing lessons, supporting personalized learning, monitoring student progress, creating learning resources, assisting with classroom management, and providing instructional recommendations.
2. Collaboration helps students solve problems together, communicate effectively, appreciate different viewpoints, and prepare for future careers.
3. Cybersecurity protects school networks, student records, educational systems, and personal information from unauthorized access or misuse.

4. Teachers understand students personally, exercise professional judgment, provide ethical guidance, build relationships, and create supportive learning environments.
5. Possible answers include designing sustainable communities, solving environmental challenges, creating engineering prototypes, conducting scientific investigations, or developing community improvement projects.

Quiz Answers

1. **B**
2. **D**
3. **A**
4. **D**
5. **B**
6. **False**
7. **True**
8. **True**
9. **True**
10. **True**

Chapter 6

Curriculum for the AGI Generation

Education has always prepared students for the future. Every generation has learned the knowledge, skills, and values needed to succeed in the world they would eventually enter as adults. As society changed, school curriculum changed as well. New discoveries in science, advances in mathematics, developments in technology, and changes in communication all influenced what students learned in the classroom. Today, Artificial General Intelligence (AGI) presents another opportunity to rethink how schools prepare young people for tomorrow. The purpose of curriculum has never been simply to fill students with information. Instead, curriculum exists to help learners understand the world, develop practical skills, think independently, solve meaningful problems, and become responsible citizens. In an age where intelligent systems may one day access and organize information almost instantly, education must place even greater emphasis on the uniquely human abilities that enable people to create, innovate, lead, and make ethical decisions.

The curriculum designed for the AGI generation should continue teaching strong foundations in reading, writing, mathematics, science, history, and the arts. These subjects remain essential because they provide the knowledge students need to understand the world around them. However, future curriculum should also help students connect these disciplines rather than viewing them as completely separate subjects. Real-world problems rarely belong to only one academic field. Solving environmental challenges requires knowledge of science, mathematics, engineering, economics, communication, and public policy. Developing new medical technologies involves biology, chemistry, computer science, ethics, and collaboration. Future curriculum should encourage students to recognize these connections so they can apply knowledge across multiple disciplines instead of memorizing isolated facts.

One of the most significant changes in future curriculum may involve shifting the focus from remembering information to understanding how to use knowledge wisely. Students will continue learning important facts because knowledge provides the foundation for deeper thinking. However, schools may spend more instructional time helping learners analyze information, ask thoughtful questions, evaluate evidence, compare multiple perspectives, and solve authentic problems. Instead of simply asking students to repeat what they have memorized, teachers may increasingly encourage them to explain ideas, defend conclusions with evidence, design creative solutions, and reflect on the consequences of their decisions. These experiences prepare students to think independently while using intelligent technologies responsibly rather than depending upon them unquestioningly.

Critical thinking should become one of the central goals of curriculum for the AGI generation. Intelligent systems may provide quick answers to many questions, but students must still determine whether those answers are accurate, complete, ethical, and appropriate for the situation. They should learn how to recognize misinformation, identify reliable sources, understand bias, evaluate evidence, and distinguish between facts, opinions, and assumptions. These skills strengthen informed decision-making and prepare students to participate responsibly in democratic societies where thoughtful judgment is essential. Teachers play a vital role in helping students develop these habits through classroom discussions, research projects, debates, case studies, and problem-solving activities that encourage careful analysis rather than simple acceptance of information.

Communication will remain another essential component of future curriculum. Throughout history, the ability to express ideas clearly has influenced leadership, innovation, and collaboration. Students should continue developing strong speaking, listening, writing, reading, and presentation skills regardless of technological advancement. AGI may assist with grammar, translation, organization, or editing, but students still need to communicate original ideas effectively and respectfully. Employers consistently value individuals who can explain complex concepts, collaborate with diverse teams, resolve disagreements professionally, and present thoughtful solutions to challenging problems. Future curriculum should therefore provide many opportunities for students to practice communication through discussions, presentations, writing assignments, collaborative projects, and community engagement.

Creativity also deserves a central place in education for the AGI generation. Intelligent technologies may generate images, music, text, and computer programs, but creativity involves much more than producing content. Creative thinking requires curiosity, imagination, experimentation, persistence, and the willingness to explore new possibilities. Students should be encouraged to invent, design, compose, build, perform, and create original work that reflects their unique perspectives and experiences. Arts education, engineering design, scientific inquiry, entrepreneurship, and project-based learning all help students develop creative confidence. Teachers nurture this creativity by encouraging exploration, supporting risk-taking, and helping students view mistakes as opportunities for growth rather than reasons to stop trying.

Ethics should become an increasingly important part of future curriculum as intelligent technologies become more capable. Students need opportunities to discuss fairness, privacy, cybersecurity, responsible technology use, academic integrity, intellectual property, environmental responsibility, and the social impact of emerging innovations. Ethical reasoning helps learners understand that technological capability does not automatically determine whether something should be done. Every technological advancement carries responsibilities that require thoughtful consideration of how decisions affect individuals, communities, and society. Through discussions, case studies, service-learning experiences, and collaborative problem-solving, students develop the judgment needed to become responsible citizens in an increasingly intelligent world.

Another important feature of curriculum for the AGI generation is adaptability. The careers today's students will pursue may change significantly during their lifetimes as new technologies emerge and industries evolve. Schools cannot predict every future occupation, but they can prepare students to adapt successfully by developing lifelong learning habits. Students should learn how to set goals, seek feedback, manage their time, collaborate effectively, embrace continuous improvement, and remain curious throughout their lives. These transferable skills allow graduates to continue learning long after formal schooling ends. The most successful curriculum will not simply prepare students for their first job. It will prepare them for decades of learning, growth, and meaningful contribution in a rapidly changing world.

Curriculum for the AGI generation is ultimately about preparing students to become thoughtful, capable, compassionate human beings. Technology may transform how information is delivered, how learning is organized, and how classrooms operate, but education's highest purpose remains unchanged. Schools exist to develop knowledge, wisdom, character, responsibility, and hope. The curriculum of tomorrow should strengthen these qualities while embracing innovation responsibly. By combining strong academic foundations with critical thinking, communication, creativity, ethics, collaboration, and lifelong learning, schools can prepare students not only to succeed in an age of Artificial General Intelligence but also to lead it with confidence, integrity, and purpose.

Chapter 6 (Part 2)

As education continues evolving, schools may introduce new learning experiences that reflect the realities of an AGI-powered world. While traditional academic subjects will remain essential, future curriculum may also include courses that help students understand intelligent technologies, digital ethics, data literacy, cybersecurity, entrepreneurship, systems thinking, and responsible innovation. These additions are not intended to replace mathematics, science, language arts, history, or the arts. Instead, they expand the curriculum by helping students understand how these subjects connect to the technologies and challenges they will encounter throughout their lives. A well-rounded education prepares students not only to understand academic concepts but also to apply them responsibly in changing environments.

Project-based learning may become an even more important instructional approach for the AGI generation. Rather than studying each subject separately, students can investigate meaningful questions that require knowledge from multiple disciplines. For example, a project focused on improving water quality in a local community may combine environmental science, chemistry, mathematics, geography, economics, engineering, public speaking, and civic engagement. Students research the problem, collect and analyze data, develop possible solutions, evaluate environmental and financial impacts, and present recommendations to classmates or community members. AGI may help organize research materials, model possible outcomes, and summarize information from multiple sources, but students remain responsible for asking questions, making decisions, evaluating evidence, and communicating their conclusions. This type of learning prepares students for future careers where solving complex problems often requires teamwork across many fields of knowledge.

Career preparation will also become more flexible as technology reshapes the workforce. Many occupations will continue changing, while entirely new careers will emerge. Instead of preparing students for one specific profession, curriculum should help them develop transferable skills that remain valuable across many different industries. Communication, collaboration, creativity, leadership, adaptability, ethical reasoning, digital literacy, and critical thinking are examples of abilities that support success regardless of how technology evolves. Students should also develop confidence in learning new skills throughout their lives because future careers may require continuous professional growth. Schools that emphasize lifelong learning prepare graduates who remain adaptable even as industries transform.

Financial literacy may also become increasingly important in future curriculum. Students should understand budgeting, saving, investing, responsible borrowing, entrepreneurship, and the economic impact of emerging technologies. As intelligent systems automate some routine tasks while creating new opportunities, individuals will benefit from understanding how economic decisions influence personal financial well-being and broader society. Entrepreneurship education encourages students to identify problems, recognize opportunities, develop innovative solutions, and understand the responsibilities involved in creating products or services that improve people's lives. AGI may provide valuable business insights and market analysis, but successful entrepreneurship continues to depend upon human creativity, ethical leadership, perseverance, and sound decision-making.

Assessment methods may also continue changing in the AGI generation. Traditional examinations will likely remain one way of measuring student learning, but schools may increasingly evaluate students through projects, presentations, research investigations, engineering challenges, portfolios, performances, collaborative activities, and real-world problem-solving experiences. These assessments allow students to demonstrate understanding by applying knowledge rather than simply recalling memorized information. AGI may assist teachers by organizing evidence of student progress, identifying learning trends, and providing instructional recommendations, but educators continue evaluating qualities such as originality, communication, teamwork, ethical reasoning, and creativity. Assessment becomes an ongoing process that supports learning rather than serving only as a final measurement of achievement.

Curriculum leaders will play a critical role in helping schools navigate these changes. District curriculum directors, instructional coaches, principals, and teacher leaders must regularly review educational standards, evaluate new instructional resources, and ensure that curriculum remains relevant while maintaining high academic expectations. Curriculum should evolve thoughtfully rather than changing simply because new technologies become available. Educational leaders should ask important questions before adopting innovations. Does this curriculum help students think more deeply? Does it prepare learners for responsible citizenship? Does it strengthen communication, collaboration, and creativity? Does it promote fairness, accessibility, and inclusion? Responsible curriculum design balances innovation with educational purpose.

Parents also remain important partners in curriculum development. Families help reinforce classroom learning by encouraging reading, supporting homework, discussing current events, promoting curiosity, and modeling lifelong learning. As new topics related to AGI, ethics, cybersecurity, and digital citizenship become part of school curriculum, parents and guardians provide valuable opportunities to continue these conversations at home. Strong partnerships between schools and families help students see that learning extends beyond classroom walls. When educators and families work together, students receive consistent encouragement that strengthens both academic achievement and personal development.

Another important goal of curriculum for the AGI generation is helping students become responsible global citizens. Intelligent technologies connect people across cultures, languages, and countries more easily than ever before. Future graduates will likely collaborate with individuals from diverse backgrounds while addressing international challenges such as environmental sustainability, public health, scientific research, humanitarian efforts, and economic development. Curriculum should therefore encourage cultural understanding, empathy, respect for diverse perspectives, and responsible global citizenship. Students who appreciate different viewpoints become better collaborators, leaders, and problem-solvers in an increasingly connected world.

Although curriculum will continue evolving, one principle should never change: education is fundamentally about developing people rather than simply delivering information. Knowledge remains important, but character, integrity, compassion, resilience, curiosity, and wisdom ultimately determine how knowledge is used. Schools should continue helping students become honest individuals who care about others, respect different ideas, accept responsibility for their actions, and contribute positively to society. AGI may expand educational possibilities in remarkable ways, but technology should always support these larger human purposes rather than replace them.

The curriculum of the future will not be measured by the number of digital tools used in classrooms or the sophistication of intelligent technologies. Its success will be measured by the graduates it produces—young people who think critically, communicate effectively, solve meaningful problems, embrace lifelong learning, demonstrate ethical leadership, and use technology responsibly to improve the lives of others. The AGI generation will inherit opportunities and challenges unlike any previous generation. By designing curriculum that combines academic excellence with creativity, compassion, adaptability, and responsible innovation, schools can prepare students not merely to participate in the future but to lead it with confidence, wisdom, and purpose.

Chapter 6 Summary

Curriculum for the AGI Generation

Curriculum has always changed as society has evolved. As Artificial General Intelligence (AGI) becomes part of the future, schools will continue teaching strong academic foundations while expanding learning to include the knowledge, skills, and values students need in a rapidly changing world.

This chapter explained that reading, writing, mathematics, science, history, and the arts will remain essential subjects. However, future curriculum will place greater emphasis on connecting these disciplines through interdisciplinary learning, project-based experiences, and real-world problem solving. Students will learn not only what to know but also how to apply knowledge responsibly in different situations.

The chapter also emphasized the importance of critical thinking, creativity, communication, collaboration, ethical decision-making, adaptability, digital literacy, financial literacy, and lifelong learning. These human-centered skills will help students succeed even as intelligent technologies continue advancing.

Teachers, curriculum leaders, parents, and school administrators all have important roles in preparing students for the AGI generation. Curriculum should evolve thoughtfully while maintaining high academic standards, protecting student well-being, and encouraging responsible innovation.

Ultimately, the purpose of curriculum is not simply to prepare students for future jobs. It is to prepare thoughtful, compassionate, knowledgeable, ethical, and adaptable individuals who can contribute positively to their communities and use technology wisely throughout their lives.

Chapter 6 Reflection

Take time to think about the ideas discussed in this chapter. Answer each question using complete sentences.

1. Why should curriculum continue changing as technology evolves?
2. Which subject do you believe will become more important in the AGI generation? Explain your answer.
3. Why is critical thinking more valuable than simply memorizing information?

4. How can project-based learning prepare students for future careers?
5. Why should ethics become an important part of every curriculum?
6. What lifelong learning habits should students develop before graduating?
7. How can parents support the goals of future curriculum at home?
8. If you could add one new subject to your school's curriculum, what would it be and why?
9. What responsibilities do curriculum leaders have as AGI becomes more common?
10. After reading this chapter, how has your understanding of future curriculum changed?

Chapter 6 Worksheet

Part A – Vocabulary Matching

Match each term with the correct definition.

A. Curriculum

B. Project-Based Learning

C. Critical Thinking

D. Digital Literacy

E. Financial Literacy

F. Lifelong Learning

G. Interdisciplinary Learning

H. Ethics

1. _____ Learning that combines knowledge from multiple academic subjects.
2. _____ The plan that outlines what students learn in school.
3. _____ Understanding how to use digital technology responsibly.
4. _____ Learning through meaningful projects that solve real-world problems.
5. _____ Carefully evaluating information before making decisions.
6. _____ Understanding money management and financial decision-making.
7. _____ Continuing to learn throughout life.
8. _____ Principles that help guide responsible decisions.

Part B – Short Answer

1. Why should schools continue teaching strong academic foundations?

2. Name four future-ready skills students should develop.

3. Why is adaptability important in the AGI generation?

4. How can project-based learning improve student understanding?

5. Why should curriculum prepare students for lifelong learning instead of only one career?

Part C – Critical Thinking

Imagine you are the superintendent of a school district redesigning curriculum for the AGI generation.

Describe three major changes you would make to prepare students for the future while preserving strong academic standards and important human values.

Chapter 6 Quiz

Multiple Choice

1. What is the primary purpose of curriculum?

A. Memorizing information only.

B. Preparing students with knowledge, skills, and values for life.

C. Replacing teachers with technology.

D. Eliminating traditional subjects.

2. Which instructional approach encourages students to solve real-world problems?

A. Project-based learning.

B. Memorization only.

C. Silent reading only.

D. Copying notes.

3. Which skill will remain valuable regardless of technological advancement?

A. Critical thinking.

B. Creativity.

C. Communication.

D. All of the above.

4. Why should ethics be included in future curriculum?

A. To help students make responsible decisions.

B. To replace science classes.

C. To eliminate technology.

D. To reduce collaboration.

5. Which group shares responsibility for preparing students for the AGI generation?

A. Teachers only.

B. Parents only.

C. Curriculum leaders only.

D. Teachers, students, parents, school leaders, and communities.

True or False

6. _____ Traditional academic subjects will remain important in future curriculum.
7. _____ Lifelong learning prepares students for changing careers.
8. _____ Technology alone should determine curriculum decisions.
9. _____ Financial literacy can help students make responsible economic decisions.
10. _____ The future curriculum should balance innovation with human values.

Chapter 6 Answer Key

Worksheet Answers

Part A – Vocabulary Matching

1. **G**
2. **A**
3. **D**
4. **B**
5. **C**
6. **E**
7. **F**
8. **H**

Part B – Suggested Responses

1. Strong academic foundations provide the knowledge students need to think critically, communicate effectively, solve problems, and continue learning throughout life.
2. Possible answers include critical thinking, creativity, communication, collaboration, adaptability, digital literacy, ethical reasoning, leadership, financial literacy, and lifelong learning.
3. Adaptability helps students respond successfully to new technologies, changing careers, and unexpected challenges throughout their lives.
4. Project-based learning helps students apply knowledge to authentic situations, work collaboratively, solve complex problems, and develop deeper understanding.
5. Many future careers will change over time, so students need the ability to continue learning, developing new skills, and adapting throughout their lives.

Quiz Answers

1. **B**
2. **A**
3. **D**
4. **A**
5. **D**
6. **True**
7. **True**
8. **False**
9. **True**
10. **True**

Chapter 6 Answer Key

Worksheet Answers

Part A – Vocabulary Matching

1. **G**
2. **A**
3. **D**
4. **B**
5. **C**
6. **E**
7. **F**
8. **H**

Part B – Suggested Responses

1. Strong academic foundations provide the knowledge students need to think critically, communicate effectively, solve problems, and continue learning throughout life.
2. Possible answers include critical thinking, creativity, communication, collaboration, adaptability, digital literacy, ethical reasoning, leadership, financial literacy, and lifelong learning.
3. Adaptability helps students respond successfully to new technologies, changing careers, and unexpected challenges throughout their lives.
4. Project-based learning helps students apply knowledge to authentic situations, work collaboratively, solve complex problems, and develop deeper understanding.
5. Many future careers will change over time, so students need the ability to continue learning, developing new skills, and adapting throughout their lives.

Quiz Answers

1. **B**
2. **A**
3. **D**
4. **A**
5. **D**
6. **True**
7. **True**
8. **False**
9. **True**
10. **True**

Chapter 7

Teaching Critical Thinking in the Age of AGI

One of the greatest responsibilities of education has always been teaching students how to think. Schools certainly help students learn facts, formulas, historical events, scientific principles, and vocabulary, but education has never been limited to memorizing information. The true purpose of learning is helping people understand ideas, ask meaningful questions, solve problems, make informed decisions, and contribute positively to society. As Artificial General Intelligence (AGI) continues advancing, these abilities become even more important. Intelligent systems may provide answers within seconds, generate reports, summarize research, translate languages, and solve increasingly complex problems. However, no matter how advanced technology becomes, students must still determine whether information is accurate, ethical, reliable, complete, and appropriate. This ability to analyze, evaluate, and reason carefully is known as critical thinking, and it may become one of the most valuable skills any student can develop in the twenty-first century.

Critical thinking begins with curiosity. Curious students naturally ask questions because they want to understand how the world works. They do not simply accept information because someone presents it confidently. Instead, they investigate evidence, compare different viewpoints, consider possible explanations, and seek deeper understanding before reaching conclusions. Throughout history, curiosity has led to some of humanity's greatest discoveries. Scientists questioned accepted beliefs about the universe. Engineers imagined new ways to solve problems. Medical researchers challenged existing treatments in search of better solutions. Inventors improved everyday life by asking simple questions such as, "Can this be done differently?" or "Is there a better way?" Every important advancement began with someone willing to think beyond what was already known. Schools encourage this mindset by creating classrooms where questions are welcomed and exploration becomes part of the learning process.

The arrival of AGI makes curiosity even more valuable because intelligent systems may often provide immediate answers. While quick access to information offers tremendous educational benefits, it can also create the temptation to stop thinking once an answer appears on a screen. Students may assume that information generated by advanced technology is always correct simply because it sounds convincing. However, responsible learners understand that intelligent systems, regardless of how advanced they become, should never replace thoughtful human judgment. Students should continue asking important questions. Where did this information come from? Is it supported by reliable evidence? Are there alternative viewpoints? Does this conclusion make sense? Could bias or missing information affect the answer? These questions help students become active thinkers instead of passive recipients of information.

Critical thinking also requires students to recognize the difference between information and understanding. Memorizing facts may help students answer questions on an examination, but genuine understanding allows them to apply knowledge in unfamiliar situations. Consider a student learning about renewable energy. Memorizing the definitions of solar, wind, and hydroelectric power represents one level of learning. Understanding how these technologies affect the environment, influence economies, create engineering challenges, and support sustainable communities requires much deeper thinking. Students who understand concepts can apply knowledge to new problems, evaluate possible solutions, and explain their reasoning clearly. Teachers play an essential role in helping students move beyond memorization toward meaningful understanding through discussion, investigation, experimentation, and reflection.

Another important element of critical thinking is recognizing bias. Every source of information reflects certain perspectives, assumptions, experiences, or limitations. Books, websites, news reports, research studies, and even intelligent technologies may present information differently depending on how they were created or trained. Students should learn to examine information carefully by comparing multiple reliable sources rather than depending upon a single explanation. They should recognize that responsible decision-making often requires considering evidence from different viewpoints before reaching conclusions. Teachers help students practice these skills by encouraging respectful discussions, evaluating multiple perspectives, and emphasizing the importance of evidence over opinion. These habits prepare students to become informed citizens who make thoughtful decisions throughout their lives.

Problem-solving represents another important aspect of critical thinking. Every day, people encounter situations that require careful analysis rather than immediate answers. Engineers design safer bridges. Doctors diagnose illnesses with similar symptoms. Business leaders make financial decisions under uncertain conditions. Community leaders address environmental challenges, transportation needs, and public safety concerns. These situations rarely have one simple solution. Instead, they require gathering information, evaluating alternatives, predicting possible outcomes, and selecting the most responsible course of action. AGI may assist by organizing information, modeling possible scenarios, or identifying patterns within large datasets, but people remain responsible for making final decisions based upon ethical considerations, human values, and long-term consequences.

Teachers encourage critical thinking by asking open-ended questions rather than questions with only one correct answer. Instead of asking students simply to remember dates or definitions, educators may ask why historical events occurred, how scientific discoveries changed society, or what solutions students would recommend for current global challenges. Classroom discussions become opportunities to explain reasoning, defend conclusions with evidence, respectfully challenge ideas, and learn from different perspectives. Students develop confidence by expressing their ideas while remaining willing to revise their thinking when presented with stronger evidence. These experiences teach intellectual humility—the understanding that learning continues throughout life and that thoughtful people remain open to new information.

Perhaps one of the greatest benefits of critical thinking is that it helps students become independent learners. Rather than depending entirely on teachers, textbooks, or intelligent technologies for every answer, students develop the confidence to investigate questions on their own. They learn how to identify reliable resources, organize information, evaluate evidence, recognize logical errors, and communicate conclusions clearly. These abilities remain valuable regardless of technological advancement because every generation encounters new questions that previous generations could not fully anticipate. Students who think critically are prepared not only to understand the world they inherit but also to improve it.

As Artificial General Intelligence continues developing, schools have an extraordinary opportunity to strengthen one of education's oldest and most important goals: teaching students how to think wisely. Technology may continue becoming faster, more accurate, and more capable, but wisdom remains a uniquely human responsibility. Critical thinking helps students use intelligent systems responsibly while preserving their independence, creativity, ethical judgment, and curiosity. These qualities will prepare them to become thoughtful leaders, responsible citizens, and lifelong learners in an increasingly intelligent world.

Chapter 7 (Part 2)

Developing strong critical thinkers requires more than asking students to memorize information or complete worksheets with predetermined answers. It requires classrooms where questioning is encouraged, evidence is valued, and thoughtful discussion becomes part of everyday learning. In an AGI-ready classroom, teachers create opportunities for students to investigate problems that do not have simple solutions. Instead of immediately providing answers, educators encourage students to examine information carefully, identify possible options, compare evidence, and explain the reasoning behind their conclusions. This process helps students recognize that learning is not simply about finding the fastest answer but about understanding how decisions are made and why certain conclusions are supported by stronger evidence than others.

One effective strategy for developing critical thinking is presenting students with authentic real-world situations. Imagine a community facing a severe drought. Students are asked to recommend how limited water supplies should be managed. An AGI system may quickly provide rainfall data, population statistics, agricultural needs, and historical records of previous droughts. However, deciding how to distribute limited resources requires more than information. Students must consider fairness, environmental sustainability, public health, economic impact, and the needs of future generations. They must weigh competing priorities, recognize that every decision has consequences, and explain why they selected one solution over another. The technology provides valuable information, but thoughtful human reasoning determines how that information is used.

Teachers also help students recognize common thinking errors that can influence decision-making. People sometimes accept information simply because it confirms their existing beliefs. Others may assume that a statement is true because many people repeat it or because it appears convincing online. Critical thinkers learn to slow down before reaching conclusions. They ask whether reliable evidence supports a claim, whether important information may be missing, and whether different explanations deserve consideration. In the age of AGI, these habits become increasingly important because intelligent systems may generate responses that sound persuasive even when they contain inaccuracies or incomplete information. Students who carefully evaluate evidence become more confident decision-makers and more responsible users of technology.

Another important classroom practice involves encouraging respectful disagreement. Critical thinking does not require everyone to reach identical conclusions. Instead, it teaches students how to discuss different viewpoints while remaining respectful and open to learning. During classroom debates, discussions, and collaborative projects, students learn to support their opinions with facts, listen carefully to opposing ideas, ask clarifying questions, and revise their thinking when stronger evidence is presented. These experiences develop communication skills, intellectual humility, and empathy. Students discover that changing one's opinion after considering better evidence is not a weakness but a sign of thoughtful learning. This mindset prepares them for future workplaces where collaboration often involves evaluating multiple perspectives before making important decisions.

AGI can become a valuable tool for strengthening critical thinking when used responsibly. For example, students may ask an intelligent system to explain a scientific concept in several different ways, summarize multiple viewpoints on a historical event, or compare possible solutions to an engineering challenge. Instead of accepting the first response immediately, students evaluate the information by consulting textbooks, academic sources, classroom discussions, and teacher guidance. They compare evidence, identify differences between sources, and determine which explanations are most reliable. This process transforms AGI from a source of automatic answers into a learning partner that encourages investigation, reflection, and independent reasoning.

Critical thinking also plays an essential role in ethical decision-making. Many future technologies will present questions that do not have simple right-or-wrong answers. Should autonomous vehicles always prioritize passenger safety, or should they consider the safety of pedestrians equally? How should intelligent medical systems assist doctors without replacing professional judgment? How can schools use personalized learning technologies while protecting student privacy? These questions involve values as well as technology. Students should practice examining ethical dilemmas by identifying stakeholders, considering short-term and long-term consequences, recognizing competing interests, and explaining how fairness, responsibility, and compassion influence their decisions. Teachers guide these discussions while encouraging respectful dialogue and careful reasoning rather than quick conclusions.

Future careers will increasingly reward individuals who think critically because many routine tasks may become automated. Jobs that require creativity, leadership, collaboration, innovation, complex problem-solving, and ethical judgment will continue depending upon human intelligence. Engineers must evaluate design options that balance safety, cost, and sustainability. Healthcare professionals interpret medical information while considering the unique needs of individual patients. Business leaders make strategic decisions under uncertain conditions. Scientists investigate questions that have never been answered before. Educators design meaningful learning experiences that inspire future generations. In each of these professions, technology provides valuable assistance, but people remain responsible for making thoughtful, informed decisions. Schools therefore prepare students not only for examinations but also for lifelong careers requiring sound judgment and continuous learning.

Families also play an important role in developing critical thinking. Parents and guardians encourage thoughtful conversations by asking children to explain their ideas, discuss current events, evaluate advertisements, compare information from different sources, and reflect on everyday decisions. Simple questions such as "Why do you think that?" or "What evidence supports your opinion?" encourage children to think more deeply about their conclusions. When families model curiosity, honesty, respectful disagreement, and lifelong learning, they reinforce the habits students develop in school. Critical thinking becomes part of everyday life rather than remaining limited to classroom assignments.

School leaders can strengthen critical thinking by creating learning environments where inquiry, innovation, and thoughtful discussion are valued across every subject area. Professional development should help teachers design lessons that encourage reasoning, analysis, collaboration, and reflection rather than relying exclusively on memorization. Curriculum should provide opportunities for students to investigate authentic problems, conduct research, evaluate evidence, communicate ideas, and apply knowledge creatively. Assessment should measure not only what students know but also how effectively they think, reason, and solve problems. When schools consistently value thoughtful inquiry, students begin seeing critical thinking as a lifelong habit rather than a skill used only during examinations.

As we look toward the future, one truth becomes increasingly clear: intelligent technologies may become faster, more knowledgeable, and more capable, but they should never replace thoughtful human judgment. The greatest value of education has always been helping students become wise rather than simply well informed. Wisdom grows through experience, reflection, ethical reasoning, curiosity, empathy, and a willingness to continue learning. Critical thinking brings all of these qualities together by teaching students to ask meaningful questions, evaluate evidence carefully, solve problems responsibly, and make decisions that improve both their own lives and the lives of others. In the age of Artificial General Intelligence, these abilities will not become less important—they will become the foundation upon which every successful learner, leader, and citizen builds the future.

Chapter 7 Summary

Teaching Critical Thinking in the Age of AGI

Critical thinking is one of the most valuable skills students can develop in an age where Artificial General Intelligence (AGI) can quickly generate information and solve many types of problems. While intelligent technologies may provide answers in seconds, students must still evaluate information carefully, recognize reliable evidence, ask meaningful questions, and make responsible decisions.

This chapter explained that critical thinking begins with curiosity. Students who ask questions, explore different viewpoints, compare evidence, and remain open to learning develop a deeper understanding of the world around them. Critical thinking also helps students distinguish between facts, opinions, assumptions, and misinformation while encouraging thoughtful analysis instead of simply accepting information at face value.

Teachers play an essential role in developing critical thinkers by creating classrooms where questioning, discussion, investigation, collaboration, and problem-solving are encouraged. Instead of focusing only on memorization, educators help students explain their reasoning, support conclusions with evidence, and respectfully consider different perspectives.

The chapter also explored the importance of ethical decision-making, recognizing bias, solving authentic problems, and using AGI as a learning partner rather than as a replacement for independent thinking. Parents, teachers, and school leaders all contribute to developing students who think carefully before making decisions.

Ultimately, critical thinking prepares students not only for future careers but also for responsible citizenship, lifelong learning, and ethical leadership. As AGI continues advancing, the ability to think independently, evaluate information wisely, and solve complex problems will become even more valuable.

Chapter 7 Worksheet

Part A – Vocabulary Matching

Match each term with its correct definition.

A. Critical Thinking

B. Evidence

C. Bias

D. Curiosity

E. Reasoning

F. Ethical Decision-Making

G. Perspective

H. Problem-Solving

1. ______ Carefully analyzing information before reaching conclusions.
2. ______ Information that supports a claim or conclusion.
3. ______ A personal viewpoint or way of seeing a situation.
4. ______ A preference or opinion that may influence judgment.
5. ______ The desire to learn, ask questions, and explore new ideas.
6. ______ Using logical thinking to reach conclusions.
7. ______ Finding effective solutions to challenges.
8. ______ Choosing actions based on fairness, honesty, and responsibility.

Part B – Short Answer

1. Why is curiosity the foundation of critical thinking?

____

____

2. Explain why students should verify information generated by AGI.

____

____

3. Name four skills that strong critical thinkers demonstrate.

4. Why is ethical reasoning important when solving problems?

5. How can respectful disagreement improve learning?

Part C – Critical Thinking Activity

Imagine your class is asked to solve a community problem, such as reducing traffic congestion, improving recycling, or conserving water.

Describe how you would use critical thinking, evidence, collaboration, and AGI responsibly to develop the best possible solution.

Chapter 7 Quiz

Multiple Choice

1. What is the primary goal of critical thinking?

A. Memorizing information.

B. Carefully evaluating information before making decisions.

C. Completing assignments more quickly.

D. Depending entirely on technology.

2. Why should students verify information generated by AGI?

A. AGI can sometimes produce inaccurate or incomplete information.

B. Technology never makes mistakes.

C. Teachers no longer matter.

D. Students should avoid technology completely.

3. Which classroom activity best develops critical thinking?

A. Memorizing definitions only.

B. Asking questions, evaluating evidence, and discussing different viewpoints.

C. Copying notes without discussion.

D. Reading without reflection.

4. Which skill remains essential even when AGI becomes more advanced?

A. Ethical judgment.

B. Communication.

C. Independent reasoning.

D. All of the above.

5. Why should students consider multiple perspectives before making decisions?

A. To better understand complex issues.

B. To evaluate stronger evidence.

C. To make more informed decisions.

D. All of the above.

True or False

6._____ Critical thinking encourages students to ask thoughtful questions.

7._____ Students should always accept the first answer provided by technology.

8._____ Teachers help students evaluate information and develop independent thinking.

9._____ Ethical reasoning is part of critical thinking.

10._____ Lifelong learners continue asking questions throughout their lives.

Chapter 7 Answer Key

Worksheet Answers

Part A – Vocabulary Matching

1. **A**
2. **B**
3. **G**
4. **C**
5. **D**
6. **E**
7. **H**
8. **F**

Part B – Suggested Responses

1. Curiosity encourages students to ask questions, investigate ideas, and seek deeper understanding instead of accepting information without thinking.
2. Students should verify AGI-generated information because intelligent systems can occasionally provide inaccurate, incomplete, outdated, or biased responses.

3. Possible answers include asking questions, evaluating evidence, solving problems, communicating clearly, recognizing bias, ethical reasoning, logical analysis, collaboration, and open-mindedness.
4. Ethical reasoning helps students consider fairness, responsibility, honesty, and the impact of decisions on others before choosing a solution.
5. Respectful disagreement encourages students to examine different viewpoints, strengthen their reasoning, and develop better-supported conclusions.

Quiz Answers

1. **B**
2. **A**
3. **B**
4. **D**
5. **D**
6. **True**
7. **False**
8. **True**
9. **True**
10. **True**

Chapter 8

Human Intelligence and Artificial Intelligence Working Together

Throughout history, people have invented tools that extended human abilities. The wheel made transportation easier. The printing press made knowledge more accessible. Electricity transformed homes, schools, hospitals, and industries. Computers changed how information was created, stored, and shared. The internet connected people across the world in ways that were once impossible. Each technological breakthrough increased what humans could accomplish, but none of these inventions replaced the need for human intelligence. Instead, they expanded human potential. Artificial General Intelligence (AGI) represents another important technological milestone. Rather than viewing AGI as a replacement for people, it is more helpful to understand it as a powerful tool that may work alongside humans to solve problems, improve decision-making, and create new opportunities. The future of education and society will depend not on choosing between human intelligence and artificial intelligence but on learning how both can work together responsibly and effectively.

Human intelligence is remarkably diverse. People learn from experience, recognize emotions, develop relationships, imagine possibilities, create works of art, understand humor, demonstrate compassion, and make ethical decisions that consider the well-being of others. Human intelligence also includes intuition, curiosity, resilience, imagination, cultural understanding, and the ability to adapt when situations change unexpectedly. These qualities develop through years of learning, personal experiences, family relationships, education, and participation in communities. Every individual brings unique perspectives that influence how problems are understood and how solutions are developed. This diversity of human thought has been responsible for scientific discoveries, artistic achievements, medical advances, technological innovation, and social progress throughout history.

Artificial Intelligence, including future AGI systems, contributes different strengths. Intelligent systems can analyze enormous amounts of information in seconds, identify patterns that might be difficult for people to recognize, organize complex data, perform repetitive calculations without becoming tired, and assist with tasks that require speed and consistency. In healthcare, intelligent systems may help physicians review medical images and identify patterns associated with disease. In engineering, they may assist with testing thousands of possible design options before construction begins. In environmental science, they may analyze climate information collected from satellites around the world. In education, AGI may help teachers personalize instruction, organize learning resources, and identify students who may benefit from additional support. These capabilities complement human intelligence by providing tools that increase efficiency and expand opportunities for discovery.

The greatest achievements often occur when human intelligence and technology complement one another instead of competing. Consider the work of a physician caring for a patient with a complex illness. An AGI system may quickly analyze medical records, compare millions of research findings, identify possible diagnoses, and recommend treatment options based on current scientific knowledge. However, the physician still speaks with the patient, understands family history, explains treatment choices, answers questions, provides emotional reassurance, and makes professional decisions based on both medical evidence and human compassion. Technology supports the physician's work, but the responsibility for patient care remains with a skilled professional. This partnership demonstrates how intelligent systems can strengthen human decision-making without replacing human judgment.

Education provides another excellent example of this partnership. Imagine a classroom where students are studying the causes of climate change. AGI assists by organizing scientific research, creating interactive simulations, translating information into multiple languages, and helping students visualize complex environmental systems. Meanwhile, the teacher encourages discussion, asks challenging questions, helps students evaluate evidence, facilitates teamwork, and guides conversations about ethical responsibilities related to environmental stewardship. Students use both technological tools and human reasoning to understand a complex issue from multiple perspectives. They learn that knowledge becomes more valuable when combined with critical thinking, collaboration, and thoughtful discussion.

One important lesson students should learn is that intelligent systems do not eliminate the need for human responsibility. Even when technology provides useful recommendations, people remain accountable for making final decisions. An AGI system may suggest several possible engineering designs for a bridge, but engineers evaluate safety standards, environmental conditions, construction costs, and community needs before selecting the final design. Intelligent software may recommend financial strategies, but business leaders remain responsible for considering employees, customers, legal requirements, and long-term organizational goals. Technology can organize information and provide valuable insights, but people must continue exercising judgment, integrity, and ethical responsibility.

As students prepare for future careers, they will increasingly work in environments where collaboration with intelligent systems becomes routine. Some professions may rely heavily on data analysis, while others emphasize communication, leadership, creativity, or problem-solving. Regardless of the career they choose, students will benefit from understanding both the strengths and limitations of AGI. They should know when technology can improve efficiency and when situations require careful human observation, empathy, or ethical reflection. Learning how to work effectively with intelligent systems will become as important as learning how to work effectively with other people. Schools therefore have an opportunity to teach not only technological skills but also the judgment required to use those skills wisely.

Another important aspect of this partnership is trust. People should trust intelligent systems only after understanding how they work, what information they use, and where their limitations exist. Responsible users verify important information, consult multiple reliable sources when appropriate, and recognize that no technology is perfect. Healthy trust is based on understanding rather than blind acceptance. Teachers help students develop this balanced perspective by encouraging thoughtful questions, careful evaluation of evidence, and responsible technology use. Students learn that confidence grows not from assuming technology is always correct but from knowing how to evaluate information carefully before making decisions.

Perhaps the greatest strength of humanity has always been the ability to combine knowledge with compassion. Throughout history, people have cared for one another during times of difficulty, celebrated achievements together, solved community problems through cooperation, and imagined better futures through creativity and determination. Artificial General Intelligence may become one of the most powerful tools ever developed, but it cannot replace the importance of kindness, empathy, courage, integrity, or hope. These qualities give purpose to knowledge and direction to innovation. As AGI becomes more capable, the partnership between human intelligence and artificial intelligence should always be guided by values that place people first.

The future will not belong solely to those who build the most advanced intelligent systems. It will belong to those who understand how human intelligence and artificial intelligence can work together to improve lives, strengthen communities, expand opportunities, and solve meaningful problems responsibly. Students who develop both technological understanding and strong human values will be well prepared to lead in an increasingly intelligent world. Education therefore has an important mission: helping young people recognize that technology is at its best when it serves humanity, and humanity is at its best when it uses knowledge with wisdom, compassion, and purpose.

Chapter 8 (Part 2)

As Artificial General Intelligence becomes more capable, the relationship between people and intelligent systems will continue to evolve. The most successful future workplaces, classrooms, hospitals, research laboratories, businesses, and government organizations will likely be those where human intelligence and AGI complement one another rather than compete. Instead of asking whether machines or people are better, society will increasingly ask how each can contribute its unique strengths toward solving important problems. This cooperative approach recognizes that technology and humanity each have valuable roles that become even more powerful when combined responsibly.

Consider the work of scientists searching for treatments for complex diseases. Research teams often examine enormous amounts of biological information collected over many years. An AGI system may analyze millions of scientific articles, identify patterns hidden within medical data, and recommend promising directions for future research. This process could save researchers countless hours by organizing information that would otherwise require years to examine manually. However, scientists still design experiments, evaluate results, question unexpected findings, consider ethical implications, and determine whether discoveries are safe enough to test with patients. Scientific progress depends upon curiosity, creativity, collaboration, and careful judgment—qualities that remain deeply human even when intelligent technologies provide extraordinary analytical support.

Engineers provide another example of successful collaboration. Imagine designing a bridge that must safely carry thousands of vehicles every day while withstanding earthquakes, strong winds, and changing weather conditions. AGI may generate hundreds of possible design options, calculate structural stress, estimate construction costs, and model how different materials perform over time. Engineers then review these recommendations by considering environmental conditions, community needs, public safety, legal requirements, and practical construction challenges. Human experience and professional responsibility guide the final decision because every engineering project affects real people and real communities. Technology increases efficiency, but accountability remains with qualified professionals.

Education will also benefit from thoughtful collaboration between teachers and intelligent systems. Students may use AGI to explore historical events through interactive simulations, investigate scientific concepts using virtual laboratories, receive personalized practice activities, or analyze complex mathematical problems. Teachers transform these experiences into meaningful learning by encouraging students to ask questions, compare ideas, evaluate evidence, communicate effectively, and apply knowledge responsibly. A classroom becomes stronger when technology supports learning while teachers continue developing curiosity, confidence, empathy, resilience, and ethical judgment. Students learn that success depends not only on understanding technology but also on understanding themselves and others.

One of the greatest responsibilities humans will continue carrying is accountability. Intelligent systems may provide recommendations, predictions, or possible solutions, but people remain responsible for the decisions they make. A judge considering legal information, a physician selecting medical treatments, a school principal implementing educational policies, or a business leader making financial decisions cannot simply transfer responsibility to technology. Every important decision requires careful evaluation of evidence, ethical reasoning, and consideration of how outcomes affect individuals and communities. Accountability ensures that people remain actively involved in decision-making rather than allowing technology to become the final authority.

Communication will become another essential skill in this partnership. People will need to explain complex ideas clearly to both other people and intelligent systems. Asking thoughtful questions, providing accurate instructions, interpreting information carefully, and communicating conclusions effectively will help students become successful collaborators. Technology can generate reports or organize information, but people must still explain recommendations, persuade others using evidence, resolve disagreements respectfully, and inspire teamwork toward shared goals. Strong communication strengthens every profession because it builds understanding, trust, and cooperation.

Trust should always be earned through understanding rather than assumed automatically. As AGI systems become more advanced, people may sometimes feel tempted to accept recommendations without careful review. Responsible users recognize that technology should support human thinking instead of replacing it. Students should learn to ask important questions whenever they interact with intelligent systems. How was this conclusion reached? What evidence supports it? Are there alternative explanations? Could important information be missing? What are the possible risks of following this recommendation? These habits encourage thoughtful decision-making while reducing the likelihood of mistakes caused by unquestioned reliance on technology.

The future partnership between people and AGI also depends upon continuous learning. Technology will continue changing throughout the lives of today's students, creating new opportunities as well as new challenges. Graduates who remain curious, adaptable, and willing to learn will be better prepared to work alongside intelligent systems than those who depend only upon existing knowledge. Lifelong learning allows people to understand emerging technologies, evaluate new information, develop additional skills, and respond confidently to changing professional environments. Schools therefore prepare students not only by teaching current knowledge but also by helping them become independent learners capable of adapting throughout their lives.

Families also contribute to preparing students for responsible collaboration with AGI. Parents encourage children to ask thoughtful questions, discuss current events, solve everyday problems, and reflect on the ethical consequences of decisions. Conversations at home about honesty, responsibility, kindness, fairness, and respect provide a strong foundation for using powerful technologies wisely. When schools and families work together, students receive consistent guidance that helps them understand both the possibilities and the responsibilities associated with intelligent systems. These shared values remain important regardless of how rapidly technology advances.

School leaders have an equally important responsibility. Principals, district administrators, curriculum specialists, and technology leaders must create learning environments where innovation serves educational goals rather than distracting from them. They establish policies that protect student privacy, encourage responsible technology use, provide professional development for teachers, and ensure that every student has equitable access to high-quality learning opportunities. Strong leadership recognizes that successful implementation of AGI depends not only on purchasing advanced technology but also on building a culture of trust, ethics, collaboration, and continuous improvement throughout the entire school community.

Perhaps the most important lesson students can learn is that technology should always strengthen humanity rather than replace it. The future needs people who demonstrate compassion when others struggle, courage when difficult decisions must be made, creativity when new ideas are needed, integrity when ethical choices become challenging, and leadership when communities face uncertainty. AGI may become an extraordinary partner in solving problems, discovering knowledge, and improving efficiency, but it cannot replace the values that give human life meaning and purpose. Every generation inherits powerful tools, yet history reminds us that the character of the people using those tools ultimately determines whether society benefits from them.

The future will be shaped by partnerships—between students and teachers, families and schools, communities and innovators, and humans and intelligent systems. The most successful individuals will not be those who compete against technology, nor those who depend upon it completely. They will be those who understand how to combine the speed and analytical power of AGI with the wisdom, empathy, creativity, ethical judgment, and resilience that define human intelligence. When these strengths work together, education fulfills its highest purpose by preparing students not only to succeed in an increasingly intelligent world but also to improve that world for future generations.

Chapter 8 Summary

Human Intelligence and Artificial Intelligence Working Together

Human intelligence and Artificial General Intelligence (AGI) each have unique strengths. Human intelligence includes creativity, empathy, ethical judgment, communication, curiosity, leadership, and the ability to build meaningful relationships. AGI can analyze large amounts of information, recognize patterns, organize complex data, and assist people with solving difficult problems more efficiently.

This chapter explained that the future is not about choosing between humans and intelligent machines. Instead, it is about learning how people and AGI can work together responsibly. In fields such as education, medicine, engineering, science, business, and environmental research, AGI can serve as a powerful assistant while humans continue making ethical decisions, exercising professional judgment, and taking responsibility for outcomes.

Students will increasingly work alongside intelligent systems throughout their education and future careers. To succeed, they must understand both the strengths and limitations of AGI. They should learn to evaluate information carefully, verify important facts, ask thoughtful questions, and use technology responsibly rather than depending on it completely.

The chapter also emphasized that teachers, parents, school leaders, and communities all play important roles in helping students develop the knowledge, character, and values needed to work successfully with intelligent technologies.

The future belongs to individuals who combine the analytical power of AGI with the uniquely human qualities of wisdom, compassion, creativity, integrity, resilience, and ethical leadership. Together, human intelligence and artificial intelligence can help solve meaningful problems and improve the lives of people around the world.

Chapter 8 Reflection

Think about the ideas presented in this chapter. Answer each question using complete sentences.

1. Why is it better to think of AGI as a partner rather than a replacement for human intelligence?
2. Which human qualities do you believe will always remain important, even in an AGI-powered world?
3. How can AGI help professionals such as doctors, teachers, engineers, and scientists?
4. Why should humans remain responsible for important decisions even when AGI provides recommendations?
5. How can students prepare to work successfully with intelligent systems in the future?
6. Why is trust important when people use AGI?
7. What responsibilities do schools have when preparing students for collaboration with intelligent technologies?
8. How can families help children develop responsible technology habits?
9. If you worked with an AGI system in your future career, how would you make sure it was helping you make good decisions?
10. What is the most important lesson you learned from this chapter about the relationship between humans and AGI?

Chapter 8 Worksheet

Part A – Vocabulary Matching

Match each term with its correct definition.

A. Collaboration

B. Human Intelligence

C. Artificial General Intelligence (AGI)

D. Accountability

E. Ethical Judgment

F. Communication

G. Trust

H. Lifelong Learning

1. _____ Working together toward a shared goal.
2. _____ The responsibility for decisions and actions.
3. _____ The ability to reason, create, empathize, and solve problems.
4. _____ A future intelligent system capable of learning across many different tasks.
5. _____ Confidence based on understanding, honesty, and reliability.
6. _____ Sharing ideas clearly with others.
7. _____ Making decisions based on fairness, honesty, and responsibility.
8. _____ Continuing to learn throughout life.

Part B – Short Answer

1. Explain why human intelligence and AGI work best together.

____

____

2. Name four human qualities that AGI cannot fully replace.

____

____

3. Give three examples of professions that may benefit from collaboration with AGI.

____

____

4. Why is accountability important when using intelligent systems?

____

____

5. Why should students continue developing communication skills even as AGI becomes more advanced?

Part C – Critical Thinking Activity

Imagine you are leading a team that includes both people and AGI systems to solve an important community problem.

Describe how you would divide responsibilities between people and AGI while ensuring fairness, safety, ethical decision-making, and human accountability.

Chapter 8 Quiz

Multiple Choice

1. What is the main idea of this chapter?

A. AGI should replace all human workers.

B. Human intelligence and AGI should work together responsibly.

C. Technology should make every decision.

D. Human intelligence is no longer important.

2. Which is considered a uniquely human strength?

A. Empathy.

B. Ethical judgment.

C. Creativity.

D. All of the above.

3. Why should humans remain responsible for important decisions?

A. Because technology cannot replace human accountability.

B. Because AGI never provides useful information.

C. Because technology should never be used.

D. Because computers cannot process information.

4. Which profession could benefit from collaboration with AGI?

A. Teachers.

B. Doctors.

C. Engineers.

D. All of the above.

5. Why is lifelong learning important in an AGI-powered future?

A. Technology will continue changing throughout our lives.

B. Students only need to learn once.

C. Careers will never change.

D. AGI eliminates the need for education.

True or False

6. _____ Human intelligence includes empathy and ethical reasoning.
7. _____ AGI should always make final decisions without human involvement.
8. _____ Trust should be based on understanding and careful evaluation.
9. _____ Families help prepare students to use technology responsibly.
10. _____ Human values remain important even as technology becomes more advanced.

Chapter 8 Answer Key

Worksheet Answers

Part A – Vocabulary Matching

1. **A**
2. **D**
3. **B**
4. **C**
5. **G**
6. **F**
7. **E**
8. **H**

Part B – Suggested Responses

1. Human intelligence provides creativity, empathy, ethical reasoning, and judgment, while AGI contributes speed, pattern recognition, data analysis, and information processing. Together they create stronger solutions than either could achieve alone.
2. Possible answers include empathy, compassion, creativity, ethical judgment, integrity, leadership, wisdom, resilience, communication, and emotional understanding.
3. Possible answers include teachers, doctors, engineers, scientists, business leaders, architects, environmental researchers, and healthcare professionals.
4. Humans remain accountable because intelligent systems provide recommendations, but people must consider ethics, safety, fairness, legal responsibilities, and the impact of decisions on others.
5. Communication helps people explain ideas, work in teams, build trust, solve problems, and lead others—skills that remain essential even when using AGI.

Quiz Answers

1. **B**
2. **D**

3. **A**
4. **D**
5. **A**
6. **True**
7. **False**
8. **True**
9. **True**
10. **True**

Chapter 9

Ethics and Responsibility in the AGI Era

Every major technological advancement in history has brought both opportunities and responsibilities. The discovery of electricity transformed homes, businesses, hospitals, and schools, but people also learned the importance of electrical safety. Automobiles changed transportation forever, but society created traffic laws, driver's education, and safety standards to protect lives. The internet connected billions of people around the world, creating remarkable opportunities for communication, education, and business, while also introducing challenges involving privacy, cybersecurity, misinformation, and responsible online behavior. Artificial General Intelligence (AGI) represents another important step in human progress. Like every powerful technology before it, AGI offers extraordinary possibilities, but its greatest benefits will only be realized if people use it responsibly, ethically, and with careful consideration for its impact on individuals, communities, and society.

Ethics refers to the principles and values that guide people in deciding what is right, fair, honest, and responsible. Ethics helps individuals consider not only what can be done but also what should be done. Every day, people make ethical decisions, whether they realize it or not. Students decide whether to complete their own assignments honestly. Teachers decide how to treat students fairly. Doctors decide how to recommend treatments that place patients' well-being first. Business leaders consider how their decisions affect employees, customers, and communities. These decisions involve more than technical knowledge; they require integrity, compassion, accountability, and respect for others. As AGI becomes more capable, ethical thinking becomes increasingly important because technology may influence decisions that affect education, healthcare, transportation, finance, scientific research, public safety, and countless other aspects of daily life.

One of the most important ethical principles in the AGI era is human responsibility. Intelligent systems may provide recommendations, analyze information, or identify possible solutions, but people remain responsible for the decisions they make. A school principal deciding whether to adopt a new educational technology cannot rely only on computer-generated reports. The principal must also consider student privacy, teacher readiness, educational effectiveness, accessibility, and community expectations. Likewise, a physician using intelligent diagnostic tools continues evaluating patient needs, explaining treatment options, and making professional decisions based on both scientific evidence and human compassion. Technology may assist decision-making, but accountability remains with people.

Fairness is another essential ethical consideration. Every student deserves equal opportunities to learn regardless of background, language, disability, family income, or geographic location. As AGI becomes more common in education, schools must ensure that intelligent technologies benefit all learners rather than creating new inequalities. Students in rural communities, urban districts, and underserved schools should all have opportunities to access high-quality educational resources. Teachers should receive appropriate training so they can use new technologies effectively, and instructional materials should be accessible to students with diverse learning needs. Ethical education recognizes that innovation should expand opportunities rather than limit them.

Privacy also becomes increasingly important in an AGI-powered world. Many educational technologies collect information about student progress, learning preferences, attendance, classroom participation, and academic performance. While this information may help teachers personalize instruction, it must be handled carefully and responsibly. Students and families have the right to understand what information is collected, why it is needed, who can access it, and how it is protected. Schools must establish clear policies that safeguard personal information while complying with privacy laws and ethical standards. Trust grows when educational institutions communicate openly and demonstrate respect for every learner's personal information.

Honesty remains another important ethical principle in the age of AGI. Intelligent systems may generate essays, solve mathematical problems, summarize articles, or answer complex questions. While these capabilities provide valuable educational support, students must understand the difference between using technology as a learning tool and allowing technology to complete work dishonestly. Academic integrity means taking responsibility for one's own learning, acknowledging the work of others, and using intelligent systems appropriately. Teachers play an important role by explaining ethical expectations, encouraging original thinking, and helping students recognize that genuine learning occurs when they actively engage with ideas rather than simply copying answers generated by technology.

Transparency is equally important as intelligent systems become more advanced. Students, teachers, parents, and school leaders should understand how educational technologies function, what information they use, and how recommendations are generated whenever possible. People are more likely to trust intelligent systems when they understand how decisions are made. Transparency encourages thoughtful evaluation rather than blind acceptance of technology. Students should develop the habit of asking questions such as: How was this recommendation created? What information was considered? Could important details be missing? Does this recommendation align with ethical principles and human values? These questions strengthen responsible decision-making while helping students become informed users of intelligent technologies.

Ethical decision-making also requires empathy. Every technological decision ultimately affects people. A new educational system influences students and teachers. A medical innovation affects patients and healthcare professionals. An intelligent transportation system influences drivers, pedestrians, and communities. Before implementing new technologies, responsible leaders consider how different groups may experience both the benefits and the challenges of innovation. Empathy encourages people to think beyond efficiency and ask whether technology improves people's lives while respecting their dignity, rights, and well-being. This human-centered approach ensures that technological progress remains focused on serving society rather than simply demonstrating technical capability.

Education has an important responsibility to prepare students for these ethical challenges. Schools should create opportunities for students to discuss real-world situations involving privacy, fairness, cybersecurity, responsible technology use, intellectual property, environmental responsibility, and the social impact of emerging innovations. Through classroom discussions, debates, case studies, collaborative projects, and community service, students learn how ethical principles apply to practical situations. They discover that many important questions do not have simple answers and that thoughtful decision-making requires balancing competing priorities while remaining committed to honesty, fairness, and respect for others.

As Artificial General Intelligence continues evolving, ethics will become one of the most valuable subjects students can study. Technology will continue advancing, but human values provide the direction that determines how these advancements shape society. Intelligence without integrity can create harm, while intelligence guided by ethics creates opportunities to improve lives, strengthen communities, and solve meaningful problems responsibly. By teaching students to combine technological understanding with compassion, fairness, accountability, and wisdom, schools prepare future leaders who can use AGI not only effectively but also ethically for the benefit of humanity.

Chapter 9 (Part 2)

Understanding ethics becomes easier when students examine situations that people may actually face in the future. Imagine a school using an AGI system to recommend students for advanced academic programs. The system analyzes grades, attendance, classroom participation, and assessment results before identifying students who appear ready for more challenging courses. At first, the recommendations seem reasonable. However, teachers notice that some students who have shown remarkable creativity, leadership, or determination are not being recommended because those qualities are difficult to measure using numerical data alone. School leaders must then decide whether to rely entirely on the technology or include teacher observations, student interviews, family input, and additional evidence. This example demonstrates why human judgment remains essential. Ethical decision-making requires considering the complete picture rather than depending only on automated recommendations.

Consider another example involving healthcare. An AGI system reviews thousands of medical records and recommends a treatment plan for a patient with a serious illness. The technology identifies the option that has produced the highest success rate according to available research. Before accepting the recommendation, however, the physician meets with the patient and family to discuss medical history, personal values, possible risks, quality of life, and individual preferences. The physician may ultimately choose a different treatment because the patient's unique circumstances require a more personalized approach. This situation illustrates an important ethical principle: technology can organize knowledge, but people remain responsible for applying that knowledge with compassion, wisdom, and professional judgment.

Bias is another challenge that requires careful attention in the AGI era. Bias occurs when decisions or recommendations unfairly favor or disadvantage certain individuals or groups. Sometimes bias reflects historical patterns contained within training data. Other times it may result from incomplete information or unintended assumptions built into a system. Students should understand that intelligent technologies are created by people, trained using information collected from the real world, and therefore may reflect imperfections found within that information. Recognizing bias does not mean rejecting technology. Instead, it encourages careful evaluation, continuous improvement, and responsible oversight. Schools should teach students how to identify potential bias, compare multiple sources of information, ask thoughtful questions, and recommend fairer solutions whenever concerns arise.

Ethical leadership becomes increasingly important as intelligent technologies become more powerful. Leaders in education, healthcare, government, business, engineering, and science make decisions that influence many people's lives. Responsible leaders understand that success is measured not only by efficiency or innovation but also by fairness, transparency, accountability, and public trust. Before introducing new technologies, ethical leaders ask important questions. Will this technology improve people's lives? Does it protect privacy? Is it accessible to everyone who needs it? Could unintended consequences harm individuals or communities? How will decisions be reviewed if problems arise? These questions demonstrate that leadership involves careful reflection as well as confident decision-making.

Students themselves can begin practicing ethical leadership long before entering professional careers. Every day, they make choices about honesty, responsibility, kindness, respect, and academic integrity. When students complete their own assignments, give proper credit to others, treat classmates fairly, and use technology responsibly, they develop habits that prepare them for future leadership roles. Ethics is not learned only through reading textbooks. It develops through daily decisions that demonstrate character and personal responsibility. Schools help strengthen these habits by creating learning environments where honesty, respect, perseverance, and fairness are recognized and encouraged.

Teachers also serve as ethical role models. Students observe how educators treat every learner with dignity, resolve disagreements respectfully, admit mistakes honestly, and make thoughtful decisions that place student learning first. These everyday actions teach powerful lessons about integrity that extend far beyond academic content. In an AGI-supported classroom, teachers continue modeling responsible technology use by demonstrating how intelligent systems should support learning without replacing independent thinking, creativity, or ethical judgment. Students learn that responsible technology use depends as much on character as it does on technical skill.

Parents and families remain essential partners in developing ethical decision-makers. Conversations at home about honesty, digital citizenship, online safety, respect for others, and responsible technology use reinforce the lessons students learn at school. Families help children understand that every online action, every digital communication, and every technological decision affects real people. By discussing current events, encouraging empathy, and modeling responsible behavior, parents strengthen the ethical foundation that children will carry into adulthood. Education becomes most effective when schools and families work together to develop both knowledge and character.

Communities also share responsibility for promoting ethical innovation. Technology companies, universities, government agencies, nonprofit organizations, and community leaders all influence how intelligent systems are developed and used. Collaboration among these groups helps establish standards that protect public safety, encourage fairness, support innovation, and promote responsible use of emerging technologies. Students should understand that ethical technology development is not the responsibility of one profession alone. It requires cooperation among many individuals who share a commitment to improving society while protecting human rights and dignity.

One of the most valuable habits students can develop is the willingness to pause before making important decisions. In a world where intelligent systems may produce answers almost instantly, thoughtful people recognize the importance of reflection. They ask whether information is accurate, whether different perspectives deserve consideration, whether decisions align with ethical principles, and whether outcomes will benefit others as well as themselves. Taking time to think carefully often leads to wiser decisions than acting quickly without sufficient understanding. This habit of thoughtful reflection becomes increasingly valuable as technology continues accelerating the speed at which information is created and shared.

As society enters the AGI era, ethics will become one of the strongest foundations for responsible innovation. Advanced technology alone cannot guarantee a better future. A better future depends upon people who use knowledge wisely, lead with integrity, respect the dignity of every individual, and remain committed to fairness, compassion, and accountability. Artificial General Intelligence may provide extraordinary capabilities, but it is human character that determines how those capabilities are used. Students who combine technological understanding with ethical leadership will become the innovators, educators, scientists, healthcare professionals, engineers, entrepreneurs, and public servants who shape the future responsibly. In the end, the greatest achievement of the AGI era will not be creating more intelligent machines—it will be preparing wiser, more compassionate people who understand that every technological advancement should ultimately serve humanity with integrity, responsibility, and hope.

Chapter 9 Summary

Ethics and Responsibility in the AGI Era

Artificial General Intelligence (AGI) has the potential to improve education, healthcare, science, business, engineering, and many other areas of society. However, with greater technological power comes greater responsibility. This chapter explained that ethics provides the foundation for making fair, honest, and responsible decisions when using intelligent technologies.

Ethics is not only about what technology can do but also about what people should do. Human judgment, accountability, compassion, integrity, and fairness remain essential because AGI can provide recommendations but cannot replace human responsibility. People must continue making important decisions while considering the impact those decisions have on individuals, families, communities, and society.

The chapter explored several important ethical principles, including privacy, transparency, honesty, fairness, accountability, empathy, and responsible innovation. Students learned that educational technologies should protect personal information, support equal opportunities, and encourage academic integrity rather than replacing genuine learning.

The chapter also discussed bias, explaining that intelligent systems can sometimes reflect limitations found in the information used to develop them. Students were encouraged to evaluate evidence carefully, compare multiple perspectives, and recognize that technology should always be monitored and improved through thoughtful human oversight.

Finally, the chapter emphasized that ethical leadership begins with everyday decisions. Teachers, parents, school leaders, technology developers, and students all share responsibility for ensuring that AGI serves humanity responsibly. By combining technological understanding with strong moral values, future generations can use AGI to improve lives while protecting human dignity, fairness, and trust.

Chapter 9 Reflection

Take time to reflect on what you learned in this chapter. Answer each question using complete sentences.

1. Why is ethics important as AGI becomes more advanced?
2. Why should humans remain responsible for important decisions even when AGI provides recommendations?
3. How can schools protect student privacy while using intelligent technologies?
4. What does fairness mean in an AGI-powered society?
5. Why is honesty important when students use AGI to complete school assignments?
6. How can teachers help students become ethical technology users?
7. Describe a situation where empathy should influence an important technological decision.
8. Why should students learn to recognize bias in information and intelligent systems?

9. How can families help children develop strong ethical values when using technology?
10. After reading this chapter, what ethical principle do you believe is most important, and why?

Chapter 9 Worksheet

Part A – Vocabulary Matching

Match each term with the correct definition.

A. Ethics

B. Accountability

C. Transparency

D. Privacy

E. Bias

F. Empathy

G. Integrity

H. Fairness

1. _____ Protecting personal information and respecting confidentiality.
2. _____ Taking responsibility for decisions and actions.
3. _____ Understanding and caring about another person's feelings and experiences.
4. _____ Moral principles that guide responsible decisions.
5. _____ Being honest and doing what is right even when no one is watching.
6. _____ Being open about how decisions are made.
7. _____ Treating people equally and justly.
8. _____ A preference or unfair influence that may affect decisions.

Part B – Short Answer

1. Explain why ethics is important in the AGI era.

____

____

2. Why should schools protect student data?

3. Name four ethical principles discussed in this chapter.

4. Why should people verify recommendations made by AGI?

5. How can ethical leadership improve the future of society?

Part C – Critical Thinking Activity

Imagine you are the principal of a school introducing an AGI-powered learning system.

Write one paragraph explaining the ethical rules you would establish to protect students, support teachers, encourage fairness, maintain privacy, and ensure responsible use of intelligent technology.

Chapter 9 Quiz

Multiple Choice

1. What is the primary purpose of ethics?

A. To improve computer speed.

B. To guide responsible decisions and actions.

C. To replace teachers.

D. To eliminate technology.

2. Why should humans remain accountable when using AGI?

A. Because technology cannot replace human responsibility.

B. Because AGI never provides useful information.

C. Because computers cannot process data.

D. Because technology should never be used.

3. Which ethical principle helps protect personal information?

A. Privacy.

B. Curiosity.

C. Memorization.

D. Competition.

4. Why is transparency important when using intelligent systems?

A. It helps people understand how decisions are made.

B. It eliminates the need for teachers.

C. It replaces ethical leadership.

D. It prevents collaboration.

5. Which group shares responsibility for ethical technology use?

A. Teachers only.

B. Technology companies only.

C. Students only.

D. Students, teachers, families, school leaders, developers, and communities.

True or False

6. _____ AGI can replace human ethics.
7. _____ Bias can affect intelligent systems.
8. _____ Honesty remains important when using AGI.
9. _____ Ethical leadership helps build public trust.
10. _____ Responsible innovation combines technology with human values.

Chapter 9 Answer Key

Worksheet Answers

Part A – Vocabulary Matching

1. **D**
2. **B**
3. **F**
4. **A**
5. **G**
6. **C**
7. **H**
8. **E**

Part B – Suggested Responses

1. Ethics helps people make responsible, fair, honest, and compassionate decisions when using powerful technologies such as AGI.
2. Schools must protect student data to respect privacy, maintain trust, comply with laws and policies, and ensure educational information is used responsibly.
3. Possible answers include privacy, fairness, accountability, honesty, transparency, empathy, integrity, respect, responsibility, and ethical leadership.
4. People should verify AGI recommendations because intelligent systems can sometimes produce inaccurate, incomplete, or biased information. Human judgment remains essential.

5. Ethical leadership encourages fairness, honesty, transparency, accountability, and responsible innovation, helping technology improve society while protecting people's rights and well-being.

Quiz Answers

1. **B**
2. **A**
3. **A**
4. **A**
5. **D**
6. **False**
7. **True**
8. **True**
9. **True**
10. **True**

Chapter 10

Preparing Students for Careers in the AGI Economy

For many generations, schools have prepared students for the careers of their time. During the Industrial Revolution, education emphasized reading, writing, mathematics, and practical skills that supported manufacturing, transportation, and commerce. As computers became common in homes and businesses, schools gradually introduced technology education, computer literacy, and digital skills to help students succeed in an increasingly connected world. Today, society stands at the beginning of another major transformation. Artificial General Intelligence (AGI) has the potential to reshape many industries, create entirely new professions, and change the way people work together. While no one can predict every future occupation, schools have an important responsibility to prepare students with the knowledge, skills, character, and adaptability needed to succeed in an economy influenced by intelligent technologies. The goal is not simply to prepare students for their first job but to prepare them for a lifetime of learning, growth, and meaningful contribution.

One of the greatest changes brought by AGI may involve the relationship between people and work. Throughout history, technology has often automated repetitive tasks while creating opportunities for new forms of employment. Machines reduced much of the physical labor required in factories, yet new careers emerged in engineering, manufacturing, design, maintenance, logistics, and technology development. Computers automated many office tasks while creating professions in software development, cybersecurity, digital marketing, data analysis, and information technology. Similarly, AGI may perform certain routine cognitive tasks more efficiently, allowing people to focus on work that requires creativity, leadership, communication, innovation, ethical reasoning, and complex decision-making. Students should understand that technological change does not simply eliminate jobs; it also transforms existing careers and creates opportunities that previous generations could not imagine.

Future careers will likely require individuals to work alongside intelligent systems rather than compete against them. A teacher may use AGI to personalize instruction while continuing to mentor students and build meaningful relationships. A physician may rely on intelligent systems to analyze medical information while remaining responsible for diagnosis, patient communication, and compassionate care. Engineers may use AGI to evaluate thousands of design possibilities before selecting the safest and most practical solution. Scientists may accelerate research by using intelligent systems to analyze enormous amounts of data while continuing to ask original questions and design innovative experiments. In every profession, technology becomes a valuable partner, but human judgment remains essential.

Because the future workforce will continue changing, schools should emphasize transferable skills that remain valuable across many professions. Communication allows people to explain ideas clearly, collaborate with diverse teams, and build trust with colleagues and clients. Critical thinking helps individuals evaluate information, solve unfamiliar problems, and make responsible decisions. Creativity encourages innovation by helping people imagine new products, services, and solutions that improve society. Collaboration teaches students how to work effectively with others, appreciate different perspectives, and contribute toward shared goals. Adaptability prepares individuals to respond confidently as technology, industries, and workplaces continue evolving. These human-centered skills remain valuable regardless of how advanced intelligent systems become because they support meaningful relationships, thoughtful leadership, and continuous innovation.

Digital literacy will become increasingly important for every career, not only for technology professionals. Students should understand how intelligent systems function, how information is analyzed, how digital tools support decision-making, and how technology should be used responsibly. They should recognize the importance of cybersecurity, data privacy, responsible communication, and ethical technology use. Digital literacy also includes understanding the limitations of intelligent systems and recognizing when human judgment should guide important decisions. Schools prepare students most effectively when they teach technology as a tool that supports human intelligence rather than replacing it.

Entrepreneurship may also become a more significant part of education in the AGI economy. Intelligent technologies lower many barriers that previously prevented individuals from creating new businesses or solving community problems. Students with creative ideas may use AGI to conduct market research, organize business plans, analyze customer needs, develop marketing strategies, and improve products or services. However, successful entrepreneurship still depends upon identifying meaningful problems, building trust with customers, demonstrating integrity, leading teams effectively, and adapting when challenges arise. Technology can accelerate many business processes, but long-term success continues to depend on human creativity, perseverance, ethical leadership, and strong communication.

Career preparation in the AGI era should also encourage interdisciplinary learning. Future professionals may combine knowledge from several fields rather than specializing exclusively in one discipline. A healthcare innovator may understand medicine, computer science, ethics, and engineering. An environmental scientist may combine biology, geography, economics, data analysis, and public policy. An educator may integrate psychology, technology, communication, curriculum design, and leadership. Schools help students prepare for these careers by encouraging connections between academic subjects and providing opportunities to solve authentic problems that require knowledge from multiple disciplines. Students learn that the world's most important challenges rarely belong to a single subject area.

Another important goal of career preparation is developing confidence. Many students worry about choosing the "perfect" career, especially as technology changes rapidly. Education should reassure students that they do not need to predict every future occupation. Instead, they should focus on becoming adaptable learners who are willing to continue developing new knowledge and skills throughout their lives. Employers consistently value individuals who demonstrate curiosity, initiative, responsibility, integrity, teamwork, and a willingness to learn. These qualities allow graduates to adjust successfully as new opportunities emerge and industries continue evolving. Lifelong learning becomes one of the greatest career advantages any student can possess.

Preparing students for careers in the AGI economy is ultimately about preparing them for meaningful lives rather than simply productive employment. Careers provide opportunities to solve problems, serve communities, support families, contribute to scientific discovery, improve healthcare, protect the environment, educate future generations, create works of art, and strengthen society. Technology may change how these goals are accomplished, but the purpose of meaningful work remains deeply human. Schools therefore have the responsibility to prepare students not only with technical knowledge but also with character, compassion, resilience, ethical judgment, and the confidence to continue learning throughout their lives. These qualities will help students succeed in any economy because they represent the enduring strengths of human intelligence working alongside intelligent technology.

Chapter 10 (Part 2)

As Artificial General Intelligence continues to develop, many careers that students will one day pursue may not yet exist. History provides many examples of occupations that were once unimaginable. Before the internet, there were no web designers, social media managers, mobile application developers, cloud computing specialists, or cybersecurity analysts. As technology advanced, entirely new industries emerged, creating millions of employment opportunities around the world. The AGI economy will likely follow a similar pattern. While some routine tasks may become automated, new professions will appear that focus on designing, managing, improving, regulating, securing, and ethically applying intelligent technologies. Students should view these changes as opportunities rather than obstacles, recognizing that education prepares them to adapt successfully to careers that continue evolving throughout their lives.

Some future careers may focus directly on Artificial General Intelligence itself. Organizations may employ AGI systems designers, human-AI collaboration specialists, AI ethics officers, intelligent systems auditors, algorithm transparency analysts, digital trust consultants, AI safety researchers, educational technology architects, robotic systems coordinators, and intelligent infrastructure managers. These professionals may help ensure that intelligent technologies operate safely, fairly, securely, and responsibly while supporting human goals. At the same time, many existing careers will simply incorporate AGI as another professional tool. Teachers, nurses, engineers, architects, scientists, lawyers, accountants, artists, journalists, entrepreneurs, and public servants will continue serving society while using intelligent systems to improve efficiency, analyze information, and support decision-making.

Regardless of future job titles, employers will continue valuing qualities that technology cannot easily replace. Leadership remains one of these qualities. Effective leaders inspire others, build trust, communicate a clear vision, encourage teamwork, resolve conflicts, and make difficult decisions during uncertain situations. Leadership depends upon emotional intelligence, integrity, accountability, empathy, and courage. AGI may organize information or evaluate possible strategies, but people motivate others through relationships, shared purpose, and personal example. Schools should therefore provide students with opportunities to lead classroom projects, participate in student organizations, mentor younger learners, and solve community problems so they develop leadership skills before entering the workforce.

Another quality that will become increasingly valuable is innovation. Innovation is more than inventing new technologies; it involves improving existing ideas, discovering better solutions, and recognizing opportunities where others see obstacles. Students develop innovative thinking by asking questions, experimenting with ideas, learning from mistakes, and approaching problems with curiosity rather than fear. Project-based learning, scientific investigations, engineering challenges, entrepreneurial activities, and creative arts all encourage innovation because they require students to think independently while applying knowledge in meaningful ways. AGI may generate ideas quickly, but human creativity determines which ideas are practical, ethical, and beneficial to society.

Communication will remain one of the strongest career skills in every profession. Employees work with customers, patients, colleagues, supervisors, community members, and international partners every day. They explain ideas, negotiate solutions, provide presentations, write reports, resolve misunderstandings, and collaborate toward common goals. As AGI becomes more common, communication may become even more important because people will need to explain technology clearly to others who have different levels of understanding. A healthcare professional may explain how an intelligent diagnostic system supports patient care. A teacher may help parents understand how AGI personalizes instruction while protecting student privacy. An engineer may present technical solutions to community leaders. Strong communication builds confidence, trust, and successful collaboration.

The future workforce will also require resilience. Change can sometimes create uncertainty, especially when new technologies transform familiar ways of working. Resilient individuals respond by learning new skills, adapting to changing circumstances, maintaining positive attitudes, and continuing to move forward despite setbacks. Students should understand that learning does not end when they graduate from high school or college. Throughout their careers they may complete professional certifications, attend workshops, participate in continuing education, and develop entirely new areas of expertise. Lifelong learning becomes one of the most valuable career habits because it allows people to remain confident and capable in a rapidly changing world.

Schools cannot prepare students for the AGI economy alone. Partnerships between educators, families, businesses, colleges, universities, and community organizations create valuable learning opportunities that connect classroom instruction with real-world experiences. Students benefit from internships, career exploration programs, mentorships, guest speakers, job shadowing experiences, research partnerships, entrepreneurship competitions, and service-learning projects. These experiences help students understand how academic knowledge applies beyond the classroom while introducing them to careers they may never have previously considered. Strong partnerships also help schools adjust curriculum as industries evolve, ensuring that education remains relevant to future workforce needs.

Families continue playing an important role in career preparation. Parents and guardians encourage responsibility, perseverance, curiosity, honesty, and confidence by supporting educational goals, discussing career interests, celebrating effort, and modeling lifelong learning. Conversations about work, leadership, financial responsibility, community service, and personal values help students understand that successful careers involve more than earning an income. Meaningful work also involves contributing positively to society, helping others, solving important problems, and developing talents that benefit both individuals and communities.

Another important lesson for students is understanding that success cannot be measured solely by salary or job title. Careers become meaningful when individuals use their abilities to improve the lives of others while continuing to grow personally and professionally. A teacher inspiring future generations, a nurse providing compassionate care, an engineer designing safer transportation systems, an entrepreneur creating jobs within a community, or a scientist developing life-saving discoveries all contribute to society in important ways. AGI may increase productivity and efficiency, but purpose continues coming from human values, relationships, and service.

The AGI economy will reward those who combine technical knowledge with wisdom, adaptability, and strong character. Students who communicate effectively, think critically, solve problems creatively, lead responsibly, collaborate respectfully, and continue learning throughout life will remain valuable regardless of how technology changes. Schools therefore prepare students most successfully when they develop both professional competence and personal character. These qualities create graduates who are ready not only to enter the workforce but also to shape its future responsibly.

Looking ahead, today's students will become tomorrow's innovators, educators, scientists, engineers, entrepreneurs, healthcare professionals, artists, public servants, and community leaders. They will inherit technologies more powerful than any previous generation has known. Yet the qualities that define outstanding professionals will remain remarkably familiar: honesty, compassion, curiosity, resilience, responsibility, creativity, and integrity. Artificial General Intelligence may transform industries and create remarkable opportunities, but it will always be people who provide vision, purpose, and ethical leadership. By preparing students with knowledge, skills, values, and confidence, education ensures that the future workforce will not simply adapt to the AGI economy—it will lead it with wisdom, innovation, and a commitment to improving the world for generations to come.

Chapter 10 Summary

Preparing Students for Careers in the AGI Economy

Artificial General Intelligence (AGI) is expected to transform many industries and create new career opportunities that do not yet exist. While some routine tasks may become automated, new professions will emerge that require people to work alongside intelligent systems while applying human creativity, ethical judgment, communication, leadership, and critical thinking.

This chapter explained that schools should prepare students not only for their first job but also for a lifetime of learning. Because technology will continue changing throughout their careers, students need adaptable skills that remain valuable regardless of future technological advancements. These skills include communication, collaboration, creativity, critical thinking, problem-solving, leadership, resilience, digital literacy, entrepreneurship, and lifelong learning.

The chapter also explored how AGI will support professionals in fields such as education, healthcare, engineering, science, business, and public service. Technology will become a valuable partner, but people will continue making important decisions, building relationships, solving complex problems, and demonstrating ethical leadership.

Career preparation extends beyond classroom instruction. Families, schools, businesses, colleges, and community organizations all contribute by providing mentorship, internships, career exploration opportunities, and real-world learning experiences that connect education with future employment.

Ultimately, successful careers in the AGI economy will depend on more than technical knowledge. Students who combine professional skills with integrity, compassion, adaptability, curiosity, and a commitment to lifelong learning will be well prepared to lead in an increasingly intelligent world.

Chapter 10 Reflection

Reflect on what you learned in this chapter. Answer each question using complete sentences.

1. Why is lifelong learning essential in the AGI economy?
2. Which future-ready skill discussed in this chapter do you believe is most important? Explain your answer.
3. How can AGI support professionals without replacing them?
4. Why should students develop leadership skills before entering the workforce?
5. How can entrepreneurship create new opportunities in an AGI-powered economy?
6. Why are communication and collaboration valuable in every profession?
7. How can schools better prepare students for careers that do not yet exist?
8. What role do families play in preparing students for future careers?
9. If you could choose any future career in the AGI economy, what would it be and why?
10. After reading this chapter, how has your view of future careers changed?

Chapter 10 Worksheet

Part A – Vocabulary Matching

Match each term with the correct definition.

A. Lifelong Learning

B. Adaptability

C. Entrepreneurship

D. Leadership

E. Digital Literacy

F. Collaboration

G. Innovation

H. Career Readiness

1. _____ Continuing to learn and develop new skills throughout life.
2. _____ The ability to adjust successfully to change.
3. _____ Starting or developing new business ideas and opportunities.
4. _____ Guiding and inspiring others toward shared goals.
5. _____ Understanding how to use technology responsibly and effectively.
6. _____ Working successfully with other people.
7. _____ Creating new ideas or improving existing solutions.
8. _____ Having the knowledge, skills, and attitudes needed for employment.

Part B – Short Answer

1. Explain why career preparation is changing in the AGI economy.

2. Name four skills employers will continue valuing even as AGI becomes more advanced.

3. Why should students become lifelong learners?

4. How can internships, mentorships, and career exploration help students?

5. Why should schools teach both technical skills and strong character?

Part C – Career Planning Activity

Imagine you are graduating ten years from now and beginning your career in an AGI-powered world.

Describe the career you hope to pursue, the skills you will need, how AGI might assist you, and the human qualities that will make you successful.

Chapter 10 Quiz

Multiple Choice

1. What is the primary goal of career preparation in the AGI economy?

A. Preparing students for only one lifelong job.

B. Preparing students for continuous learning and changing careers.

C. Eliminating traditional education.

D. Replacing workers with technology.

2. Which skill will remain valuable in every profession?

A. Communication.

B. Critical thinking.

C. Leadership.

D. All of the above.

3. How will AGI most likely affect future careers?

A. It will replace every worker.

B. It will become a tool that supports professionals while creating new opportunities.

C. It will eliminate education.

D. It will prevent innovation.

4. Why are internships and mentorships valuable?

A. They connect classroom learning with real-world experience.

B. They replace school.

C. They eliminate the need for teachers.

D. They reduce lifelong learning.

5. Which human quality remains essential in every career?

A. Integrity.

B. Responsibility.

C. Adaptability.

D. All of the above.

True or False

6. _____ Many future careers have not yet been created.
7. _____ Lifelong learning helps people adapt to changing technology.
8. _____ Schools alone are responsible for preparing students for future careers.
9. _____ AGI will likely support professionals rather than replace every occupation.
10. _____ Strong character is just as important as technical knowledge.

Chapter 10 Answer Key

Worksheet Answers

Part A – Vocabulary Matching

1. **A**
2. **B**
3. **C**
4. **D**
5. **E**
6. **F**
7. **G**
8. **H**

Part B – Suggested Responses

1. Career preparation is changing because AGI is transforming industries, creating new occupations, automating some routine tasks, and increasing the importance of adaptable, human-centered skills.
2. Possible answers include communication, leadership, creativity, collaboration, critical thinking, adaptability, resilience, ethical judgment, problem-solving, and lifelong learning.
3. Lifelong learning helps people develop new knowledge, adapt to changing technologies, pursue new career opportunities, and remain successful throughout their professional lives.
4. These experiences provide real-world knowledge, develop professional skills, introduce career options, build confidence, and connect classroom learning to future employment.
5. Technical knowledge helps students perform their jobs, while strong character ensures they use their knowledge responsibly, ethically, and in ways that benefit others.

Quiz Answers

1. **B**
2. **D**
3. **B**
4. **A**
5. **D**
6. **True**
7. **True**
8. **False**
9. **True**
10. **True**

Chapter 11

Leadership in the Age of AGI

Throughout history, every generation has looked to leaders during times of change. Whether guiding communities through scientific discoveries, economic challenges, technological revolutions, or social transformation, effective leaders have always helped people navigate uncertainty while building hope for the future. The emergence of Artificial General Intelligence (AGI) represents one of the most significant technological developments in modern history, and it will require thoughtful leadership at every level of society. Schools, businesses, governments, healthcare organizations, nonprofit institutions, and local communities will all depend upon individuals who can combine technological understanding with ethical judgment, compassion, vision, and the ability to bring people together. Leadership in the AGI era is not simply about understanding intelligent technology. It is about helping people use that technology wisely while preserving the values that strengthen families, schools, workplaces, and communities.

Many people believe that leadership belongs only to presidents, chief executive officers, school superintendents, or elected officials. In reality, leadership begins much earlier and appears in everyday situations. A student who encourages classmates during a difficult project demonstrates leadership. A teacher who inspires curiosity and confidence in young learners practices leadership every day. A parent who models honesty, responsibility, and kindness provides leadership within the family. A volunteer organizing a neighborhood service project also leads by helping others work toward a common goal. Leadership is not defined by a job title or position of authority. Instead, it is demonstrated through actions that positively influence others, solve problems, and encourage people to achieve shared goals. This understanding becomes especially important in the AGI era because every individual has opportunities to influence how technology is used within their own community.

One of the most important qualities of effective leadership is vision. Vision means seeing possibilities that others may not yet recognize and helping people move toward meaningful goals. As AGI transforms education, healthcare, transportation, manufacturing, agriculture, communication, and countless other industries, leaders must look beyond today's challenges and prepare for tomorrow's opportunities. School leaders may imagine new ways of teaching that combine intelligent technologies with meaningful human relationships. Business leaders may develop innovative products that improve people's lives while protecting privacy and promoting fairness. Community leaders may identify ways intelligent systems can improve public services while ensuring that every resident benefits from technological progress. Vision allows leaders to guide change with purpose rather than simply reacting to events as they occur.

Leadership also requires excellent communication. During periods of rapid technological change, people naturally have questions, concerns, and differing opinions. Some individuals become excited about innovation, while others worry about uncertainty or possible risks. Effective leaders listen carefully before responding. They explain complex ideas clearly, encourage respectful conversations, answer questions honestly, and build trust by communicating openly with others. Communication involves more than speaking confidently; it also requires listening with empathy, understanding different perspectives, and helping people work together despite disagreements. In schools, teachers demonstrate these skills daily by guiding classroom discussions where students respectfully exchange ideas while learning from one another.

Trust forms the foundation of every successful leader. People willingly follow leaders whom they believe are honest, responsible, fair, and dependable. Trust develops gradually through consistent actions rather than promises alone. Leaders earn trust by admitting mistakes, accepting responsibility, treating people respectfully, keeping commitments, and making decisions that place the well-being of others above personal gain. As AGI becomes increasingly involved in important decisions, trust will become even more valuable. Communities will expect leaders to explain how intelligent technologies are being used, protect privacy, ensure fairness, and remain accountable for outcomes. Technology may support leadership, but character determines whether people choose to follow.

Another essential leadership quality is adaptability. Throughout history, successful leaders have adjusted to changing circumstances without losing sight of their core values. New challenges often require new ideas, different strategies, and continuous learning. The AGI era will introduce opportunities and problems that no previous generation has experienced. Leaders who remain curious, open-minded, and willing to learn will be better prepared to guide others through uncertainty. Adaptability does not mean abandoning important principles. Instead, it means finding responsible ways to apply enduring values within changing environments. Schools help students develop adaptability by encouraging curiosity, problem-solving, creativity, collaboration, and resilience.

Decision-making becomes increasingly important as leaders encounter more complex situations involving intelligent technologies. Every important decision involves balancing multiple priorities. School administrators may consider educational quality, student privacy, teacher training, accessibility, and financial resources before adopting new technologies. Business leaders evaluate innovation, customer trust, employee well-being, cybersecurity, and long-term sustainability. Community leaders consider public safety, fairness, environmental impact, and responsible use of public resources. AGI may assist by organizing information, analyzing possible outcomes, and identifying patterns within large datasets, but leaders remain responsible for evaluating ethical consequences and making final decisions. Wisdom involves recognizing that accurate information is valuable only when combined with thoughtful human judgment.

Leaders in the AGI era must also inspire lifelong learning. Because technology continues evolving rapidly, effective leaders recognize that education does not end with graduation. They encourage employees, students, colleagues, and community members to continue developing new knowledge and skills throughout their lives. Schools model this principle by supporting professional development for teachers, encouraging student curiosity, and creating learning environments where asking questions is valued. Businesses invest in employee training while communities provide educational opportunities for citizens of all ages. Lifelong learning strengthens organizations because it prepares people to adapt confidently as new technologies and new opportunities emerge.

Perhaps the greatest responsibility of leadership in the AGI era is ensuring that technology serves humanity rather than controlling it. Leaders must continually ask important questions before implementing powerful new technologies. Will this innovation improve people's lives? Does it protect human dignity? Is it fair to everyone? Does it strengthen education, healthcare, public safety, or community well-being? Are appropriate safeguards in place? These questions remind us that technology should always remain a tool that supports human goals rather than becoming the goal itself. Great leadership keeps people at the center of every important decision.

As students prepare for their futures, they should understand that leadership is not reserved for a select few. Every student has opportunities to develop leadership qualities through daily choices that demonstrate responsibility, honesty, kindness, perseverance, and respect. Whether leading a classroom project, serving on a student council, helping a classmate understand a difficult lesson, or organizing a community service activity, students build habits that prepare them for greater responsibilities in adulthood. In the age of Artificial General Intelligence, the world will need leaders who understand both technology and humanity—individuals who combine knowledge with wisdom, innovation with integrity, and confidence with compassion. These are the leaders who will guide society toward a future where technological progress benefits everyone.

Chapter 11 (Part 2)

Leadership in the age of Artificial General Intelligence will require more than technical knowledge. Future leaders must understand how to balance innovation with responsibility while helping people adapt to rapid technological change. Every new technology brings excitement, but it can also create uncertainty. Some people welcome change quickly, while others may worry about how new systems will affect their jobs, privacy, education, or daily lives. Effective leaders recognize these concerns and respond with patience, honesty, and empathy. Instead of forcing change without explanation, they involve people in the decision-making process, listen carefully to questions, provide accurate information, and encourage collaboration. When people feel respected and included, they are far more willing to support positive change.

One important leadership style that will become increasingly valuable in the AGI era is servant leadership. A servant leader focuses first on helping others succeed rather than seeking personal recognition or authority. Teachers demonstrate servant leadership every day by placing student learning above personal recognition. Principals serve teachers by providing resources, encouragement, and professional development. Community leaders strengthen neighborhoods by listening to residents and addressing shared concerns. In the future, organizations using AGI most successfully will likely be led by individuals who understand that technology should improve people's lives rather than simply increase efficiency. Servant leadership reminds us that every technological advancement should ultimately benefit humanity.

School leaders will have especially important responsibilities as AGI becomes part of education. They must create clear visions for how intelligent technologies will support teaching and learning while protecting student privacy, promoting educational equity, and maintaining high academic standards. Effective principals and district administrators encourage teachers to experiment with new instructional approaches while providing training, technical support, and opportunities for collaboration. They also communicate openly with families, helping parents understand how AGI supports learning without replacing the essential role of teachers. Strong educational leadership creates confidence because it demonstrates that innovation is guided by thoughtful planning rather than by technology alone.

Leadership also requires the courage to make difficult decisions. Sometimes leaders must choose between several reasonable options, each with advantages and disadvantages. Imagine a school district deciding whether to adopt an advanced AGI learning platform. The technology promises personalized instruction and improved efficiency, but implementing it requires significant financial investment, teacher training, and careful attention to student privacy. Responsible leaders evaluate educational benefits, consult teachers, families, technology specialists, and students, review research, and consider both short-term and long-term consequences before making a final decision. Courage does not mean making quick decisions. It means making thoughtful decisions even when the answers are not simple.

Another essential leadership responsibility involves building strong teams. Great leaders recognize that no individual possesses every skill or every answer. They value diverse perspectives because people with different experiences often identify creative solutions that others may overlook. In an AGI-powered workplace, successful teams may include educators, engineers, software developers, healthcare professionals, researchers, business specialists, cybersecurity experts, and community leaders working together toward shared goals. Leaders encourage respectful communication, recognize individual strengths, resolve conflicts constructively, and create environments where everyone feels valued. Collaboration becomes even more powerful when intelligent technologies support human teamwork rather than replacing it.

Resilience is another quality that distinguishes effective leaders. Unexpected challenges will continue appearing as technology evolves. New discoveries may require organizations to revise policies, redesign training programs, improve cybersecurity, or rethink existing practices. Resilient leaders remain calm during uncertainty. They acknowledge difficulties honestly while maintaining confidence that solutions can be found through teamwork, careful planning, and continuous learning. Students can begin developing resilience by viewing mistakes as opportunities for growth rather than reasons to give up. Every challenge becomes a chance to strengthen problem-solving skills, perseverance, and self-confidence.

Student leadership will also become increasingly important in the AGI generation. Schools provide many opportunities for young people to practice leadership long before entering professional careers. Students lead by encouraging classmates, organizing service projects, participating in student government, mentoring younger learners, resolving conflicts respectfully, and contributing positively to school culture. Leadership is demonstrated through daily actions rather than special titles. A student who welcomes a new classmate, helps another student understand difficult material, or speaks respectfully during discussions demonstrates qualities that will remain valuable throughout life. The AGI era will reward individuals who combine technological knowledge with compassion, responsibility, integrity, and a willingness to serve others.

Ethical leadership becomes especially important when intelligent systems influence important decisions. Leaders should establish clear expectations regarding privacy, fairness, transparency, cybersecurity, and responsible technology use. They should encourage regular evaluation of intelligent systems to identify possible improvements and ensure that technology continues serving educational and organizational goals. Ethical leaders admit when changes are needed, invite constructive feedback, and remain accountable for decisions. Transparency strengthens trust because people understand how decisions are made and why certain actions are taken. In every organization, trust grows when leaders consistently demonstrate honesty, fairness, and responsibility.

The leaders of tomorrow will also recognize that learning never ends. They will read widely, seek advice from mentors, attend professional development programs, participate in conferences, study emerging technologies, and remain curious throughout their careers. Continuous learning allows leaders to understand changing conditions while remaining prepared to guide others through new opportunities and unexpected challenges. Students who develop strong learning habits today will become adults who adapt confidently as technology continues advancing. Lifelong learning is not simply a professional advantage—it is an essential characteristic of effective leadership.

As Artificial General Intelligence becomes part of everyday life, society will need leaders who understand both innovation and humanity. These leaders will recognize that technology is most valuable when it strengthens education, improves healthcare, protects the environment, supports scientific discovery, expands economic opportunity, and improves the quality of life for everyone. They will measure success not only by efficiency or productivity but also by the positive impact their decisions have on people and communities. Leadership in the AGI era is ultimately about building trust, encouraging collaboration, protecting human dignity, and inspiring others to work toward a shared vision of a better future.

Every student reading this book has the potential to become one of those future leaders. Leadership begins with everyday choices—telling the truth, accepting responsibility, helping others, listening respectfully, working hard, and continuing to learn. As students develop these habits, they prepare themselves to lead classrooms, workplaces, organizations, communities, and perhaps even nations. Artificial General Intelligence will undoubtedly change many aspects of society, but the qualities that define exceptional leaders will remain remarkably consistent: wisdom, integrity, courage, compassion, humility, and a genuine commitment to serving others. When these qualities guide technological progress, the future becomes not only more intelligent but also more hopeful, more ethical, and more human.

Chapter 11 Summary

Leadership in the Age of AGI

Leadership will become one of the most important human qualities in the age of Artificial General Intelligence (AGI). As intelligent technologies continue transforming education, business, healthcare, government, and communities, society will need leaders who combine technological understanding with wisdom, integrity, compassion, and ethical decision-making.

This chapter explained that leadership is not limited to people with important titles or positions. Leadership begins with everyday actions such as encouraging others, solving problems, communicating honestly, accepting responsibility, and serving the needs of a team or community. Students can begin developing leadership skills through their daily choices at school, at home, and in their communities.

The chapter also explored several qualities of effective leaders, including vision, communication, trust, adaptability, courage, resilience, servant leadership, collaboration, and lifelong learning. These characteristics help leaders guide organizations through change while building confidence and maintaining strong relationships with the people they serve.

As AGI becomes more common, leaders must also ensure that intelligent technologies are used ethically. They must protect privacy, promote fairness, encourage transparency, support responsible innovation, and keep people at the center of every important decision. Technology should always serve humanity rather than replace human judgment.

Ultimately, leadership in the AGI era is about helping others grow, solving meaningful problems, and creating a future where technological progress improves lives while preserving the values that make society stronger. The future belongs to leaders who combine intelligence with character, innovation with compassion, and knowledge with wisdom.

Chapter 11 Reflection

Think carefully about the ideas discussed in this chapter. Answer each question using complete sentences.

1. Why is leadership important in an AGI-powered world?
2. Which leadership quality discussed in this chapter do you believe is most important? Explain your answer.
3. How can students begin developing leadership skills today?
4. Why is servant leadership valuable in schools and communities?
5. How can leaders build trust during times of technological change?
6. Why should leaders continue learning throughout their careers?
7. Describe a leader you admire. Which qualities make this person an effective leader?
8. How should leaders balance innovation with ethics?
9. If you became the principal of an AGI-ready school, what would be your top three priorities?
10. After reading this chapter, what kind of leader do you hope to become?

Chapter 11 Worksheet

Part A – Vocabulary Matching

Match each term with the correct definition.

A. Leadership

B. Vision

C. Integrity

D. Servant Leadership

E. Resilience

F. Collaboration

G. Adaptability

H. Accountability

1. _____ Inspiring and guiding others toward shared goals.
2. _____ The ability to see future possibilities and create meaningful goals.
3. _____ Being honest and doing what is right even when no one is watching.
4. _____ Leading by serving and supporting others.
5. _____ Recovering from challenges and continuing to move forward.
6. _____ Working together to accomplish common objectives.
7. _____ Adjusting successfully to changing circumstances.
8. _____ Accepting responsibility for decisions and actions.

Part B – Short Answer

1. Explain why leadership is important during times of technological change.

____

____

2. Name four qualities of effective leaders discussed in this chapter.

____

____

3. Why should leaders communicate openly with the people they serve?

____

____

4. How can schools help students develop leadership skills?

____

____

5. Why should leaders place people before technology?

____

____

____

Part C – Leadership Activity

Imagine you have been selected to lead your school's AGI Innovation Committee.

Write one paragraph describing how you would help teachers, students, parents, and school leaders work together to introduce AGI responsibly while protecting privacy, promoting fairness, encouraging collaboration, and improving student learning.

____

____

____

____

____

____

Chapter 11 Quiz

Multiple Choice

1. What is the primary purpose of leadership?

A. Controlling people.

B. Guiding and inspiring others toward meaningful goals.

C. Using technology to replace people.

D. Giving orders without listening.

2. Which leadership style focuses on helping others succeed?

A. Competitive leadership.

B. Servant leadership.

C. Authoritarian leadership.

D. Independent leadership.

3. Which leadership quality helps people adjust successfully to change?

A. Adaptability.

B. Memorization.

C. Competition.

D. Isolation.

4. Why should leaders continue learning throughout their careers?

A. Technology and society continue changing.

B. Learning ends after graduation.

C. Leaders never face new challenges.

D. AGI replaces lifelong learning.

5. Which statement best describes leadership in the AGI era?

A. Technology should make every decision.

B. Leaders should combine innovation with ethics and human values.

C. Leadership belongs only to government officials.

D. AGI eliminates the need for leadership.

True or False

6. _____ Leadership can begin at any age.
7. _____ Trust is built through honesty and consistent actions.
8. _____ AGI should replace ethical leadership.
9. _____ Collaboration strengthens leadership.
10. _____ Lifelong learning is an important leadership habit.

Chapter 11 Answer Key

Worksheet Answers

Part A – Vocabulary Matching

1. **A**
2. **B**
3. **C**
4. **D**
5. **E**
6. **F**
7. **G**
8. **H**

Part B – Suggested Responses

1. Leadership helps people navigate change by providing direction, building trust, encouraging teamwork, solving problems, and making responsible decisions.
2. Possible answers include vision, integrity, communication, adaptability, resilience, courage, servant leadership, accountability, empathy, collaboration, and lifelong learning.
3. Open communication builds trust, answers questions, reduces uncertainty, encourages collaboration, and helps people understand the reasons behind important decisions.
4. Schools develop leadership by providing opportunities through student government, classroom projects, service-learning, mentoring, teamwork, clubs, athletics, and community service.
5. Technology is a tool, but leaders must protect human dignity, support ethical decision-making, build relationships, and ensure that innovation benefits people and communities.

Quiz Answers

1. **B**
2. **B**
3. **A**
4. **A**
5. **B**
6. **True**
7. **True**
8. **False**
9. **True**
10. **True**

Chapter 12

Building a Human-Centered Future with AGI

Every generation inherits powerful tools that shape the future. Fire allowed early civilizations to cook food, create warmth, and build communities. The printing press made education available to millions of people. Electricity transformed homes, businesses, hospitals, and schools. Computers and the internet connected the world in ways previous generations could never have imagined. Today, Artificial General Intelligence (AGI) represents another remarkable step in humanity's long history of innovation. Yet history teaches an important lesson: technology alone has never determined the future. Instead, the future has always been shaped by the choices people make about how technology is used. The same will be true for AGI. Its greatest value will not come from how intelligent it becomes, but from how wisely people choose to use it to improve the lives of others.

A human-centered future begins with a simple idea: technology exists to serve people, not the other way around. Every new invention should improve human well-being, strengthen communities, expand opportunities, and help solve meaningful problems. When schools adopt AGI-powered learning tools, the goal should not be to replace teachers but to help every student receive better support and more personalized instruction. When hospitals use intelligent systems, the purpose should not be to remove physicians from patient care but to help healthcare professionals diagnose illnesses more accurately and spend more time caring for patients. When businesses introduce AGI into the workplace, success should be measured not only by increased productivity but also by how technology supports employees, improves customer experiences, and contributes positively to society.

Human-centered thinking reminds us that every technological decision affects real people. Behind every student learning with AGI is a family that hopes for educational success. Behind every patient assisted by intelligent healthcare systems is a person who deserves compassion and dignity. Behind every community using intelligent transportation systems are families who expect safe roads and reliable public services. Technology becomes meaningful only when it improves the quality of life for individuals and communities. This perspective encourages leaders, educators, engineers, scientists, and policymakers to consider not only what technology can accomplish but also how those accomplishments influence people's lives.

Education plays a central role in building a human-centered future. Schools prepare students not only to understand technology but also to understand themselves, their communities, and their responsibilities to others. Reading, writing, mathematics, science, history, the arts, and technology all contribute to developing knowledgeable individuals. Equally important, however, are qualities such as empathy, honesty, responsibility, perseverance, curiosity, kindness, and respect. These human values provide the foundation that guides responsible innovation. Students who develop strong character alongside strong academic skills become adults who use technology thoughtfully rather than carelessly.

One of the greatest strengths of humanity has always been collaboration. Throughout history, people have solved problems by working together across cultures, professions, and generations.

Scientific discoveries often result from teams of researchers sharing ideas. Engineers, architects, construction workers, and community leaders collaborate to build schools, hospitals, bridges, and transportation systems. Teachers, parents, and students work together to create successful learning environments. The AGI era will continue requiring this spirit of cooperation. Intelligent technologies may accelerate research and organize information, but meaningful progress will still depend upon people who communicate effectively, respect different perspectives, and work together toward common goals.

A human-centered future also requires inclusion. Every student should have opportunities to learn, regardless of background, language, disability, family income, or geographic location. Every community should benefit from responsible technological innovation rather than being left behind because of limited resources or unequal access. Schools must continue working toward educational equity by ensuring that intelligent technologies support all learners while respecting individual needs and differences. Inclusive education recognizes that diversity strengthens communities by bringing together different experiences, ideas, and perspectives that encourage creativity and innovation.

Another important element of a human-centered future is environmental responsibility. Technological progress should improve people's lives while protecting the natural world for future generations. Intelligent systems may help scientists monitor ecosystems, reduce energy consumption, improve recycling programs, predict natural disasters, protect endangered species, and design more sustainable cities. Students should understand that environmental stewardship is not separate from technological innovation. Instead, responsible innovation includes finding solutions that benefit both humanity and the planet. The future belongs to individuals who recognize that economic progress, scientific discovery, and environmental sustainability can work together rather than compete with one another.

Communities will also benefit when AGI strengthens human relationships rather than replacing them. Technology can help people communicate across great distances, translate languages, organize information, and connect individuals with valuable resources. However, genuine friendships, family relationships, mentorship, teamwork, and community service continue developing through personal interaction, trust, empathy, and shared experiences. Schools should continue encouraging students to participate in discussions, collaborative projects, athletics, music, art, volunteer service, and leadership opportunities that strengthen interpersonal relationships. Technology may enhance communication, but it cannot replace the importance of human connection.

Building a human-centered future also requires optimism. Throughout history, every generation has faced uncertainty when new technologies emerged. Some people feared that books would reduce memory, that calculators would eliminate mathematical thinking, or that computers would replace human creativity. While every technological change created challenges, people also learned to adapt, develop new skills, and discover opportunities that had previously been impossible. AGI will likely follow a similar path. Students should approach the future with thoughtful optimism—recognizing both the responsibilities and the remarkable possibilities that intelligent technologies may bring. Confidence grows when people prepare themselves through education, ethical leadership, lifelong learning, and a commitment to serving others.

Ultimately, building a human-centered future is not the responsibility of governments, technology companies, or schools alone. Every individual contributes through daily choices that demonstrate honesty, kindness, responsibility, fairness, curiosity, and respect. Students who help classmates succeed, teachers who inspire lifelong learning, parents who encourage good character, entrepreneurs who solve community problems, scientists who pursue discoveries responsibly, and leaders who place people before technology all contribute to shaping a future where innovation benefits everyone. Artificial General Intelligence may become one of the most powerful technologies humanity has ever created, but its greatest success will always be measured by one question: Does it help people live healthier, wiser, safer, and more meaningful lives? When the answer is yes, technology fulfills its highest purpose by serving humanity with integrity, compassion, and hope.

Chapter 12 (Part 2)

Building a human-centered future with Artificial General Intelligence also requires cooperation beyond individual schools, businesses, or communities. Many of the opportunities and challenges created by AGI will extend across national borders. Climate change, healthcare, cybersecurity, scientific research, disaster response, food security, and economic development are global issues that benefit from international collaboration. Intelligent systems may help researchers analyze worldwide data, identify emerging health concerns, improve agricultural production, and coordinate emergency responses during natural disasters. However, these accomplishments depend upon people from different countries working together with mutual respect and shared purpose. Students who develop cultural understanding, communication skills, and appreciation for diverse perspectives will be better prepared to participate in this increasingly connected world.

Global citizenship will become an important part of education in the AGI era. Being a global citizen does not mean abandoning one's own community or culture. Instead, it means recognizing that our actions often influence people beyond our immediate surroundings. A scientific discovery made in one country may improve healthcare around the world. An educational innovation developed in one school district may help students in many other communities. A technological breakthrough designed to reduce pollution may benefit future generations across the globe. Students should understand that responsible innovation carries both local and global responsibilities. Every thoughtful decision contributes to a larger network of people working together to improve life for everyone.

Another important responsibility involves protecting future generations. The choices people make today will influence the opportunities available to children and grandchildren many years from now. Building a human-centered future means asking whether today's decisions create a better tomorrow. Schools teach this perspective by encouraging students to think beyond immediate results and consider long-term consequences. Engineers designing sustainable buildings, scientists developing renewable energy technologies, educators preparing future leaders, healthcare professionals improving medical treatments, and policymakers creating responsible regulations all contribute to a future that benefits those who have not yet been born.

AGI should support these long-term goals by helping society solve problems while preserving opportunities for future generations.

Innovation should always be accompanied by thoughtful reflection. Throughout history, some inventions produced unexpected consequences because people focused only on short-term benefits. Responsible innovators pause to ask important questions before introducing powerful new technologies. How might this innovation affect families? Could it create unintended risks? Does it protect privacy and human dignity? Will it benefit people fairly? Can it be improved before widespread use? Reflection encourages careful planning rather than impulsive action. In the AGI era, thoughtful reflection becomes one of humanity's greatest strengths because intelligent systems may accelerate technological development much faster than previous generations experienced.

Education prepares students to become responsible innovators by encouraging curiosity alongside accountability. Students should feel excited about discovering new ideas while also understanding that every invention carries responsibilities. A future engineer may design intelligent transportation systems that improve public safety. A scientist may develop medical technologies that save lives. A software developer may create educational tools that help millions of children learn more effectively. An entrepreneur may build businesses that strengthen local economies while creating meaningful employment opportunities. Every innovation begins with a person who believes positive change is possible, but lasting success depends upon using knowledge responsibly and ethically.

Communities become stronger when people actively participate in shaping the future rather than simply observing change. Students should understand that they are not passive observers of the AGI era. They are future teachers, researchers, healthcare professionals, engineers, artists, entrepreneurs, community leaders, scientists, public servants, and parents. Their ideas, decisions, and actions will influence how intelligent technologies are developed and used. Schools help students recognize this responsibility by providing opportunities for leadership, community service, collaborative problem-solving, civic engagement, and creative innovation. These experiences build confidence while showing young people that they already possess the ability to contribute positively to society.

Another essential characteristic of a human-centered future is resilience. New technologies will undoubtedly bring unexpected challenges that require patience, flexibility, and continuous learning. Some solutions will succeed immediately, while others will require revision and improvement. Resilient individuals understand that setbacks are part of progress rather than signs of failure. They learn from mistakes, seek advice from others, adapt to changing circumstances, and continue moving forward with determination. Students who develop resilience today will become adults capable of leading organizations, solving community problems, and responding confidently to future technological changes.

Hope also plays a powerful role in building the future. History demonstrates that humanity has repeatedly overcome difficult challenges through cooperation, innovation, education, and perseverance. Diseases once considered untreatable now have effective medical treatments. Communication that once required weeks now occurs instantly across continents. Scientific discoveries continue improving agriculture, transportation, environmental protection, and countless other aspects of daily life. AGI represents another opportunity to improve human well-being, provided it is guided by wisdom, compassion, and ethical leadership. Students should recognize that they have reasons to approach the future with confidence because every generation has the opportunity to make meaningful contributions that improve society.

Perhaps the most important lesson of this chapter is that people remain at the center of every technological advancement. Machines may become faster, more accurate, and more capable, but they do not replace the qualities that define humanity. Compassion comforts those facing hardship. Creativity imagines possibilities that have never existed before. Integrity builds trust within families, schools, workplaces, and communities. Courage inspires people to confront difficult challenges. Wisdom helps leaders balance innovation with responsibility. These qualities give direction to technological progress and ensure that knowledge serves purposes greater than efficiency alone.

Schools therefore have one of the most important missions in the AGI era. They are not simply preparing students to use intelligent technology. They are preparing future citizens who understand how to improve society through knowledge, character, service, and responsible leadership. Every lesson in mathematics, science, literature, history, the arts, technology, and citizenship contributes to this larger purpose by helping students become thoughtful, ethical, and compassionate individuals capable of building a better world.

The future will not be determined solely by the intelligence of machines. It will be determined by the wisdom of the people who design them, teach with them, regulate them, improve them, and use them every day. Students reading this book represent the generation that will shape that future. They have the opportunity to build schools where every learner is supported, businesses that create meaningful opportunities, communities that care for one another, scientific discoveries that improve health and protect the environment, and governments that promote fairness and opportunity. Artificial General Intelligence may become one of humanity's greatest achievements, but its greatest success will always depend upon people who choose to lead with compassion, think with integrity, serve with humility, and innovate with purpose. When human values remain at the center of technological progress, the future becomes brighter not only because our machines become more intelligent, but because our societies become wiser, stronger, and more united.

Chapter 12 Summary

Building a Human-Centered Future with AGI

Artificial General Intelligence (AGI) has the potential to improve education, healthcare, science, business, transportation, environmental protection, and many other areas of society. However, technology alone cannot create a better future. A truly successful future depends on people using AGI responsibly, ethically, and with a commitment to improving the lives of others.

This chapter explained that a human-centered future places people at the heart of every technological decision. Intelligent systems should support teachers, doctors, engineers, scientists, business leaders, families, and communities rather than replace human relationships, ethical judgment, or compassion.

The chapter emphasized several important ideas, including collaboration, inclusion, environmental responsibility, global citizenship, lifelong learning, resilience, innovation, and service. Students learned that responsible innovation requires balancing technological progress with human dignity, fairness, sustainability, and the well-being of future generations.

The chapter also explained that schools have a unique responsibility to prepare students not only to understand AGI but also to become ethical leaders, thoughtful problem-solvers, compassionate citizens, and lifelong learners. Every student has the opportunity to help shape the future through everyday decisions that reflect honesty, kindness, responsibility, and respect.

Ultimately, the future will not be measured by how intelligent machines become. It will be measured by how wisely people use those technologies to strengthen communities, solve meaningful problems, protect the planet, and improve the quality of life for everyone.

Chapter 12 Reflection

Think carefully about the ideas presented in this chapter. Answer each question using complete sentences.

1. What does it mean to build a human-centered future?
2. Why should technology always serve people instead of replacing them?
3. How can students contribute to a better future today?
4. Why is collaboration important when solving global challenges?
5. How can AGI help protect the environment?
6. Why should schools continue teaching empathy, kindness, and responsibility?
7. What responsibilities do future innovators have when creating new technologies?
8. How can global citizenship help improve the world?
9. If you could create one AGI-powered solution to improve your community, what would it be?
10. After reading this chapter, what human value do you believe is most important for shaping the future, and why?

Chapter 12 Worksheet

Part A – Vocabulary Matching

Match each term with its correct definition.

A. Human-Centered Innovation

B. Global Citizenship

C. Sustainability

D. Collaboration

E. Resilience

F. Inclusion

G. Stewardship

H. Innovation

1. _____ Creating technology that improves people's lives.
2. _____ Working together toward shared goals.
3. _____ Caring for natural resources and protecting the environment.
4. _____ Respecting and including people from different backgrounds.
5. _____ Recovering from challenges and continuing to grow.
6. _____ Thinking beyond local communities to care about the world.
7. _____ Developing new ideas that solve meaningful problems.
8. _____ Using resources responsibly so future generations can benefit.

Part B – Short Answer

1. Explain why people should remain at the center of technological innovation.

___

___

2. Name four human qualities discussed in this chapter that technology cannot replace.

___

___

3. Why is protecting future generations an important responsibility?

___

___

4. How can schools prepare students to build a better future?

___

___

5. Why should innovation always be guided by ethics?

Part C – Future Builder Activity

Imagine you are part of an international team designing AGI solutions to improve life around the world.

Write one paragraph describing how your team would use AGI to solve a global challenge while protecting human dignity, promoting fairness, respecting the environment, and serving future generations.

Chapter 12 Quiz

Multiple Choice

1. What is the primary goal of a human-centered future?

A. Making machines more important than people.

B. Using technology to improve people's lives.

C. Eliminating human decision-making.

D. Replacing teachers and families.

2. Which human quality remains essential in the AGI era?

A. Compassion.

B. Integrity.

C. Wisdom.

D. All of the above.

3. Why is global cooperation important in the AGI era?

A. Many challenges affect people around the world.

B. Countries should work independently.

C. Technology only benefits one community.

D. Schools no longer matter.

4. Why should innovation include environmental responsibility?

A. To protect natural resources for future generations.

B. To reduce education.

C. To eliminate scientific research.

D. To replace human leadership.

5. Which statement best summarizes this chapter?

A. Technology should always make every decision.

B. Human values should guide technological progress.

C. AGI should replace human creativity.

D. Schools should focus only on technology.

True or False

6. _____ Human-centered innovation places people first.
7. _____ Students can help shape the future through responsible decisions.
8. _____ Collaboration helps solve complex global challenges.
9. _____ Sustainability is important for future generations.

10. _____ The future depends on both technological advancement and strong human values.

Chapter 12 Answer Key

Worksheet Answers

Part A – Vocabulary Matching

1. **A**
2. **D**
3. **G**
4. **F**
5. **E**
6. **B**
7. **H**
8. **C**

Part B – Suggested Responses

1. People should remain at the center of innovation because technology is a tool designed to improve human life, strengthen communities, and solve meaningful problems while respecting dignity and human rights.
2. Possible answers include compassion, empathy, integrity, creativity, ethical judgment, wisdom, resilience, leadership, kindness, responsibility, and courage.
3. Today's decisions affect tomorrow's opportunities. Protecting future generations means making responsible choices that preserve resources, encourage sustainability, and create a better world.
4. Schools prepare students by teaching academic knowledge, ethical leadership, critical thinking, collaboration, creativity, responsible technology use, and lifelong learning.
5. Ethics ensures that innovation is fair, responsible, transparent, safe, and focused on improving people's lives rather than causing harm.

Quiz Answers

1. **B**
2. **D**
3. **A**
4. **A**
5. **B**
6. **True**

7. **True**
8. **True**
9. **True**
10. **True**

Chapter 13

The Future of Schools in an AGI World

Schools have always reflected the needs of society. As communities changed, education changed with them. During the agricultural age, children often learned practical skills that supported farming and local communities. During the Industrial Revolution, schools introduced more structured classrooms that prepared students for manufacturing, business, and expanding cities. The Information Age brought computers, the internet, digital learning, and global communication into classrooms around the world. Today, education stands at the beginning of another important transformation as Artificial General Intelligence (AGI) becomes increasingly capable. This new era offers opportunities to improve teaching and learning in ways that previous generations could only imagine. However, the purpose of schools remains the same: helping every student develop the knowledge, skills, character, and confidence needed to build successful and meaningful lives.

The future school will not simply contain more technology. Instead, it will become a learning community where technology supports personalized education while teachers continue guiding students academically, socially, and emotionally. AGI may help educators analyze learning progress, identify areas where students need additional support, recommend instructional resources, translate lessons into multiple languages, and create learning experiences tailored to individual needs. These capabilities allow teachers to spend less time performing repetitive administrative tasks and more time mentoring students, encouraging critical thinking, building relationships, and inspiring curiosity. Rather than replacing teachers, AGI has the potential to strengthen one of education's most important human relationships—the connection between teacher and student.

Personalized learning may become one of the defining characteristics of future schools. Every student learns differently. Some understand mathematical concepts quickly but need additional support in writing. Others excel in science while developing reading comprehension more gradually. Some students learn best through visual demonstrations, while others benefit from discussion, hands-on activities, or independent exploration. AGI may help teachers recognize these differences by organizing assessment information, identifying learning patterns, and suggesting instructional strategies that address individual strengths and challenges. Teachers then use their professional judgment to design meaningful learning experiences that encourage every student to reach his or her fullest potential. Personalization does not mean lowering expectations; it means providing appropriate support so all learners have opportunities to succeed.

The physical classroom may also continue evolving. Future learning environments could become more flexible, allowing students to work independently, collaborate in small groups, conduct research, participate in discussions, create multimedia presentations, and solve authentic problems using both traditional resources and intelligent technologies. Furniture, instructional materials, and classroom layouts may become more adaptable to support different learning activities throughout the school day. Technology should enhance these experiences without becoming the center of attention. The classroom remains a place where students ask questions, build friendships, practice leadership, develop confidence, and learn how to work respectfully with others.

Teachers will continue serving as instructional leaders, mentors, and role models. While AGI may organize information quickly, teachers understand students as individuals with unique personalities, interests, strengths, challenges, and aspirations. Educators recognize when students need encouragement after experiencing disappointment. They celebrate personal growth, help resolve conflicts, inspire perseverance, and create classroom cultures where every learner feels respected and valued. These human qualities cannot be automated because they depend upon empathy, trust, patience, and meaningful relationships developed over time. The future school succeeds not because technology becomes more intelligent, but because teachers use technology to strengthen human learning.

Assessment practices will likely continue changing as schools place greater emphasis on demonstrating understanding rather than simply recalling information. Traditional examinations may remain one part of the evaluation process, but students may increasingly demonstrate learning through research projects, engineering challenges, scientific investigations, presentations, digital portfolios, artistic performances, community service, and collaborative problem-solving. AGI may help teachers organize evidence of student progress, identify learning trends, and recommend additional practice when needed. However, educators continue evaluating qualities such as creativity, communication, ethical reasoning, leadership, resilience, and collaboration—abilities that reflect authentic learning and prepare students for future success.

The curriculum of future schools will likely expand to include topics that help students understand intelligent technologies while strengthening essential human skills. Students may study artificial intelligence, digital citizenship, cybersecurity, data literacy, ethics, entrepreneurship, environmental sustainability, financial literacy, and global citizenship alongside mathematics, science, history, language arts, physical education, and the arts. Rather than replacing traditional academic subjects, these additions help students understand how knowledge connects across disciplines and applies to real-world challenges. Schools prepare students most effectively when they integrate technological understanding with critical thinking, creativity, communication, and responsible citizenship.

Future schools will also strengthen partnerships with families and local communities. Parents remain children's first teachers, and their involvement continues influencing academic success, character development, and lifelong learning. AGI may help schools communicate more effectively with families by providing timely updates, translating information into multiple languages, organizing educational resources, and identifying opportunities for additional support.

Even with these improvements, strong family relationships continue depending upon trust, communication, and shared commitment to student success. Schools become strongest when educators, parents, students, and community members work together toward common educational goals.

School leadership will become increasingly important as educational systems adopt new technologies. Principals, district administrators, curriculum specialists, instructional coaches, and school boards must evaluate educational innovations carefully before implementation. Responsible leaders ask important questions. Does this technology improve student learning? Does it protect student privacy? Is it accessible to all learners? Does it support teachers rather than replacing professional judgment? Is adequate training available? These questions help ensure that technological decisions remain focused on educational quality rather than novelty alone.

As education continues evolving, one truth remains constant: schools exist to help students become knowledgeable, ethical, compassionate, and capable individuals who contribute positively to society. Artificial General Intelligence may transform many aspects of teaching and learning, but it does not change education's deeper purpose. Students still need encouragement, meaningful relationships, opportunities to discover their talents, and guidance from caring adults who believe in their potential. The future of schools will therefore be defined not by technology itself but by how wisely educators use technology to strengthen learning, inspire hope, and prepare every student to thrive in an increasingly intelligent world.

Chapter 13 (Part 2)

The future of schools will be shaped not only by new technologies but also by the people who use them. Teachers, administrators, support staff, students, parents, and community partners each play an essential role in creating learning environments where innovation supports educational excellence. Technology alone cannot create outstanding schools. Successful schools are built upon strong relationships, thoughtful leadership, high academic expectations, and a shared commitment to helping every student succeed. AGI becomes valuable only when it strengthens these foundations rather than distracting from them.

Teachers will continue serving as the heart of every successful school. Although AGI may organize lesson materials, analyze student performance, recommend instructional resources, and automate certain administrative tasks, educators remain responsible for guiding learning, encouraging curiosity, providing emotional support, and helping students develop confidence. Teachers understand that every student has a unique story, different strengths, personal challenges, and individual goals. They know when a student needs encouragement after struggling with a difficult assignment, when a classroom discussion should explore a deeper question, or when a lesson should be adjusted because students require additional support. These decisions require professional experience, empathy, flexibility, and genuine care for students—qualities that remain uniquely human.

The role of the principal will also continue evolving. Future school leaders must understand both educational leadership and emerging technologies. They will create school cultures that encourage innovation while protecting student privacy, supporting teacher growth, and maintaining high academic standards. Effective principals help teachers explore new instructional strategies, encourage collaboration among staff members, and ensure that technology aligns with educational goals rather than becoming an end in itself. They also communicate openly with parents and community members, building trust by explaining how AGI supports learning while preserving the central role of educators.

Students themselves will become increasingly active participants in their own learning. Rather than waiting passively for information, they will investigate meaningful questions, conduct research, collaborate with classmates, develop creative solutions, and reflect on their own progress. AGI may provide personalized guidance, immediate feedback, and access to vast educational resources, but students remain responsible for setting goals, managing their learning, asking thoughtful questions, and applying knowledge responsibly. Education becomes most powerful when students view themselves as active learners who take ownership of their academic growth.

Future classrooms may place greater emphasis on solving authentic problems connected to real communities. Students might work together to design environmentally sustainable neighborhoods, develop emergency response plans for natural disasters, improve local transportation systems, create community health awareness campaigns, or propose solutions for reducing food waste. AGI may assist by organizing research, analyzing data, modeling possible outcomes, and helping students visualize complex systems. Teachers guide students through collaboration, ethical reasoning, communication, and critical thinking while ensuring that projects remain connected to meaningful learning objectives. These experiences help students recognize that education extends beyond textbooks into the challenges and opportunities of everyday life.

Partnerships between schools and families will become even more valuable in the AGI era. Parents provide encouragement, reinforce learning habits, and help children develop responsibility, perseverance, honesty, and respect. Schools provide academic instruction, guidance, and opportunities for intellectual growth. When these partnerships remain strong, students receive consistent support that strengthens both academic achievement and personal development. AGI may improve communication by translating messages, organizing progress reports, and providing educational resources for families, but trust continues developing through respectful relationships and shared commitment to student success.

Community organizations, businesses, colleges, universities, libraries, museums, and nonprofit agencies will also contribute to future education. These partnerships create opportunities for internships, mentorships, research experiences, service-learning projects, career exploration, and community engagement. Students benefit by seeing how classroom knowledge applies to real-world professions and community challenges. Schools that build strong partnerships prepare graduates who understand not only academic concepts but also how to contribute meaningfully to society through service, leadership, innovation, and collaboration.

Educational equity must remain a priority as schools adopt AGI technologies. Every student deserves access to high-quality learning opportunities regardless of family income, geographic location, language, disability, or cultural background. Responsible school systems work to ensure that technology reduces educational barriers rather than creating new inequalities. This includes providing reliable access to digital resources, offering appropriate teacher training, supporting students with diverse learning needs, and ensuring that instructional materials remain accessible to all learners. Equity also means recognizing that every student brings valuable experiences and perspectives that enrich classroom learning.

Professional development for educators will remain essential. Teachers cannot effectively integrate new technologies without opportunities to learn, practice, collaborate, and reflect on their instructional strategies. Schools should provide ongoing professional learning that helps educators understand both the technical capabilities and the educational implications of AGI. Teachers benefit from sharing successful classroom experiences, discussing challenges, exploring new instructional methods, and collaborating with colleagues. Continuous professional growth strengthens the entire educational system because confident teachers create confident learners.

Future schools will also encourage lifelong learning beyond graduation. Communities increasingly recognize that education does not end with a high school diploma or university degree. Adults will continue developing new knowledge and skills throughout their professional lives as technology evolves. Schools may expand partnerships with colleges, workforce training programs, community education centers, and online learning organizations to support learners of all ages. This broader vision transforms schools into lifelong learning centers that serve entire communities rather than only children and adolescents.

The future school will measure success by more than standardized test scores. Academic achievement remains important, but schools will also celebrate creativity, collaboration, leadership, resilience, ethical decision-making, civic responsibility, innovation, and service to others. Students who graduate from AGI-ready schools should possess not only strong academic knowledge but also the confidence to solve problems, communicate effectively, adapt to change, and contribute positively to their communities. These qualities prepare graduates for meaningful careers as well as responsible citizenship.

As we imagine the schools of tomorrow, one truth remains unchanged. Education has always been about unlocking human potential. Artificial General Intelligence may provide remarkable new tools, but it cannot replace the encouragement of an inspiring teacher, the guidance of caring parents, the friendship of classmates, or the satisfaction of discovering something through personal effort. Schools will continue shaping future generations by combining the best of technological innovation with the timeless values of curiosity, integrity, compassion, perseverance, and service. Students entering these schools will not simply learn about the future—they will become the generation that creates it. Through responsible leadership, thoughtful innovation, and unwavering commitment to human dignity, the schools of the AGI era will prepare young people to build a world that is not only more intelligent but also more just, more compassionate, and more hopeful for everyone.

Chapter 13 Summary

The Future of Schools in an AGI World

The schools of the future will continue preparing students for successful lives while using Artificial General Intelligence (AGI) to improve teaching, learning, and educational opportunities. Although technology will become more advanced, the mission of education will remain the same: helping every student develop knowledge, character, confidence, and the ability to contribute positively to society.

This chapter explained that AGI can personalize learning by helping teachers identify student strengths, provide additional support, organize instructional materials, and create engaging learning experiences. However, teachers will continue serving as mentors, role models, instructional leaders, and trusted adults who inspire students through encouragement, empathy, and meaningful relationships.

The chapter also described how classrooms may become more flexible, collaborative, and project-based. Students will work on authentic problems, apply knowledge across multiple subjects, and develop important future-ready skills such as critical thinking, creativity, communication, leadership, collaboration, and ethical decision-making.

Strong partnerships among schools, families, businesses, colleges, and community organizations will remain essential. Educational leaders must ensure that AGI is introduced responsibly by protecting student privacy, promoting educational equity, providing teacher training, and keeping learning focused on student success rather than technology alone.

Ultimately, the future of schools will be measured not only by academic achievement but also by how well they prepare students to become ethical leaders, lifelong learners, responsible citizens, and compassionate individuals. The best schools will combine the power of intelligent technology with the timeless human values that have always defined outstanding education.

Chapter 13 Reflection

Reflect on the ideas presented in this chapter. Answer each question using complete sentences.

1. How do you imagine schools changing during the AGI era?
2. Why will teachers remain important even as AGI becomes more advanced?
3. How can personalized learning help students succeed?
4. Why should future schools focus on more than standardized test scores?
5. How can schools and families work together to improve student learning?
6. Why is educational equity important when introducing AGI into schools?
7. Which future-ready skill discussed in this chapter do you believe will help students the most? Explain your answer.
8. How can community partnerships strengthen education?

9. If you could design the perfect AGI-ready classroom, what would it include?
10. After reading this chapter, what excites you most about the future of education?

Chapter 13 Worksheet

Part A – Vocabulary Matching

Match each term with its correct definition.

A. Personalized Learning

B. Educational Equity

C. Collaboration

D. Lifelong Learning

E. Community Partnership

F. Innovation

G. Professional Development

H. Student-Centered Learning

1. _____ Instruction designed to meet the needs of individual students.
2. _____ Providing every student with fair opportunities to succeed.
3. _____ Working together toward common educational goals.
4. _____ Continuing education throughout life.
5. _____ Schools working together with families, businesses, and organizations.
6. _____ Developing and applying new ideas to improve education.
7. _____ Ongoing learning and training for educators.
8. _____ Learning that actively involves students in their own education.

Part B – Short Answer

1. Explain how AGI can help teachers improve student learning.

____

____

2. Why should schools continue emphasizing human relationships?

3. Name four future-ready skills students should develop.

4. Why are school-community partnerships valuable?

5. How can schools prepare students for careers that may not yet exist?

Part C – School Design Activity

Imagine you have been asked to design a new AGI-ready school for your community.

Describe your vision for the school, including classrooms, technology, teachers, student activities, partnerships with families and businesses, and the values that would guide learning.

Chapter 13 Quiz

Multiple Choice

1. What is the primary purpose of future schools?

A. Replacing teachers with AGI.

B. Preparing students with knowledge, skills, character, and confidence.

C. Eliminating traditional education.

D. Teaching only technology.

2. How can AGI best support teachers?

A. By replacing classroom instruction.

B. By helping personalize learning and reducing routine administrative tasks.

C. By eliminating communication with parents.

D. By replacing school leaders.

3. Which future-ready skill is emphasized throughout this chapter?

A. Critical thinking.

B. Collaboration.

C. Creativity.

D. All of the above.

4. Why are partnerships with families important?

A. They strengthen student learning and development.

B. They reduce the need for teachers.

C. They eliminate classroom instruction.

D. They replace schools.

5. Which statement best summarizes the future of schools?

A. Technology is more important than people.

B. Human relationships and technology should work together to improve learning.

C. AGI will replace education.

D. Schools should focus only on standardized testing.

True or False

6. _____ Teachers will continue playing an essential role in education.
7. _____ Personalized learning can help students with different learning needs.
8. _____ Educational equity ensures all students have opportunities to succeed.
9. _____ Schools should encourage lifelong learning.
10. _____ The best schools combine technological innovation with strong human values.

Chapter 13 Answer Key

Worksheet Answers

Part A – Vocabulary Matching

1. **A**
2. **B**
3. **C**
4. **D**
5. **E**
6. **F**
7. **G**
8. **H**

Part B – Suggested Responses

1. AGI can help teachers personalize instruction, analyze student progress, organize educational resources, identify learning needs, and reduce administrative tasks so they have more time to teach and mentor students.
2. Human relationships provide encouragement, empathy, trust, guidance, motivation, and emotional support that technology cannot replace.
3. Possible answers include critical thinking, creativity, communication, collaboration, leadership, adaptability, ethical decision-making, resilience, digital literacy, and lifelong learning.

4. Community partnerships connect classroom learning with real-world experiences through internships, mentorships, guest speakers, service-learning projects, career exploration, and educational resources.
5. Schools prepare students by emphasizing adaptable skills, lifelong learning, leadership, creativity, collaboration, ethical decision-making, problem-solving, and the ability to work with emerging technologies.

Quiz Answers

1. **B**
2. **B**
3. **D**
4. **A**
5. **B**
6. **True**
7. **True**
8. **True**
9. **True**
10. **True**

Chapter 14

Students as the Architects of the AGI Future

Every generation inherits a world shaped by the people who came before it. At the same time, every generation also has the opportunity to improve that world for those who follow. Today's students are growing up during one of the most significant technological transformations in human history. Artificial General Intelligence (AGI) has the potential to influence education, healthcare, transportation, scientific research, business, communication, environmental protection, and many other areas of daily life. While engineers, scientists, educators, and technology companies continue developing these intelligent systems, it is today's students who will eventually decide how AGI is used in the decades ahead. They will become the teachers who educate future generations, the doctors who care for patients, the engineers who design new technologies, the entrepreneurs who build businesses, the researchers who make scientific discoveries, and the public leaders who establish policies that guide society. In many ways, students are not simply preparing for the future—they are preparing to build it.

The word "architect" usually describes a person who designs buildings. Before construction begins, architects create detailed plans that consider safety, purpose, appearance, durability, accessibility, and the needs of the people who will use the building. In a similar way, students become architects of the future by helping design the world they want future generations to inherit. Their decisions today influence the kind of society that exists tomorrow. Students who value honesty, fairness, compassion, curiosity, and responsibility will help build communities where intelligent technologies strengthen education, healthcare, economic opportunity, and quality of life. Just as architects carefully plan every detail before construction begins, students should learn to think carefully about how technology can best serve humanity.

Education provides students with the foundation needed to shape this future responsibly. Mathematics teaches logical reasoning and problem-solving. Science encourages observation, experimentation, and evidence-based thinking. History helps students understand how societies have changed over time and why responsible leadership matters. Language arts develops communication, reading comprehension, writing, and critical analysis. The arts encourage imagination, creativity, and self-expression. Technology education introduces students to digital tools, computational thinking, and responsible innovation. Together, these subjects prepare students to understand complex problems while developing the knowledge and skills necessary to solve them. Every lesson learned in school contributes to the larger goal of preparing thoughtful citizens capable of making informed decisions in an increasingly intelligent world.

One of the greatest opportunities students will have is improving lives through innovation. Innovation does not always require inventing entirely new technologies. Sometimes innovation means improving existing systems so they become more useful, more accessible, more affordable, or more environmentally responsible. A future teacher may develop new ways to personalize learning with AGI. A physician may improve healthcare by combining intelligent diagnostic systems with compassionate patient care. An engineer may design safer transportation systems that reduce accidents while protecting the environment. A software developer may create educational tools that help children with different learning needs succeed in school. Students should understand that innovation begins by identifying real problems and asking thoughtful questions about how those problems might be solved.

Curiosity remains one of the most valuable qualities future innovators can develop. Every important scientific discovery and technological breakthrough began with someone asking questions that others had not considered. Why does this happen? Is there a better way? What problem still needs solving? Curiosity encourages exploration, investigation, experimentation, and lifelong learning. In the AGI era, students should continue asking questions rather than simply accepting answers provided by intelligent systems. Technology may accelerate research and organize information, but meaningful discoveries still depend upon people who remain curious enough to explore new possibilities.

Students will also become responsible decision-makers. Throughout their lives they will encounter situations where technology offers several possible solutions. Choosing wisely requires more than technical knowledge. It requires ethical reasoning, empathy, fairness, accountability, and consideration of long-term consequences. Imagine a future city using AGI to improve transportation, manage energy consumption, and coordinate emergency services. Community leaders must ensure that these systems protect privacy, serve every neighborhood fairly, remain secure against cyber threats, and continue functioning during emergencies. Students who develop strong ethical foundations today will become leaders capable of making these important decisions tomorrow.

Another important responsibility involves collaboration. Few significant achievements occur through individual effort alone. Scientists work together across universities and research laboratories. Healthcare teams include physicians, nurses, pharmacists, therapists, and specialists. Engineers collaborate with architects, environmental scientists, construction professionals, and community leaders. Teachers partner with parents, counselors, administrators, and community organizations to support student success. The AGI era will require even greater collaboration because solving complex challenges often demands knowledge from multiple disciplines. Students should therefore develop communication skills, respect different perspectives, resolve disagreements constructively, and contribute positively to team efforts. These abilities strengthen innovation because diverse perspectives often lead to stronger solutions.

Resilience will become another defining quality of future architects of the AGI world. Not every idea succeeds immediately. Scientific experiments sometimes fail before leading to important discoveries. Businesses occasionally encounter setbacks before developing successful products. Engineers revise designs repeatedly before achieving safe and effective solutions. Educators continually improve lessons based on student learning. Students should understand that mistakes are not evidence of failure but opportunities for learning and growth. Resilient individuals respond to challenges by reflecting, adapting, seeking advice, and continuing to move forward with determination.

Character ultimately determines how knowledge is used. Intelligent technologies may become increasingly powerful, but human values continue guiding every important decision. Honesty builds trust. Compassion strengthens communities. Integrity encourages responsible leadership. Respect promotes cooperation. Humility allows people to continue learning from others. These qualities help students become individuals who use technology to improve lives rather than simply demonstrating technical skill. The future needs professionals who combine intelligence with wisdom and innovation with responsibility.

As students prepare for adulthood, they should recognize that they already possess the ability to influence the future. Every classroom discussion, community service project, scientific investigation, leadership opportunity, artistic creation, and act of kindness contributes to developing the habits that will guide future decisions. Artificial General Intelligence may transform many aspects of society, but it is today's students who will determine whether that transformation creates a future that is more equitable, compassionate, sustainable, innovative, and hopeful. By embracing learning, developing strong character, and remaining committed to serving others, students become the architects who design not only smarter technologies but also a better world for everyone.

Chapter 14 (Part 2)

As students prepare to become the architects of the AGI future, they should understand that leadership begins long before entering a profession. Every opportunity to solve a classroom problem, organize a community service project, help a classmate, or participate in student government develops skills that prepare young people to lead in adulthood. Leadership is not reserved for people with impressive job titles or positions of authority. Instead, it grows through daily actions that demonstrate responsibility, honesty, perseverance, and a willingness to serve others. These experiences help students build confidence while showing them that meaningful change often begins with small acts of initiative and cooperation.

Innovation will continue depending upon individuals who are willing to imagine better solutions for society. Many future breakthroughs may come from students who are sitting in classrooms today. Some may develop intelligent systems that improve healthcare by identifying diseases earlier or making medical treatment more accessible in underserved communities. Others may create educational technologies that help every child receive personalized instruction regardless of language or location. Future engineers may design transportation systems that reduce traffic congestion, improve safety, and decrease environmental pollution. Environmental scientists may develop AGI-powered tools that protect forests, conserve water, monitor wildlife, and improve renewable energy production. Entrepreneurs may establish businesses that solve community challenges while creating meaningful employment opportunities. Every innovation begins with someone who believes positive change is possible and is willing to work diligently toward that vision.

Students should also recognize that responsible citizenship remains essential in the AGI era. Citizenship involves more than obeying laws or participating in elections. Responsible citizens contribute positively to their communities by respecting others, protecting public resources, volunteering their time, supporting fairness, and helping solve local problems. Intelligent technologies may assist governments and communities by improving transportation, emergency response, environmental monitoring, public health, and educational services, but citizens remain responsible for ensuring that these technologies are used ethically and for the benefit of everyone. Students who participate in community projects, volunteer organizations, school leadership activities, and civic discussions begin developing habits that strengthen democracy and community life.

Entrepreneurship offers another exciting opportunity for future architects of the AGI world. Throughout history, entrepreneurs have recognized problems that others overlooked and created innovative solutions that improved everyday life. AGI may help future entrepreneurs analyze markets, organize business information, predict customer needs, and improve operational efficiency. However, successful businesses continue depending upon qualities such as honesty, creativity, perseverance, ethical leadership, customer service, and strong communication. Students who develop entrepreneurial thinking learn to identify opportunities, solve meaningful problems, adapt to changing circumstances, and contribute positively to local and global economies.

Lifelong learning will remain one of the greatest advantages students can possess. The technologies available when today's students graduate from school may differ significantly from those they use twenty or thirty years later. Successful professionals continually update their knowledge, develop new skills, attend training programs, read current research, participate in professional organizations, and remain curious throughout their careers. Students who enjoy learning today will be well prepared to adapt confidently as new discoveries and opportunities emerge. Lifelong learning transforms education from a temporary experience into a permanent habit that supports personal growth throughout life.

Another responsibility future architects must embrace is protecting human dignity. Every technological advancement should respect the value of every individual regardless of age, background, language, culture, disability, or economic circumstances. Students should understand that intelligent systems should increase opportunities rather than create barriers. Future leaders, educators, engineers, healthcare professionals, and policymakers must continue asking whether innovations are fair, inclusive, accessible, and beneficial for all members of society. Protecting human dignity requires empathy, respect, and a sincere commitment to ensuring that progress benefits everyone rather than only a small portion of the population.

Students should never underestimate the importance of creativity. While AGI may generate designs, organize information, and identify patterns, human creativity remains essential for imagining entirely new possibilities. Creativity inspires scientific discoveries, artistic expression, technological innovation, literature, music, architecture, engineering, and entrepreneurship. Schools strengthen creativity by encouraging exploration, experimentation, imagination, collaboration, and thoughtful risk-taking. Students who develop creative confidence become adults capable of solving challenges that previous generations could not have anticipated.

Strong relationships will continue shaping the future as much as technological progress. Families provide encouragement and values. Teachers inspire learning and confidence. Friends offer support and collaboration. Mentors share wisdom gained through experience. Community leaders create opportunities for service and growth. AGI may strengthen communication and improve access to information, but lasting success continues depending upon trust, respect, cooperation, and meaningful human relationships. Students should therefore invest not only in developing technical knowledge but also in building character and strengthening connections with others.

The future will also require courage. There will be times when students become adults who must make difficult decisions involving new technologies, unexpected challenges, or uncertain outcomes. Courage allows people to defend ethical principles even when doing so is not easy. It encourages leaders to protect privacy, promote fairness, reject dishonesty, and place human well-being above convenience or financial gain. Courage also inspires innovation because meaningful progress often requires exploring ideas that have never been attempted before. Students who practice courage today by speaking honestly, accepting responsibility, and standing up for what is right prepare themselves for greater leadership responsibilities tomorrow.

Every generation leaves a legacy. Some generations are remembered for scientific discoveries. Others transformed transportation, medicine, communication, education, or civil rights. The generation growing up during the emergence of Artificial General Intelligence has the opportunity to shape one of the most important technological transitions in history. Their legacy will not be determined solely by how advanced intelligent systems become. It will be measured by whether they use those systems to reduce suffering, expand educational opportunities, strengthen healthcare, protect the environment, encourage economic opportunity, promote justice, and improve the quality of life for people around the world.

As this chapter concludes, one message stands above all others: the future is not waiting for students—it is waiting to be built by them. Every lesson they learn, every challenge they overcome, every question they ask, every act of kindness they demonstrate, and every goal they pursue prepares them for that responsibility. Artificial General Intelligence will undoubtedly become an important part of tomorrow's world, but the direction of that world will always depend upon human character. Students who combine knowledge with wisdom, creativity with responsibility, ambition with compassion, and innovation with integrity will become the architects of a future where technology strengthens humanity and where every advancement reflects the highest values of education, leadership, and service. The greatest achievement of the AGI era will not simply be creating more intelligent machines—it will be empowering a generation of thoughtful, ethical, and courageous people who use intelligence, both human and artificial, to build a better world for everyone.

Chapter 14 Summary

Students as the Architects of the AGI Future

Today's students will become tomorrow's innovators, educators, engineers, scientists, healthcare professionals, entrepreneurs, public servants, and community leaders. As Artificial General Intelligence (AGI) continues transforming society, students will play an important role in deciding how these powerful technologies are developed and used.

This chapter explained that students are the architects of the future because their knowledge, character, creativity, and leadership will shape the world for future generations. Like architects who carefully design buildings before construction begins, students must carefully consider how technology can improve education, healthcare, environmental sustainability, business, transportation, and everyday life while protecting human dignity and promoting fairness.

The chapter emphasized the importance of curiosity, innovation, resilience, ethical decision-making, entrepreneurship, lifelong learning, collaboration, and responsible citizenship. Students learned that meaningful innovation begins by identifying real problems, asking thoughtful questions, and creating solutions that benefit individuals and communities.

The chapter also highlighted the importance of strong character. Honesty, integrity, compassion, courage, responsibility, and respect remain essential because technology alone cannot determine what is right or wrong. Human values guide every important decision involving AGI.

Ultimately, the future will not be created by technology alone. It will be created by students who combine knowledge with wisdom, creativity with ethics, leadership with service, and innovation with compassion. These future leaders will help ensure that AGI improves lives while strengthening schools, families, communities, and society.

Chapter 14 Reflection

Think about the ideas discussed in this chapter. Answer each question using complete sentences.

1. Why are students called the architects of the AGI future?
2. How can education prepare students to become responsible innovators?
3. Which human quality discussed in this chapter do you believe will be most important in the future? Explain your answer.
4. Why is curiosity essential for innovation?
5. How can entrepreneurship help solve community problems?
6. Why should future leaders protect human dignity when using AGI?
7. How can students begin developing leadership skills while still in school?
8. Why is lifelong learning important in a rapidly changing world?
9. If you could create one AGI innovation to improve people's lives, what would it be?
10. After reading this chapter, what role do you hope to play in shaping the future?

Chapter 14 Worksheet

Part A – Vocabulary Matching

Match each term with the correct definition.

A. Innovation

B. Entrepreneurship

C. Leadership

D. Curiosity

E. Human Dignity

F. Lifelong Learning

G. Citizenship

H. Resilience

1. _____ Creating new ideas or improving existing solutions.
2. _____ The desire to ask questions and explore new knowledge.
3. _____ Starting new ventures that solve problems and create value.
4. _____ Respecting the value and worth of every individual.
5. _____ Continuing to learn throughout life.
6. _____ Participating responsibly in and contributing to society.

7. _____ Recovering from challenges and continuing to grow.
8. _____ Inspiring and guiding others toward positive goals.

Part B – Short Answer

1. Explain why students have an important role in shaping the AGI future.

____

____

2. Name four qualities that future innovators should develop.

____

____

3. Why is ethical decision-making important when creating new technologies?

____

____

4. How can collaboration improve innovation?

____

____

5. Why should students prepare for careers that may not yet exist?

____

____

____

Part C – Future Architect Activity

Imagine you are leading a team that has been asked to design an AGI-powered solution for a major community challenge.

Describe your project, the problem it solves, how AGI helps, how people remain responsible for important decisions, and how your solution improves the lives of others while protecting fairness, privacy, and human dignity.

____

____

____

____

Chapter 14 Quiz

Multiple Choice

1. Why are students considered the architects of the AGI future?

A. They will help shape how technology is used in society.

B. They will only study technology.

C. They will replace teachers.

D. They will eliminate traditional careers.

---

2. Which quality encourages innovation and discovery?

A. Curiosity.

B. Isolation.

C. Memorization.

D. Competition.

---

3. Why is ethical leadership important in the AGI era?

A. It helps ensure technology serves people responsibly.

B. It replaces human judgment.

C. It eliminates difficult decisions.

D. It prevents technological progress.

4. Which statement best describes lifelong learning?

A. Learning ends after graduation.

B. People continue learning throughout their lives.

C. Technology eliminates education.

D. Students only learn in classrooms.

5. Which combination best prepares students for the future?

A. Technical knowledge only.

B. Human values only.

C. Technical knowledge combined with ethics, creativity, leadership, and lifelong learning.

D. Memorization alone.

True or False

6. _____ Innovation often begins with curiosity and thoughtful questions.
7. _____ Human dignity should remain a priority when developing AGI.
8. _____ Students can begin developing leadership skills before entering the workforce.
9. _____ Lifelong learning helps people adapt to technological change.
10. _____ The future depends on both technological innovation and strong human character.

Chapter 14 Answer Key

Worksheet Answers

Part A – Vocabulary Matching

1. **A**
2. **D**
3. **B**
4. **E**
5. **F**
6. **G**
7. **H**

8. **C**

Part B – Suggested Responses

1. Students will become the future leaders, educators, scientists, engineers, entrepreneurs, healthcare professionals, and policymakers who will guide how AGI is developed and used. Their decisions will influence society for many years.
2. Possible answers include curiosity, creativity, integrity, resilience, leadership, communication, collaboration, ethical reasoning, adaptability, compassion, and lifelong learning.
3. Ethical decision-making ensures that technology is developed and used fairly, responsibly, safely, transparently, and in ways that improve people's lives while respecting privacy and human dignity.
4. Collaboration brings together different experiences, knowledge, and perspectives, leading to stronger ideas, better problem-solving, and more innovative solutions than one person could develop alone.
5. Many future careers have not yet been created. Students who develop adaptable skills and commit to lifelong learning will be better prepared to succeed as technology and industries continue evolving.

Quiz Answers

1. **A**
2. **A**
3. **A**
4. **B**
5. **C**
6. **True**
7. **True**
8. **True**
9. **True**
10. **True**

Chapter 15

The Lifelong Journey of Learning in the AGI Age

For many years, people believed that education followed a simple path. Children attended elementary school, continued through middle and high school, perhaps attended college or technical school, found employment, and then spent decades working in the same profession. While learning certainly continued throughout life, formal education was often viewed as something that happened primarily during childhood and early adulthood. Today, that idea is changing. The emergence of Artificial General Intelligence (AGI), along with other rapidly advancing technologies, has transformed the way people think about education. In the modern world, learning is no longer a destination that ends with graduation. Instead, it has become a lifelong journey that continues throughout every stage of life. Students entering the AGI era will need curiosity, adaptability, and a willingness to continue learning long after they leave the classroom.

History demonstrates that societies have always evolved as new knowledge emerged. Farmers learned new agricultural methods. Doctors adopted improved medical treatments. Engineers developed stronger materials and safer construction techniques. Teachers introduced new instructional strategies as educational research advanced. Every generation has built upon the discoveries of those who came before it. What makes the AGI era unique is the speed at which knowledge is expanding. Scientific discoveries, technological innovations, and new career opportunities are developing more rapidly than ever before. This means that students who graduate today may work with technologies, professions, and challenges that do not yet exist. Preparing for this future requires more than memorizing information. It requires developing the ability to learn continuously, adapt confidently, and apply knowledge responsibly.

One of the greatest strengths students can develop is intellectual curiosity. Curious people naturally ask questions, investigate new ideas, and seek deeper understanding. They view learning as an exciting opportunity rather than simply a school requirement. Curiosity encourages exploration, creativity, experimentation, and innovation. Throughout history, remarkable discoveries have often begun with someone asking a simple question: "Why?" or "What if?" Scientists, inventors, educators, entrepreneurs, and artists all depend upon curiosity to inspire new ideas and solve meaningful problems. In the AGI age, curiosity becomes even more valuable because intelligent systems may provide information quickly, but human curiosity determines which questions deserve to be explored in the first place.

Adaptability is another essential quality for lifelong learners. Change has always been part of human history, but technological progress now occurs at an extraordinary pace. New software, communication tools, healthcare technologies, transportation systems, educational platforms, and workplace innovations appear regularly. Instead of fearing change, successful learners recognize that every advancement creates opportunities to develop new skills and expand their understanding. Adaptability does not require knowing everything. Rather, it means approaching unfamiliar situations with confidence, patience, and the belief that learning is always possible. Students who become comfortable learning new ideas today will find it easier to adjust to future technologies and career opportunities.

Reading continues to be one of the most powerful tools for lifelong learning. Books preserve human knowledge across generations, allowing readers to benefit from the experiences, research, and wisdom of others. Whether reading history, science, literature, biographies, technology, philosophy, or current events, students expand their understanding of the world while strengthening vocabulary, comprehension, critical thinking, and communication skills. In the

AGI era, reading becomes even more valuable because it helps individuals evaluate information thoughtfully rather than accepting every answer without question. Strong readers become strong thinkers because they compare ideas, analyze evidence, recognize different perspectives, and develop informed opinions.

Learning also becomes more meaningful when students apply knowledge in practical ways. Classroom lessons become stronger when connected to real experiences through science experiments, engineering projects, artistic creations, community service, internships, research activities, entrepreneurship, and collaborative problem-solving. AGI may provide valuable assistance by organizing information, simulating scenarios, or recommending resources, but genuine understanding develops when students actively participate in learning. Experience transforms information into wisdom because learners discover not only how something works but also why it matters.

Mistakes should also be viewed as valuable teachers throughout the lifelong learning journey. Every accomplished scientist, athlete, musician, engineer, entrepreneur, and educator has experienced setbacks while developing expertise. Errors reveal opportunities for improvement, encourage reflection, and strengthen perseverance. Students should understand that making mistakes does not mean they are incapable of success. Instead, mistakes provide important feedback that guides future growth. A growth mindset allows learners to view challenges as opportunities rather than obstacles. This perspective encourages resilience, confidence, and continuous improvement throughout life.

Another important aspect of lifelong learning involves learning from other people. Teachers, parents, mentors, classmates, colleagues, community leaders, and professionals all possess valuable experiences worth sharing. Listening carefully to others, asking thoughtful questions, accepting constructive feedback, and appreciating different perspectives enrich personal understanding. Collaboration often accelerates learning because individuals build upon one another's knowledge and experiences. The AGI age will continue emphasizing teamwork because solving complex challenges frequently requires contributions from people with diverse expertise.

Technology itself has expanded opportunities for lifelong education. People can now attend online courses, participate in virtual workshops, watch educational lectures, join professional organizations, access digital libraries, and communicate with experts around the world. These resources make learning more accessible than at any previous time in history. However, access to information alone does not guarantee wisdom. Lifelong learners develop the ability to evaluate sources carefully, verify facts, distinguish evidence from opinion, and use technology responsibly. Critical thinking remains essential because intelligent systems provide information, but people decide how that information should be interpreted and applied.

Perhaps the most inspiring aspect of lifelong learning is recognizing that human potential has no fixed limit. Every year brings opportunities to develop new skills, discover hidden talents, strengthen character, and contribute to society in meaningful ways. Students should never believe that education ends when they receive a diploma or degree. Instead, graduation marks the beginning of a new chapter filled with opportunities for continued exploration, professional growth, personal development, and service to others. In the AGI age, the individuals who thrive will not necessarily be those who know the most today. They will be those who remain curious enough to continue learning tomorrow. Lifelong learning transforms education from a temporary experience into a way of living, empowering individuals to grow continuously while helping build a wiser, more innovative, and more compassionate world.

Chapter 15 (Part 2)

The journey of lifelong learning does not always follow a straight path. There will be times when students encounter subjects that seem difficult, skills that require repeated practice, or challenges that test their patience and determination. These moments are not signs of failure. Instead, they are opportunities to become stronger, wiser, and more confident learners. Every accomplished professional has experienced setbacks while developing expertise. Scientists conduct experiments that do not produce expected results. Engineers redesign projects after discovering weaknesses. Teachers revise lessons when students need different approaches. Entrepreneurs learn from unsuccessful business ideas before creating successful companies. Lifelong learners understand that progress is built through persistence, reflection, and continuous improvement rather than immediate perfection.

A growth mindset becomes especially valuable in the AGI age. People with a growth mindset believe that intelligence, knowledge, and skills can continue developing through effort, practice, and learning. Rather than saying, "I cannot do this," they ask, "What can I learn to improve?" This attitude transforms obstacles into opportunities. Students who approach difficult assignments with curiosity instead of frustration develop resilience that benefits every area of life. They recognize that every challenge teaches valuable lessons that prepare them for future success. As technology continues evolving, this willingness to learn becomes one of the greatest advantages any individual can possess.

Artificial General Intelligence may become an important learning partner throughout life. Intelligent systems may recommend books, organize research, explain complex topics, translate languages, provide personalized practice activities, simulate professional scenarios, and help individuals develop new skills. Healthcare professionals may study emerging medical discoveries with the assistance of AGI. Engineers may learn new design methods through intelligent training systems. Teachers may explore innovative instructional strategies while improving classroom practices. Business leaders may analyze changing markets and develop new management approaches. In each case, AGI supports learning by making information more accessible, but human curiosity, critical thinking, ethical judgment, and motivation continue directing the learning process.

Continuous learning also strengthens confidence. Individuals who regularly develop new knowledge become more comfortable facing unfamiliar situations because they trust their ability to learn. Instead of fearing change, they view it as an opportunity for growth. This confidence becomes particularly important in careers where technology continues advancing. Workers who remain committed to professional development often discover new opportunities, accept greater responsibilities, and contribute innovative ideas to their organizations. Students who establish strong learning habits today prepare themselves to thrive in careers that will continue evolving throughout their lives.

Professional development extends beyond technical knowledge. Successful individuals continually strengthen communication, leadership, teamwork, emotional intelligence, cultural understanding, ethical reasoning, financial literacy, and problem-solving abilities. These human-centered skills become increasingly valuable because they complement the capabilities of intelligent technologies. AGI may analyze data efficiently, but people continue building trust, leading organizations, resolving conflicts, encouraging collaboration, and making decisions that require wisdom and compassion. Lifelong learners therefore seek growth in both professional expertise and personal character.

Reflection plays an important role in continuous improvement. Effective learners regularly evaluate their progress by asking thoughtful questions. What have I learned? Which skills have improved? What challenges remain? What goals should I pursue next? Reflection transforms experience into understanding because it encourages individuals to recognize both accomplishments and opportunities for further growth. Teachers often use reflection after lessons to improve instruction. Athletes review performances to strengthen future competitions. Scientists analyze research findings to guide future investigations. Students who develop reflective habits become more intentional learners because they understand how their own learning processes work.

Another important lesson of lifelong learning is recognizing that knowledge belongs to everyone. Learning is not limited by age, profession, or background. Children, teenagers, adults, and senior citizens all continue discovering new ideas throughout life. Grandparents learn new technologies to communicate with their families. Parents develop new skills to support changing careers. Retired professionals volunteer their expertise while continuing to study subjects that interest them. Communities become stronger when people of every generation share knowledge, experiences, and perspectives. Schools introduce this lifelong habit, but society benefits when learning continues across every stage of life.

Lifelong learners also understand the importance of teaching others. Sharing knowledge strengthens both the teacher and the learner. Students explain mathematical concepts to classmates. Older students mentor younger children. Professionals train new employees entering the workforce. Parents teach life skills to their children. Teachers inspire future generations every day. As individuals explain ideas, answer questions, and encourage others, they deepen their own understanding while contributing positively to their communities. Education becomes a cycle where every learner eventually becomes a teacher in some way.

Preparing for the future also means accepting that uncertainty will always exist. No one can predict every technological discovery, career opportunity, or global challenge that tomorrow may bring. However, individuals who continue learning remain prepared to adapt regardless of changing circumstances. They possess the confidence to acquire new knowledge, develop new skills, and respond thoughtfully to unexpected situations. Lifelong learning therefore provides more than information—it provides resilience, flexibility, confidence, and hope.

Perhaps the greatest reward of lifelong learning is personal fulfillment. Learning allows individuals to appreciate history, understand science, enjoy literature, create art, solve problems, build relationships, contribute to communities, and discover new possibilities throughout life. Education expands opportunities while helping people understand themselves and the world around them. Every book read, every skill mastered, every conversation shared, and every challenge overcome contributes to becoming a wiser and more compassionate individual.

As students prepare to enter the AGI age, they should remember that graduation is not the end of education—it is the beginning of an exciting lifelong adventure. Artificial General Intelligence will continue introducing new tools, new discoveries, and new opportunities, but the desire to learn will remain one of humanity's greatest strengths. Students who embrace curiosity, perseverance, humility, adaptability, and continuous improvement will be prepared not only to succeed professionally but also to lead meaningful lives filled with purpose and service. The future belongs to lifelong learners because they understand that education is not measured by the number of years spent in school but by a lifelong commitment to growing in knowledge, wisdom, character, and compassion. In the AGI era, those who never stop learning will never stop discovering new ways to improve themselves, strengthen their communities, and help shape a brighter future for generations to come.

Chapter 15 Summary

The Lifelong Journey of Learning in the AGI Age

Learning does not end when students graduate from high school, college, or a training program. In the age of Artificial General Intelligence (AGI), education becomes a lifelong journey that continues throughout every stage of life. As technology advances and new careers emerge, people must continue developing new knowledge, skills, and abilities to remain successful in a changing world.

This chapter explained that curiosity, adaptability, resilience, and a growth mindset are essential qualities for lifelong learners. Students who enjoy learning, ask thoughtful questions, embrace challenges, and learn from mistakes will be better prepared for careers and opportunities that may not yet exist.

The chapter also explored how AGI can become a valuable learning partner by helping individuals access information, organize research, practice new skills, and personalize learning experiences. However, human curiosity, critical thinking, ethical judgment, and motivation remain the driving forces behind meaningful education.

Lifelong learning also includes personal growth. Strong communication, leadership, emotional intelligence, collaboration, financial literacy, ethical decision-making, and service to others remain valuable throughout life. Students learned that education is not measured only by academic achievement but also by continuous improvement in character and responsibility.

Ultimately, the AGI era will reward individuals who never stop learning. Those who remain curious, adaptable, and committed to personal growth will be prepared not only to succeed professionally but also to improve their communities and contribute positively to society throughout their lives.

Chapter 15 Reflection

Take time to reflect on the ideas presented in this chapter. Answer each question using complete sentences.

1. Why is lifelong learning more important than ever in the AGI era?
2. How can a growth mindset help students succeed throughout life?
3. Why should mistakes be viewed as opportunities for learning?
4. How can AGI support lifelong learning without replacing human thinking?
5. Which lifelong learning habit do you believe will help you the most? Explain your answer.
6. Why is adaptability an important career skill?
7. How can reading continue to improve your knowledge throughout life?
8. In what ways can teaching others strengthen your own learning?
9. What new skill would you like to learn during the next five years?
10. After reading this chapter, how has your understanding of education changed?

Chapter 15 Worksheet

Part A – Vocabulary Matching

Match each term with its correct definition.

A. Lifelong Learning

B. Growth Mindset

C. Adaptability

D. Reflection

E. Curiosity

F. Professional Development

G. Resilience

H. Continuous Improvement

1. _____ Continuing to learn throughout every stage of life.
2. _____ Believing that abilities can improve through effort and learning.
3. _____ Adjusting successfully to change.
4. _____ Thinking about experiences in order to improve future performance.
5. _____ The desire to ask questions and discover new knowledge.
6. _____ Learning new knowledge and skills for your career.
7. _____ Recovering from setbacks and continuing forward.
8. _____ Regularly working to become better over time.

Part B – Short Answer

1. Explain why lifelong learning is essential in the AGI age.

2. Name four qualities of successful lifelong learners.

3. How can AGI become a helpful learning partner?

4. Why is reflection important for continuous improvement?

5. How does lifelong learning benefit both individuals and society?

Part C – Personal Learning Plan

Imagine you are graduating today and preparing for a career in an AGI-powered world.

Create a five-year personal learning plan describing the knowledge, skills, certifications, experiences, books, mentors, or educational opportunities you would pursue to continue growing professionally and personally.

____

____

____

____

____

____

Chapter 15 Quiz

Multiple Choice

1. What is the main idea of lifelong learning?

A. Education ends after graduation.

B. Learning continues throughout life.

C. Technology replaces education.

D. Schools provide all the knowledge a person will ever need.

2. Which quality helps people view challenges as opportunities to improve?

A. Growth mindset.

B. Fear of failure.

C. Memorization.

D. Avoidance.

3. How can AGI best support lifelong learning?

A. By encouraging personalized learning and access to information.

B. By replacing curiosity.

C. By eliminating the need for teachers.

D. By preventing independent thinking.

4. Why is adaptability important?

A. Technology and careers continue changing.

B. Learning never changes.

C. Students only need one career.

D. Knowledge remains the same forever.

5. Which statement best describes lifelong learners?

A. They stop learning after earning a diploma.

B. They remain curious, adaptable, and committed to continuous improvement.

C. They depend entirely on technology.

D. They avoid difficult challenges.

True or False

6. _____ Curiosity encourages lifelong learning.
7. _____ Mistakes can become valuable learning opportunities.
8. _____ Professional development ends after getting a job.
9. _____ Reflection helps people improve their knowledge and skills.
10. _____ Lifelong learning prepares people for an uncertain future.

Chapter 15 Answer Key

Worksheet Answers

Part A – Vocabulary Matching

1. **A**
2. **B**
3. **C**
4. **D**
5. **E**
6. **F**
7. **G**
8. **H**

Part B – Suggested Responses

1. Lifelong learning helps people adapt to changing technologies, develop new skills, pursue new career opportunities, solve emerging problems, and continue growing throughout life.
2. Possible answers include curiosity, adaptability, resilience, a growth mindset, critical thinking, communication, perseverance, ethical judgment, creativity, humility, and continuous improvement.
3. AGI can organize information, recommend learning resources, personalize instruction, explain complex concepts, simulate real-world situations, and help learners practice new skills while people continue making thoughtful decisions.
4. Reflection helps individuals evaluate their progress, recognize strengths, identify areas for improvement, learn from experience, and establish future learning goals.
5. Lifelong learning strengthens careers, improves communities, encourages innovation, supports responsible citizenship, and helps people continue contributing positively to society throughout their lives.

Quiz Answers

1. **B**
2. **A**
3. **A**
4. **A**
5. **B**
6. **True**
7. **True**
8. **False**
9. **True**
10. **True**

Chapter 16

A Call to Lead the AGI Generation

Every generation is remembered for the challenges it faced and the choices it made. Some generations built railroads that connected nations. Others developed electricity that transformed homes and industries. Scientists unlocked the mysteries of medicine, explorers expanded humanity's understanding of the world, and educators opened doors to knowledge for millions of students. Today, another remarkable chapter of history is being written. Artificial General Intelligence (AGI) is beginning to reshape education, healthcare, science, business, communication, transportation, and countless other areas of society. Yet the defining story of this era will not simply be about machines becoming more intelligent. It will be about people choosing how to use that intelligence to create a future that is wiser, fairer, healthier, and more compassionate. That responsibility now belongs to the AGI generation.

The AGI generation includes today's students, teachers, parents, school leaders, researchers, engineers, entrepreneurs, healthcare professionals, public servants, and community members. Unlike previous generations, they are witnessing the early development of technologies capable of learning across many different tasks, supporting complex decision-making, and helping solve problems that once required enormous amounts of human effort. These opportunities bring tremendous promise, but they also require thoughtful leadership. Every technological breakthrough creates choices about how it will be applied. Those choices will determine whether innovation strengthens education, improves healthcare, protects the environment, expands economic opportunity, and promotes fairness for everyone.

Throughout this book, one message has appeared repeatedly: technology is most valuable when it serves humanity. AGI should strengthen teachers rather than replace them. It should support healthcare professionals while preserving compassionate patient care. It should help scientists accelerate discoveries while maintaining ethical research practices. It should assist businesses in improving products and services while respecting employees and customers. Technology achieves its greatest purpose when it expands human potential instead of diminishing human responsibility. This principle should guide every future decision involving intelligent systems.

Students preparing to enter adulthood should recognize that leadership begins long before receiving a diploma, earning a degree, or accepting a professional position. Leadership begins with daily habits. Every time students demonstrate honesty during an assignment, help a classmate understand a difficult concept, accept responsibility for mistakes, or show kindness toward others, they strengthen the character needed to guide future innovations responsibly. Great leaders are not defined only by their accomplishments. They are remembered because they consistently place integrity, service, and compassion above personal recognition.

Teachers also stand at the center of the AGI generation. Every lesson taught, every encouraging conversation, every thoughtful question, and every opportunity created for students contributes to shaping future innovators and leaders. Technology may continue changing classrooms, but teachers remain the professionals who inspire confidence, encourage curiosity, nurture creativity, and help students believe in their own potential. The influence of an outstanding teacher often extends far beyond the classroom because the encouragement offered today may inspire discoveries that benefit society decades later.

Parents and families continue serving as children's first and most enduring teachers. Long before students enter classrooms, they begin learning honesty, kindness, responsibility, perseverance, respect, and compassion at home. These values become the moral foundation that guides future decisions involving powerful technologies. Families who encourage curiosity, reading, meaningful conversations, community service, and lifelong learning help prepare children not only for successful careers but also for responsible citizenship. Strong partnerships between homes and schools remain one of the greatest strengths of education because they unite academic learning with character development.

School leaders carry equally important responsibilities. Principals, superintendents, curriculum specialists, technology leaders, and school boards must guide educational innovation thoughtfully. Their decisions influence thousands of students, educators, and families. Responsible leaders evaluate new technologies carefully, provide meaningful professional development for teachers, protect student privacy, encourage educational equity, and ensure that innovation always supports learning rather than distracting from it. Leadership requires balancing excitement about new possibilities with careful consideration of ethical responsibilities and long-term educational goals.

Perhaps one of the greatest lessons students can carry into the future is understanding that intelligence alone is never enough. Throughout history, some of humanity's greatest achievements resulted from combining knowledge with wisdom, creativity with responsibility, courage with humility, and innovation with compassion. AGI may continue becoming more capable, but human character remains the force that determines whether those capabilities improve society. Honesty builds trust. Respect strengthens relationships. Compassion encourages service. Integrity protects fairness. Wisdom helps people recognize that every important decision affects real lives. These timeless values will remain just as important in the AGI era as they have been throughout history.

The future will undoubtedly include challenges that no previous generation has experienced. New ethical questions will emerge. New careers will appear. New discoveries will change how people work, communicate, learn, and solve problems. Yet students should approach these changes with confidence rather than fear. Every generation has faced uncertainty, and every generation has also discovered remarkable opportunities through education, collaboration, perseverance, and responsible leadership. The AGI generation has every reason to believe it can continue this tradition by using intelligent technologies to strengthen humanity while preserving the values that unite communities around the world.

Every student reading this book should understand one important truth: the future is not something that simply happens. The future is created every day through choices, actions, relationships, discoveries, and acts of service. Students who remain curious, continue learning, treat others with respect, think critically, communicate honestly, and lead with integrity are already shaping tomorrow. They do not need to wait until adulthood to begin making a positive difference. Their influence begins wherever they choose to improve the lives of others.

Chapter 16 (Part 2)

The future of Artificial General Intelligence will not be determined only by the scientists who design algorithms or the engineers who build intelligent systems. It will also be shaped by teachers who inspire curiosity, parents who teach strong values, school leaders who create opportunities for innovation, entrepreneurs who solve meaningful problems, healthcare professionals who care for patients with compassion, public servants who protect their communities, and students who choose to use knowledge responsibly. Every person has a role in building a future where technology serves humanity. This shared responsibility reminds us that the AGI era belongs to everyone, not just those working in technology.

One of the greatest opportunities before the AGI generation is the ability to solve problems that have challenged humanity for centuries. Intelligent systems may help researchers discover new medical treatments, improve food production, protect endangered ecosystems, strengthen disaster response, reduce energy consumption, and expand access to quality education around the world. These advances have the potential to improve millions of lives. However, achieving these goals requires more than powerful technology. It requires people who are willing to cooperate across cultures, professions, and nations while placing human well-being above personal interests. Progress is strongest when knowledge is combined with compassion and when innovation is guided by a commitment to serving others.

The classroom will remain one of the most important places where this future begins. Every lesson that encourages students to think critically, ask thoughtful questions, solve meaningful problems, and respect different perspectives helps prepare them for leadership in the AGI era. Classrooms are more than places where information is delivered. They are communities where confidence grows, friendships develop, ideas are explored, and future leaders discover their potential. Technology may become increasingly advanced, but the encouragement of a caring teacher, the support of classmates, and the guidance of families will continue shaping lives in ways that no machine can replace.

Students should never underestimate the importance of character. Throughout this book, we have explored knowledge, innovation, ethics, leadership, collaboration, creativity, lifelong learning, and responsibility. These ideas all depend upon character. Knowledge without integrity can be misused. Innovation without ethics may create unintended harm. Leadership without compassion can lose the trust of others. Intelligence without wisdom may overlook the needs of people. Character provides the moral foundation that allows every other skill to be used responsibly. It influences the decisions people make when no one is watching and guides them through situations where there may be no easy answers.

The AGI generation will inherit opportunities unlike any previous generation. Students may help build intelligent medical systems that extend healthy lives. They may create educational platforms that provide high-quality learning to children in every part of the world. They may design sustainable cities that reduce pollution while improving transportation and public safety. They may develop scientific discoveries that protect natural resources, improve agriculture, or explore new frontiers in space. Some students will become teachers who inspire future innovators. Others will become artists, engineers, researchers, entrepreneurs, community leaders, healthcare professionals, or public servants. Every profession will have opportunities to use AGI responsibly in ways that improve the lives of others.

As these opportunities continue expanding, students should remember that success is not measured only by grades, awards, job titles, or financial achievement. True success is measured by the positive impact individuals have on the lives of others. A teacher who inspires confidence in a struggling student, a scientist whose research improves public health, an engineer who designs safer bridges, a nurse who comforts a frightened patient, an entrepreneur who creates meaningful employment, or a community volunteer who serves neighbors all demonstrate success by contributing to something greater than themselves. AGI may provide remarkable tools, but people give those tools purpose through service, compassion, and responsibility.

This book has emphasized that learning never ends. Graduation is not the finish line but the beginning of a lifelong journey filled with new questions, new discoveries, new friendships, and new opportunities for growth. The students who thrive in the AGI generation will not necessarily be those who memorize the most information. They will be those who continue asking questions, embrace challenges, remain humble enough to keep learning, and adapt confidently as the world continues changing. Curiosity will remain one of humanity's greatest strengths because it inspires every scientific breakthrough, technological innovation, artistic creation, and meaningful discovery.

The future also belongs to people who work together. Some of the world's greatest achievements have come through collaboration rather than individual effort. Medical breakthroughs result from teams of researchers. Space exploration depends upon scientists, engineers, mathematicians, technicians, and educators working together. Strong schools are built through partnerships among teachers, students, families, administrators, and communities. The AGI era will continue rewarding collaboration because solving complex global challenges requires diverse perspectives, shared knowledge, mutual respect, and a willingness to learn from one another.

Perhaps the greatest lesson of all is that hope remains stronger than uncertainty. Every generation has faced moments when the future seemed difficult to predict. Yet humanity has repeatedly demonstrated resilience, creativity, perseverance, and compassion. Education has always been the bridge that carries societies from uncertainty toward opportunity. Schools prepare young people not only to understand the world as it exists today but also to imagine the world as it could become tomorrow. Artificial General Intelligence offers another opportunity to improve that world if guided by wisdom, ethics, and human-centered leadership.

As you close this book, remember that you are not simply studying the future—you are becoming part of it. Every lesson you learn, every challenge you overcome, every book you read, every question you ask, every person you encourage, and every act of integrity you demonstrate prepares you to become a leader in the AGI generation. The future is not waiting for someone else to build it. It is waiting for students who are willing to learn with curiosity, lead with courage, serve with compassion, innovate with responsibility, and act with integrity.

May you always remain a lifelong learner, a thoughtful leader, and a person of strong character. May you use knowledge to serve others, technology to improve lives, and wisdom to make decisions that strengthen your family, your school, your community, your nation, and our world. Artificial General Intelligence may become one of humanity's greatest technological achievements, but your greatest achievement will always be the kind of person you choose to become.

The future of education is not written by machines.

The future of education is written by teachers who inspire, parents who believe, leaders who serve, communities that support learning, and students who dream boldly enough to build a better tomorrow.

That future begins with you.

Chapter 16 Summary

A Call to Lead the AGI Generation

The future of Artificial General Intelligence (AGI) will be shaped not only by technology but by the people who choose how to use it. Throughout this book, students learned that AGI has the potential to improve education, healthcare, business, science, transportation, environmental protection, and many other areas of society. However, these benefits can only be achieved when intelligent technology is guided by strong human values.

This chapter emphasized that every student has the opportunity to become a leader in the AGI generation. Leadership begins with everyday choices such as demonstrating honesty, treating others with respect, accepting responsibility, showing compassion, and continuing to learn throughout life. These qualities prepare students to become future educators, engineers, scientists, healthcare professionals, entrepreneurs, community leaders, and responsible citizens.

The chapter also reinforced that technology should always serve humanity. Teachers, parents, school leaders, families, and communities all play essential roles in helping students develop knowledge, character, creativity, ethical judgment, and lifelong learning habits. These human qualities remain essential regardless of how advanced intelligent systems become.

Finally, students were encouraged to approach the future with confidence, curiosity, resilience, and hope. Every generation has faced change, and every generation has also created new opportunities through education, collaboration, innovation, and service. The AGI generation now has the opportunity to continue that tradition by building a future that is more intelligent, more compassionate, more ethical, and more inclusive for people around the world.

The future is not something students simply inherit. It is something they help create through their choices, their character, and their commitment to serving others.

Chapter 16 Reflection

Reflect on the ideas presented throughout this final chapter. Answer each question using complete sentences.

1. What does it mean to become a leader in the AGI generation?
2. Why should technology always serve humanity instead of replacing human values?
3. Which lesson from this entire book has influenced you the most? Explain your answer.
4. How can students begin demonstrating leadership today?
5. Why are honesty, integrity, and compassion important in an AGI-powered world?
6. How can education prepare students to solve future challenges?
7. In what ways can AGI improve society when used responsibly?
8. How can families, schools, and communities work together to prepare future leaders?
9. What personal goals will you set after completing this book?
10. Imagine yourself twenty years from now. How do you hope your knowledge, character, and leadership will improve the lives of others?

Chapter 16 Worksheet

Part A – Vocabulary Matching

Match each term with its correct definition.

A. Leadership

B. Integrity

C. Innovation

D. Lifelong Learning

E. Compassion

F. Responsibility

G. Collaboration

H. Human-Centered Technology

1. _____ Guiding others through positive actions and ethical decisions.
2. _____ Doing what is right even when no one is watching.
3. _____ Creating better ideas or improving existing solutions.
4. _____ Continuing to learn throughout life.
5. _____ Caring about the well-being of others.

6. _____ Being accountable for decisions and actions.
7. _____ Working together toward common goals.
8. _____ Using technology to improve people's lives while respecting human values.

Part B – Short Answer

1. Explain why character is just as important as knowledge in the AGI era.

___

___

2. Name five human qualities discussed throughout this book that will remain valuable in the future.

___

___

3. Why should students view themselves as future leaders rather than simply future workers?

___

___

4. How can AGI help improve education while preserving the role of teachers?

___

___

5. What responsibilities will future leaders have when using intelligent technologies?

___

___

___

Part C – Personal Leadership Plan

Imagine you are writing a letter to your future self ten years from today.

Describe the type of leader you hope to become, the values you want to live by, the knowledge you hope to gain, how you plan to continue learning throughout life, and how you want to use AGI to improve your family, community, and the world.

___

___

Chapter 16 Quiz

Multiple Choice

1. What is the central message of this chapter?

A. AGI should replace human leadership.

B. Students should prepare to lead the AGI generation with knowledge, ethics, and compassion.

C. Technology alone determines the future.

D. Education ends after graduation.

2. Which human quality remains essential regardless of technological progress?

A. Integrity.

B. Compassion.

C. Responsibility.

D. All of the above.

3. Why is lifelong learning important in the AGI era?

A. Technology and society continue changing.

B. Learning ends after graduation.

C. AGI eliminates education.

D. Students only need one career.

4. Which group helps prepare students for the future?

A. Schools.

B. Families.

C. Communities.

D. All of the above.

5. Which statement best summarizes this book?

A. Technology is more important than people.

B. Human values should guide the responsible use of AGI.

C. AGI replaces education.

D. Machines should make every important decision.

True or False

6. _____ Every student has the potential to become a future leader.
7. _____ Character influences how technology is used.
8. _____ Teachers will continue playing an essential role in education.
9. _____ Responsible innovation combines technology with ethics.
10. _____ The future is shaped by the choices people make.

Chapter 16 Answer Key

Worksheet Answers

Part A – Vocabulary Matching

1. **A**
2. **B**
3. **C**
4. **D**

5. **E**
6. **F**
7. **G**
8. **H**

Part B – Suggested Responses

1. Character guides how knowledge is used. Honesty, integrity, compassion, responsibility, and ethical judgment help ensure that AGI improves society while respecting human dignity and fairness.
2. Possible answers include integrity, compassion, creativity, leadership, resilience, curiosity, communication, collaboration, adaptability, ethical reasoning, responsibility, empathy, wisdom, and lifelong learning.
3. Students will become educators, scientists, engineers, entrepreneurs, healthcare professionals, policymakers, and community leaders whose decisions will shape how AGI benefits society.
4. AGI can personalize learning, organize educational resources, reduce administrative tasks, and provide additional academic support, allowing teachers to spend more time mentoring, inspiring, and building relationships with students.
5. Future leaders must protect privacy, promote fairness, ensure transparency, encourage ethical innovation, support inclusion, maintain human oversight, and use technology to improve people's lives.

Quiz Answers

1. **B**
2. **D**
3. **A**
4. **D**
5. **B**
6. **True**
7. **True**
8. **True**
9. **True**
10. **True**

GLOSSARY

Letter A

1. Access Time

The amount of time it takes for an AI system or computer to locate and retrieve data from memory or storage. Access time affects how quickly megabytes of data can be used during AI processing.

2. Activation Data

Intermediate data generated inside an AI model while it is running. Activation data is stored temporarily in memory and often measured in megabytes during model execution.

3. Adaptive Storage

A storage approach that automatically adjusts how data is stored or moved based on usage patterns. In AI systems, adaptive storage helps manage large volumes of megabytes efficiently.

4. Algorithmic Data Size

The total amount of data an algorithm needs to operate effectively. In AI, this size is often measured in megabytes or larger units, depending on model complexity.

5. Allocation (Memory Allocation)

The process of assigning a specific number of megabytes in memory or storage for an AI task, model, or dataset.

6. Analytics Dataset

A structured collection of data used for analysis or AI training. The size of an analytics dataset is commonly measured in megabytes, gigabytes, or more.

7. Annotation Storage

The space required to store labels, tags, or explanations added to AI training data. These annotations contribute additional megabytes to total dataset size.

8. Artificial Neural Network (ANN) Size

The total memory footprint of a neural network, including weights, biases, and parameters. ANN size is often described in megabytes when discussing model efficiency.

9. Asset Compression

The process of reducing the number of megabytes required to store AI-related files such as models, images, or datasets without losing essential information.

10. Available Memory

The amount of free memory, measured in megabytes, that an AI system can still use to load data, run models, or perform computations.

ANI (Artificial Narrow Intelligence)

Artificial Narrow Intelligence refers to AI systems designed to perform **one specific task or a narrow set of tasks** rather than general intelligence. ANI systems rely on data stored and processed in memory and storage measured in **megabytes, gigabytes, or more**. Examples include image recognition, speech-to-text, recommendation systems, and chatbots. ANI does not understand beyond its training scope, but it can process large amounts of data efficiently within its defined function.

Letter B

1. Bandwidth

The amount of data that can be transferred between systems in a given time. In AI systems, bandwidth determines how quickly megabytes of data can move between storage, memory, and processors.

2. Batch Processing

A method where AI systems process large groups of data all at once instead of one item at a time. Batch processing often involves handling many megabytes of data in a single operation.

3. Binary Encoding

The process of representing information using binary values (0s and 1s). All megabytes of AI data are ultimately stored and transmitted using binary encoding.**4. Bit Depth**

The number of bits used to represent a single piece of data, such as a pixel or audio sample. Higher bit depth increases data quality but also increases the number of megabytes required.

5. Bitmap Data

A type of image data where each pixel is stored as a set of bits. Bitmap images can quickly grow in size, consuming large numbers of megabytes in AI vision systems.

6. Buffer Memory

Temporary memory used to hold data while it is being transferred or processed. Buffers store data in chunks measured in megabytes to keep AI systems running smoothly.

7. Bulk Data Storage

Large-scale storage designed to hold massive datasets used for AI training or analysis. Bulk storage capacity is measured in megabytes, gigabytes, or larger units.

8. Byte Stream

A continuous flow of bytes transmitted or processed by a system. AI applications often analyze byte streams that accumulate into megabytes of data.

9. Bytecode

An intermediate form of program code that is easier for machines to execute than human-written code. Bytecode files occupy storage space measured in megabytes.

10. Byzantine Fault Tolerance (BFT)

A system property that allows AI or distributed systems to continue functioning even when some components fail or act unpredictably. Implementing BFT requires additional data handling and storage overhead measured in megabytes.

Letter C

1. Cache Memory

A small, high-speed memory area that stores frequently used data so the processor can access it faster. Cache helps reduce the time needed to move megabytes of data from main memory or storage.

2. Capacity Planning

The process of estimating how much memory and storage an AI system will need. Capacity planning ensures there are enough megabytes available to handle data, models, and future growth.

3. Checkpoint File

A saved snapshot of an AI model during training. Checkpoint files are stored in memory or storage and often consume many megabytes so training can resume without starting over.

4. Chunking

The practice of breaking large datasets into smaller pieces. Chunking helps AI systems process megabytes of data more efficiently by handling them in manageable parts.

5. Cloud Storage

A method of storing data on remote servers accessed through the internet. Cloud storage manages files measured in megabytes and allows AI systems to scale beyond local hardware limits.

6. Compression

The process of reducing the size of data so it uses fewer megabytes. Compression helps AI systems store, transfer, and process data more efficiently.

7. Compute Load

The amount of processing work required to run an AI task. Compute load often increases as the number of megabytes being processed grows.

8. Context Window

The amount of data an AI model can consider at one time. Context windows consume memory measured in megabytes, especially in language and vision models.

9. Corpus

A large collection of text or data used to train AI models. A corpus is usually measured in megabytes or larger units depending on its size.

10. CUDA Memory

Specialized memory used by GPUs to accelerate AI computations. CUDA memory holds model data and intermediate results measured in megabytes during processing.

Letter D

1. Data Allocation

The process of assigning a specific amount of memory or storage for data use. In AI systems, data allocation determines how many megabytes are reserved for datasets, models, or tasks.

2. Data Buffer

A temporary storage area that holds data while it is being transferred or processed. Data buffers manage megabytes of information to keep AI systems running smoothly.

3. Data Compression

A technique used to reduce the size of data so it consumes fewer megabytes. AI systems use data compression to save storage space and speed up data transfer.

4. Data Footprint

The total amount of data an AI system uses, including datasets, models, and temporary files. A data footprint is measured in megabytes, gigabytes, or more.

5. Data Loader

A software component that loads data into memory for AI training or inference. Data loaders handle batches of data measured in megabytes.

6. Data Migration

The process of moving data from one storage system to another. During AI system upgrades, data migration may involve transferring large numbers of megabytes.

7. Data Throughput

The rate at which data is processed or transferred by a system. Higher throughput allows AI systems to move more megabytes efficiently.

8. Dataset Size

The total amount of data in a dataset used for AI training or testing. Dataset size is commonly measured in megabytes or larger units.

9. Deep Learning Model Size

The amount of memory required to store a deep learning model, including its parameters and weights. Model size is often described in megabytes to assess efficiency.

10. Disk Storage

Long-term storage used to save files, datasets, and AI models. Disk storage capacity and usage are measured in megabytes, gigabytes, or terabytes.

Letter E

1. Edge Computing

A computing approach where data is processed closer to where it is generated rather than sent to a central server. Edge computing reduces how many megabytes must be transferred over networks.

2. Embedding Size

The amount of memory required to store vector representations used by AI models. Embedding size is often measured in megabytes and affects model performance and storage needs.

3. Encoded Data

Data that has been converted into a specific format for storage or transmission. Encoded data occupies megabytes depending on the encoding method used.

4. Encoding Scheme

A rule set that defines how data is represented digitally, such as text or images. Different encoding schemes can increase or reduce the number of megabytes required.

5. Encrypted Storage

Storage that protects data by converting it into a secure format. Encryption may slightly increase the number of megabytes used due to added security information.

6. End-to-End Data Pipeline

The full path data takes from collection to processing and storage. Each stage of the pipeline manages data volumes measured in megabytes.

7. Energy Efficiency (AI Systems)

A measure of how much energy an AI system uses to process data. Systems that move and store fewer megabytes are often more energy efficient.

8. Execution Memory

The memory required while a program or AI model is running. Execution memory usage is tracked in megabytes during runtime.

9. External Storage

Storage devices located outside a computer, such as USB drives or external hard drives. External storage capacity is measured in megabytes and larger units.

10. Extracted Features

Important data patterns identified by AI models during processing. Extracted features are stored temporarily or permanently in memory measured in megabytes.

Letter F

1. Feature Map

A structured output produced by AI models, especially in image and signal processing. Feature maps are stored in memory and can consume significant megabytes during computation.

2. Feature Scaling

The process of adjusting data values to a consistent range before training an AI model. Feature scaling affects how efficiently megabytes of data are processed and stored.

3. File Allocation Table (FAT)

A file system structure that tracks where files are stored on a disk. FAT helps manage how megabytes are organized and retrieved from storage.

4. File Compression Format

A standardized way to reduce file size so it uses fewer megabytes. Compression formats help AI systems store and transfer data efficiently.

5. File System Cache

A temporary memory area that stores frequently accessed files. File system caches reduce repeated access to storage and manage megabytes more efficiently.

6. Floating-Point Data

Numerical data that includes decimal values and is commonly used in AI calculations. Floating-point data requires more bits per value, increasing memory usage measured in megabytes.

7. Frame Buffer

A region of memory that stores image or video frames before they are displayed or processed. Frame buffers often consume large numbers of megabytes in AI vision systems.

8. Fragmentation

A condition where data is stored in scattered locations instead of one continuous block. Fragmentation can reduce storage efficiency even when megabytes appear available.

9. Free Memory

The amount of unused memory available for programs or AI tasks. Free memory is measured in megabytes and determines how much additional data can be loaded.

10. Full Dataset Load

The act of loading an entire dataset into memory at once. This approach can require large amounts of megabytes and is common in AI training scenarios.

Letter G

1. Garbage Collection

An automatic memory-management process that frees memory no longer in use. Garbage collection helps reclaim megabytes so AI programs can continue running efficiently.

2. Generalization Data

Data used to test how well an AI model performs on new, unseen inputs. Storing and evaluating generalization data requires additional megabytes beyond training data.

3. Gigabyte (GB)

A larger unit of data measurement equal to 1,024 megabytes (or commonly approximated as 1,000 MB). Gigabytes are used when datasets or models grow beyond megabyte scale.

4. Graph Data Structure

A way of organizing data using nodes and connections. Graph-based AI systems store graph data in memory and storage measured in megabytes.

5. GPU Memory

Specialized memory used by graphics processing units to accelerate AI workloads. GPU memory holds model parameters and data batches measured in megabytes.

6. Gradient Data

Numerical values calculated during AI training to update model parameters. Gradient data is stored temporarily in memory and contributes to overall megabyte usage.

7. Granularity

The level of detail at which data is stored or processed. Finer granularity often increases the number of megabytes required.

8. Greedy Algorithm

An algorithm that makes the best immediate choice at each step. Greedy algorithms may reduce memory usage by limiting how many megabytes of data must be stored at once.

9. Ground Truth Data

Correct, labeled data used to train or evaluate AI systems. Ground truth datasets are stored in files measured in megabytes or larger units.

10. Growth Rate (Data)

The speed at which data size increases over time. In AI systems, a high data growth rate means storage needs measured in megabytes can expand quickly.

Letter H

1. Hard Disk Capacity

The total amount of data a hard disk can store. Capacity is measured in megabytes and larger units.

2. Hardware Acceleration

The use of specialized hardware to speed up AI processing. Acceleration often reduces how long megabytes of data stay in memory.

3. Hash Table

A data structure that stores information for fast lookup. Hash tables occupy memory measured in megabytes in large AI systems.

4. Hierarchical Storage

A storage design that uses multiple layers such as RAM, disk, and cloud. Each layer manages data measured in megabytes.

5. High-Dimensional Data

Data with many features or variables. High-dimensional datasets often require large numbers of megabytes.

6. Host Memory

Main system memory used by the CPU. Host memory stores AI data and models measured in megabytes.

7. Hybrid Storage

A combination of different storage types working together. Hybrid storage systems manage megabytes across multiple devices.

8. Hyperparameter Storage

Memory used to store configuration values for AI models. These settings are saved in files measured in megabytes.

9. Hyperscale Data

Extremely large datasets used by major AI systems. Hyperscale data is tracked from megabytes up to much larger units.

10. Heuristic Data

Information used by AI systems to guide decision-making. Heuristic data contributes to the overall data size in megabytes.

Letter I

1. Image Dataset Size

The total amount of storage required for image data. Size is measured in megabytes or more.

2. Inference Memory

The memory used when an AI model is making predictions. Inference memory usage is tracked in megabytes.

3. Input Buffer

A temporary area where incoming data is stored. Input buffers hold megabytes before processing begins.

4. Intermediate Data

Data produced during processing steps. Intermediate data can significantly increase memory usage in megabytes.

5. Index File

A file that helps locate data quickly. Index files use additional megabytes to improve performance.

6. Information Density

The amount of useful data stored within a given size. Higher density means more information per megabyte.

7. Initialization Data

Data loaded when an AI system starts. Initialization data occupies memory measured in megabytes.

8. In-Memory Processing

Processing data directly in RAM instead of storage. This approach uses large amounts of memory measured in megabytes.

9. Input Feature Size

The amount of data required to represent input features. Feature size affects how many megabytes are needed.

10. Instruction Cache

A small memory area that stores frequently used instructions. Instruction caches manage small but critical megabytes.

Letter J

1. Job Queue

A list of tasks waiting to be processed. Job queues may store task data measured in megabytes.

2. Joint Dataset

A dataset created by combining multiple sources. Joint datasets often increase total size in megabytes.

3. JSON Data Size

The amount of storage required for data stored in JSON format. JSON files can grow quickly in megabytes.

4. Jitter Buffer

A temporary storage area that smooths data flow. Jitter buffers store megabytes during real-time processing.

5. Job Scheduler

A system that decides when tasks run. Schedulers manage memory and data measured in megabytes.

6. Just-in-Time Processing

Processing data only when needed. This approach can reduce how many megabytes are stored at once.

7. Joint Memory Allocation

Memory shared across multiple AI tasks. Joint allocation must carefully manage available megabytes.

8. Java Bytecode Size

The storage size of compiled Java programs. Bytecode files occupy megabytes on disk.

9. Job Metadata

Information describing AI tasks. Metadata adds additional megabytes to total system storage.

10. Junction Storage Point

A logical link between storage locations. Junctions help organize data measured in megabytes.

Letter K

1. Kernel Memory

Memory reserved for core system operations. Kernel memory usage is tracked in megabytes.

2. Key-Value Store

A data storage method that pairs keys with values. Large key-value stores consume many megabytes.

3. Knowledge Base Size

The total amount of stored knowledge in an AI system. Size is measured in megabytes or larger units.

4. K-Means Dataset Size

The amount of data used in clustering algorithms. Dataset size affects memory usage in megabytes.

5. Keras Model Size

The storage required for AI models built with Keras. Model size is measured in megabytes.

6. Keyframe Data

Important frames selected from video data. Keyframe storage contributes to total megabyte usage.

7. Kernel Cache

A cache used by the operating system kernel. Kernel caches store frequently used data in megabytes.

8. Knowledge Graph Storage

Memory used to store relationships between data points. Knowledge graphs require significant megabytes.

9. Kinetic Data Stream

Continuously changing data from sensors or systems. These streams generate growing megabytes over time.

10. K-Nearest Neighbor Memory Usage

The memory required by nearest-neighbor algorithms. Memory use increases as datasets grow in megabytes.

Letter L

1. **Latency**
   The delay between requesting data and receiving it. Latency affects how quickly megabytes move through AI systems.
2. **Layer Output Size**
   The amount of data produced by a neural network layer. Output size is measured in megabytes during processing.
3. **Load Balancing**
   Distributing work across systems so no single device is overloaded. Balancing helps manage megabytes efficiently.
4. **Local Storage**
   Data stored on a device rather than the cloud. Local storage capacity is measured in megabytes.
5. **Log File Size**
   The amount of storage used by system logs. Logs can accumulate many megabytes over time.
6. **Loss History Data**
   Stored values showing how model error changes during training. Loss history consumes megabytes.

7. **Low-Precision Data**
   Data stored using fewer bits per value. Low-precision formats reduce megabyte usage.
8. **Labeled Dataset**
   Data that includes tags or labels for AI training. Labels increase total dataset size in megabytes.
9. **Linear Model Size**
   The storage required for a linear AI model. Size is measured in megabytes.
10. **Load Time**
   The time required to bring data or models into memory. Load time depends on megabytes involved.

Letter M

1. **Memory Allocation**
   Assigning a specific amount of memory for tasks. Allocation is tracked in megabytes.
2. **Memory Footprint**
   The total memory an AI program uses. Footprint is measured in megabytes.
3. **Metadata Size**
   The storage used by descriptive information about data. Metadata adds extra megabytes.
4. **Mini-Batch Size**
   The amount of data processed at once during training. Batch size affects megabyte usage.
5. **Model Checkpoint Size**
   The storage required for saved training states. Checkpoints often consume many megabytes.
6. **Model Compression**
   Reducing model size while preserving performance. Compression lowers megabytes required.
7. **Model Parameters**
   Values learned by an AI model. Parameter storage contributes to total megabytes.
8. **Memory Bandwidth**
   The rate at which memory transfers data. Bandwidth affects how fast megabytes move.
9. **Multimodal Dataset**
   Data combining text, images, audio, or video. Multimodal data uses large megabytes.
10. **Mutable Data**
   Data that changes during processing. Mutable data can increase temporary megabyte usage.

Letter N

1. **Network Bandwidth**
   The capacity of a network connection. Bandwidth controls how many megabytes can be transferred.

2. **Neural Network Size**
   The total storage required for a neural network. Size is measured in megabytes.
3. **Node Memory**
   Memory available on a computing node. Node memory limits megabytes per task.
4. **Normalization Data**
   Values used to scale data consistently. Normalization adds to dataset megabytes.
5. **Non-Volatile Memory**
   Memory that retains data without power. Capacity is measured in megabytes.
6. **Numerical Precision**
   The detail level of stored numbers. Higher precision increases megabytes.
7. **Noise Data**
   Unwanted or random information in datasets. Noise increases data size in megabytes.
8. **Neural Activation Size**
   Memory used to store neuron outputs. Activation size is measured in megabytes.
9. **Network Transfer Size**
   The amount of data sent across a network. Transfer size is tracked in megabytes.
10. **Node Cache**
    Temporary storage on a node for faster access. Cache size uses megabytes.

Letter O

1. **Object Storage**
   A storage method that manages data as objects. Capacity is measured in megabytes.
2. **Offline Dataset**
   Data stored locally rather than streamed. Offline datasets occupy megabytes.
3. **On-Device Storage**
   Storage located on the AI device itself. On-device capacity is measured in megabytes.
4. **Operational Memory**
   Memory used during active AI operations. Usage is tracked in megabytes.
5. **Optimization Data**
   Information used to improve model performance. Optimization data uses megabytes.
6. **Output Buffer**
   Temporary storage for results before delivery. Buffers hold megabytes.
7. **Overhead Data**
   Extra data required for system operation. Overhead increases total megabytes.
8. **Object Detection Output Size**
   The amount of data produced by detection models. Output size is measured in megabytes.
9. **Online Storage**
   Storage accessible via the internet. Online storage limits are measured in megabytes.
10. **Open Dataset Size**
    The storage footprint of publicly available datasets. Size is measured in megabytes.

Letter P

1. **Parameter Count**
   The total number of model values. Count correlates with megabytes required.
2. **Persistent Storage**
   Long-term storage that retains data. Capacity is measured in megabytes.
3. **Pipeline Buffer**
   Temporary storage between processing stages. Buffers manage megabytes in motion.
4. **Preprocessing Data**
   Data created while preparing datasets. Preprocessing adds megabytes.
5. **Precision Reduction**
   Lowering numeric detail to save space. Reduction decreases megabyte usage.
6. **Prediction Output Size**
   The amount of data produced by model predictions. Size is measured in megabytes.
7. **Primary Memory**
   Main system memory used for processing. Capacity is measured in megabytes.
8. **Processing Overhead**
   Extra resources needed during computation. Overhead increases megabyte usage.
9. **Profiling Data**
   Information collected to analyze performance. Profiling data uses megabytes.
10. **Paged Memory**
    Memory divided into fixed-size blocks. Paging manages megabytes efficiently.

Letter Q

1. **Quantization**
   A technique that reduces numerical precision to lower memory usage. Quantization helps AI models use fewer megabytes.
2. **Query Cache**
   Stored results from previous searches or requests. Query caches save megabytes by avoiding repeated computation.
3. **Query Latency**
   The time it takes to retrieve data after a request. Latency depends on how many megabytes must be accessed.
4. **Queue Buffer**
   A temporary holding area for data waiting to be processed. Buffers store megabytes in order.
5. **Quick Access Memory**
   Memory designed for fast retrieval. It handles megabytes needed immediately by AI tasks.
6. **Quantitative Dataset**
   Data made up of numerical values. These datasets are stored and measured in megabytes.
7. **Query Result Size**
   The amount of data returned from a query. Result size is measured in megabytes.

8. **Quorum Storage**
   A distributed storage method requiring agreement across systems. Data is replicated in megabytes.
9. **Quality Metrics Data**
   Information used to measure model performance. Metrics consume storage in megabytes.
10. **Quantized Model Size**
    The reduced size of an AI model after quantization. Size is typically measured in megabytes.

Letter R

1. **RAM Usage**
   The amount of active memory in use. RAM usage is tracked in megabytes.
2. **Read Throughput**
   The speed at which data is read from storage. Throughput affects how fast megabytes are accessed.
3. **Real-Time Processing**
   Processing data immediately as it arrives. Real-time systems manage megabytes continuously.
4. **Recursive Memory Use**
   Memory consumption during repeated function calls. Usage accumulates in megabytes.
5. **Redundant Storage**
   Extra copies of data kept for reliability. Redundancy increases total megabytes stored.
6. **Resource Allocation**
   Assigning system resources like memory and storage. Allocation is measured in megabytes.
7. **Runtime Memory**
   Memory required while a program is running. Runtime memory usage is tracked in megabytes.
8. **Raw Dataset Size**
   The size of unprocessed data. Raw datasets often require many megabytes.
9. **Read-Only Memory Footprint**
   The storage space used by non-modifiable data. Footprint is measured in megabytes.
10. **Retrieval Speed**
    How quickly stored data can be accessed. Speed depends on the number of megabytes involved.

Letter S

1. **Sample Size**
   The number of data examples used in AI training. Larger samples increase megabytes.

2. **Scalable Storage**
   Storage that grows with demand. Scalability supports increasing megabytes.
3. **Serialized Data Size**
   The storage size of data converted into a transferable format. Size is measured in megabytes.
4. **Shared Memory**
   Memory accessible by multiple processes. Shared memory usage is tracked in megabytes.
5. **Snapshot Size**
   The storage required for saved system states. Snapshots consume megabytes.
6. **Sparse Data Representation**
   A storage method that saves space when data contains many empty values. Sparsity reduces megabytes.
7. **Storage Capacity**
   The total amount of data a system can store. Capacity is measured in megabytes or more.
8. **Streaming Data Buffer**
   Temporary storage for incoming data streams. Buffers handle megabytes in motion.
9. **System Cache**
   Memory that stores frequently used data. Caches manage megabytes for faster access.
10. **Synchronization Data**
    Information used to keep systems aligned. Sync data adds to total megabytes.

Letter T

1. **Temporary Storage**
   Short-term storage used during processing. Temporary storage holds megabytes briefly.
2. **Tensor Size**
   The memory required to store multidimensional data structures. Tensor size is measured in megabytes.
3. **Throughput Rate**
   The amount of data processed per unit time. Rate is often described in megabytes per second.
4. **Training Dataset Size**
   The total amount of data used to train AI models. Size is measured in megabytes.
5. **Transfer Buffer**
   Temporary memory used during data movement. Buffers hold megabytes during transfer.
6. **Transactional Storage**
   Storage that ensures data consistency. Transactions add overhead measured in megabytes.
7. **Thread Memory Usage**
   Memory consumed by execution threads. Usage is tracked in megabytes.
8. **Token Storage Size**
   The memory required to store processed tokens. Token data uses megabytes.
9. **Time-Series Data Size**
   The storage footprint of data collected over time. Size increases in megabytes.

10. **Training Checkpoint Size**
    The storage required for saved training states. Checkpoints are measured in megabytes.

Letter U

1. **Unified Memory**
   A memory system shared between CPU and GPU. Unified memory manages data in megabytes efficiently across processors.
2. **Upload Size**
   The amount of data sent to storage or the cloud. Upload size is measured in megabytes.
3. **User Data Storage**
   Storage allocated for user-generated files. Capacity is tracked in megabytes.
4. **Utilization Rate**
   The percentage of memory or storage currently in use. Utilization reflects how many megabytes are occupied.
5. **Uncompressed Data Size**
   The size of data before compression. Uncompressed data often uses more megabytes.
6. **Update Payload**
   Data sent during software or model updates. Payload size is measured in megabytes.
7. **Uptime Storage Logs**
   Logs recorded while systems run continuously. Logs accumulate megabytes over time.
8. **Unified Dataset**
   A dataset combined from multiple sources. Size is measured in megabytes.
9. **User Session Memory**
   Memory allocated for active users. Session memory uses megabytes dynamically.
10. **Usage Quota**
    A storage limit set for users or systems. Quotas are defined in megabytes or larger units.

Letter V

1. **Validation Dataset Size**
   The amount of data used to evaluate AI models. Size is measured in megabytes.
2. **Vector Embedding Size**
   The memory required to store numerical representations of data. Size is measured in megabytes.
3. **Virtual Memory**
   A system that extends RAM using disk storage. Virtual memory is managed in megabytes.
4. **Volatile Memory**
   Memory that loses data when power is off. Capacity is measured in megabytes.
5. **Video Dataset Size**
   The storage required for video data. Video datasets consume many megabytes.

6. **Versioned Storage**
   Storage that keeps multiple file versions. Versioning increases megabyte usage.
7. **Vision Model Size**
   The memory footprint of computer vision models. Size is measured in megabytes.
8. **Vector Database Storage**
   Storage used for similarity search data. Vector databases consume large megabytes.
9. **Virtualized Storage**
   Storage abstracted from physical hardware. Capacity is tracked in megabytes.
10. **Volume Capacity**
    The total size of a storage volume. Capacity is measured in megabytes or more.

Letter W

1. **Weight Parameters**
   Learned values in AI models. Weight storage contributes to megabytes used.
2. **Working Memory**
   Memory actively used during processing. Working memory usage is measured in megabytes.
3. **Write Throughput**
   The speed at which data is written to storage. Throughput affects megabytes per second.
4. **Warm Cache**
   Cached data that is already loaded. Warm caches reduce repeated megabyte transfers.
5. **Workflow Data Size**
   The total data used across an AI workflow. Size is measured in megabytes.
6. **Web Dataset Size**
   The storage required for web-based data. Size is tracked in megabytes.
7. **Weight Compression**
   Reducing model weight size to save memory. Compression lowers megabytes used.
8. **Window Size (AI Context)**
   The amount of data processed at once. Window size affects memory megabytes.
9. **Writable Storage**
   Storage that allows data modification. Capacity is measured in megabytes.
10. **Workload Memory Demand**
    The memory required for tasks. Demand is expressed in megabytes.

Letter X

1. **X-Axis Data Size**
   Data stored along one dimension of a dataset. Size contributes to megabytes used.
2. **XML Data Size**
   The storage footprint of XML-formatted data. XML files often use many megabytes.

3. **XOR Encoding**
   A binary operation used in data processing. Encoded data occupies megabytes.
4. **Execution Context Size**
   Memory required during task execution. Size is measured in megabytes.
5. **External Dataset Size**
   The size of data sourced externally. External datasets add megabytes.
6. **Expanded Memory Use**
   Memory growth during processing. Expansion increases megabytes consumed.
7. **Experimental Dataset**
   Data used for testing AI models. Size is measured in megabytes.
8. **Extraction Buffer**
   Temporary storage during data extraction. Buffers store megabytes briefly.
9. **Extended Storage Capacity**
   Additional storage added to a system. Capacity is measured in megabytes.
10. **Explainability Data Size**
    Data used to explain AI decisions. Explainability outputs consume megabytes.

Letter Y

1. **Yield Data Size**
   The amount of useful output data produced. Yield is measured in megabytes.
2. **Yearly Data Growth**
   Annual increase in stored data. Growth is tracked in megabytes.
3. **YAML File Size**
   The storage footprint of YAML configuration files. Size is measured in megabytes.
4. **Y-Axis Feature Size**
   Feature data along a dataset dimension. Size contributes to megabytes.
5. **Young Generation Memory**
   Memory area for newly created data. Usage is measured in megabytes.
6. **Yield Optimization Data**
   Data used to improve output efficiency. Stored in megabytes.
7. **YourAIStudyBuddy Dataset Size**
   The total data used by AI study tools. Size is measured in megabytes.
8. **Yottabyte Reference Scale**
   A conceptual upper scale of data measurement. Used for comparison beyond megabytes.
9. **Yield Metrics Storage**
   Storage used for performance metrics. Metrics consume megabytes.
10. **Yoked Memory Allocation**
    Linked memory regions used together. Allocation is measured in megabytes.

Letter Z

1. **Zero-Copy Memory**
   A method that avoids duplicating data. Zero-copy reduces megabytes in motion.
2. **Zipped Dataset Size**
   The storage size after compression. Zipped files use fewer megabytes.
3. **Zettabyte Scale (Reference)**
   A large-scale data concept. Used to compare growth beyond megabytes.
4. **Zone-Based Storage**
   Storage divided into regions. Zones manage megabytes efficiently.
5. **Z-Score Normalization Data**
   Statistical values used in preprocessing. Data adds megabytes.
6. **Zero Padding**
   Adding placeholder data to inputs. Padding increases memory megabytes.
7. **Zoomed Feature Maps**
   Scaled representations in vision models. Stored in megabytes.
8. **Zonal Cache**
   Cache divided by region. Cache size is measured in megabytes.
9. **Zero-Day Model Update Size**
   The storage required for emergency updates. Size is measured in megabytes.
10. **Zipped Model Archive**
    Compressed AI model files. Archives reduce megabytes required.

Teacher's Guide

The AGI-Ready Classroom

Redefining Learning for the Next Generation

By Susie Hala

IntelliGloss AI Education Series – Module 2: Artificial General Intelligence (AGI)

Welcome to the Teacher's Guide

Thank you for choosing **The AGI-Ready Classroom: Redefining Learning for the Next Generation** as part of your instructional program.

Artificial General Intelligence (AGI) represents one of the most significant technological developments of the twenty-first century. As intelligent technologies continue transforming education, healthcare, science, business, engineering, government, and everyday life, schools have an important responsibility to prepare students to understand both the opportunities and responsibilities that accompany these advances.

This Teacher's Guide is designed to help educators confidently integrate AGI education into their classrooms while promoting critical thinking, ethical decision-making, collaboration, creativity, and responsible technology use.

The goal of this book is not simply to teach students about AGI. It is to prepare thoughtful, ethical, lifelong learners who can help shape the future with wisdom, compassion, and integrity.

Purpose of the Book

This book helps students:

- Understand what Artificial General Intelligence (AGI) is.
- Distinguish AGI from today's Artificial Narrow Intelligence (ANI).
- Explore how AGI may influence education, careers, healthcare, science, business, and society.
- Develop ethical decision-making skills.
- Build critical thinking and problem-solving abilities.
- Understand the importance of lifelong learning.

- Prepare for careers in an AGI-powered economy.
- Become responsible leaders in the future of intelligent technology.

Intended Audience

This book is appropriate for:

- Middle School (Grades 6–8)
- High School (Grades 9–12)
- Career Technical Education (CTE)
- STEM Programs
- Technology Courses
- Computer Science Courses
- Digital Literacy Courses
- Artificial Intelligence Electives
- Teacher Professional Development
- Parent Education Programs

Learning Outcomes

By the end of this book, students should be able to:

- Explain the meaning of Artificial General Intelligence.
- Compare ANI and AGI.
- Describe future applications of AGI.
- Discuss ethical responsibilities associated with intelligent systems.
- Identify future-ready career skills.
- Demonstrate responsible digital citizenship.
- Evaluate both the benefits and risks of AGI.
- Collaborate respectfully with others.
- Apply critical thinking to real-world scenarios.
- Develop a personal plan for lifelong learning.

Instructional Suggestions

Each chapter is designed to be completed over approximately one week of instruction.

A suggested sequence:

Day 1

- Introduce the chapter.
- Discuss the Essential Question.
- Preview key vocabulary.
- Activate prior knowledge.

Day 2

- Read and discuss the chapter.
- Clarify important concepts.
- Encourage student questions.

Day 3

- Small-group discussions.
- Real-world case studies.
- Classroom activities.

Day 4

- Complete the Reflection and Worksheet.
- Peer collaboration.
- Teacher-guided discussion.

Day 5

- Quiz.
- Review.
- Class reflection.
- Extension project.

Classroom Discussion Strategies

Encourage students to:

- Ask thoughtful questions.
- Support opinions with evidence.
- Respect different viewpoints.
- Work collaboratively.
- Consider ethical implications.
- Connect classroom learning to current events.

Possible discussion prompts include:

- How should AGI improve education?

- What responsibilities accompany powerful technologies?
- Which human qualities will remain important?
- How should schools prepare future generations?
- What makes ethical leadership important?

Cross-Curricular Connections

English Language Arts

- Informational reading
- Research writing
- Presentations
- Debate
- Persuasive essays

Science

- Scientific innovation
- Ethics
- Data analysis
- Future technologies

Mathematics

- Logical reasoning
- Statistics
- Pattern recognition
- Computational thinking

Social Studies

- Technology and society
- Public policy
- Global citizenship
- Historical innovation

Business & Entrepreneurship

- Future careers
- Innovation
- Leadership
- Economic development

Computer Science

- Artificial Intelligence
- Machine Learning
- Robotics
- Data Systems
- Digital Citizenship

Differentiated Instruction

Support diverse learners by:

- Using cooperative learning groups.
- Providing visual organizers.
- Encouraging project-based learning.
- Offering student choice during assignments.
- Providing vocabulary support.
- Allowing multiple presentation formats.
- Connecting lessons to student interests.

Assessment Options

Use a variety of assessments, including:

- Chapter quizzes
- Reflection journals
- Research projects
- Class presentations
- Debates
- Group discussions
- Technology demonstrations
- Career exploration assignments
- Student portfolios
- Community service projects

Extension Activities

Students may:

- Research current AI developments.
- Interview professionals using AI.
- Create ethical AI guidelines.

- Design future classrooms.
- Develop AGI career pathways.
- Build innovation proposals.
- Create community awareness campaigns.
- Present future technology forecasts.

Family Engagement

Encourage families to:

- Discuss responsible technology use.
- Explore AI tools together.
- Read current technology news.
- Talk about future careers.
- Encourage curiosity.
- Model lifelong learning.
- Support responsible digital habits.

Classroom Projects

Examples include:

- Design an AGI-ready school.
- Create an AI ethics policy.
- Develop a future career portfolio.
- Research emerging technologies.
- Debate AI policy issues.
- Create community technology presentations.
- Design a sustainable smart city.
- Build innovation proposals that solve local problems.

Technology Integration

Students may responsibly use AI tools to:

- Brainstorm ideas.
- Organize research.
- Practice writing.
- Translate information.
- Generate study questions.

- Analyze data.

Teachers should emphasize:

- Academic honesty.
- Citation of sources.
- Verification of information.
- Independent thinking.
- Ethical technology use.

Classroom Expectations

Students should demonstrate:

- Respect
- Responsibility
- Integrity
- Curiosity
- Collaboration
- Critical thinking
- Creativity
- Ethical decision-making
- Lifelong learning

Capstone Project

At the conclusion of the book, students may complete a final project titled:

Leading the AGI Generation

Students will create a presentation, report, digital portfolio, or multimedia project answering the following questions:

- What is AGI?
- How will AGI change education?
- What careers may emerge?
- What ethical responsibilities exist?
- How should schools prepare students?
- What leadership qualities will future generations need?
- How will I contribute to an AGI-powered world?

Final Message to Educators

Technology will continue to evolve, but great teaching has always been about far more than information. Great teachers inspire curiosity, encourage perseverance, build confidence, nurture character, and help students believe in their own potential.

Artificial General Intelligence will introduce extraordinary opportunities into education, but the most powerful force in every classroom will continue to be the relationship between a caring teacher and a motivated student.

As educators, we are not simply preparing students to understand technology—we are preparing them to lead with wisdom, integrity, compassion, creativity, and courage.

The students sitting in today's classrooms will become tomorrow's innovators, scientists, teachers, engineers, healthcare professionals, entrepreneurs, public servants, and community leaders.

May this book help inspire them to build a future where Artificial General Intelligence strengthens humanity, expands opportunity, and reflects the highest values of education.

Learn AI. Understand AI. Shape the Future.

— Susie Hala

IntelliGloss Press

NOTE:

NOTES:

NOTES:

NOTES:

NOTES:

NOTE:

www.ingramcontent.com/pod-product-compliance
Lightning Source LLC
Chambersburg PA
CBHW041753220926
51847CB00014B/188
* 9 7 8 1 9 7 2 9 2 5 2 3 2 *